IMAGES
of America

AROUND MILTON

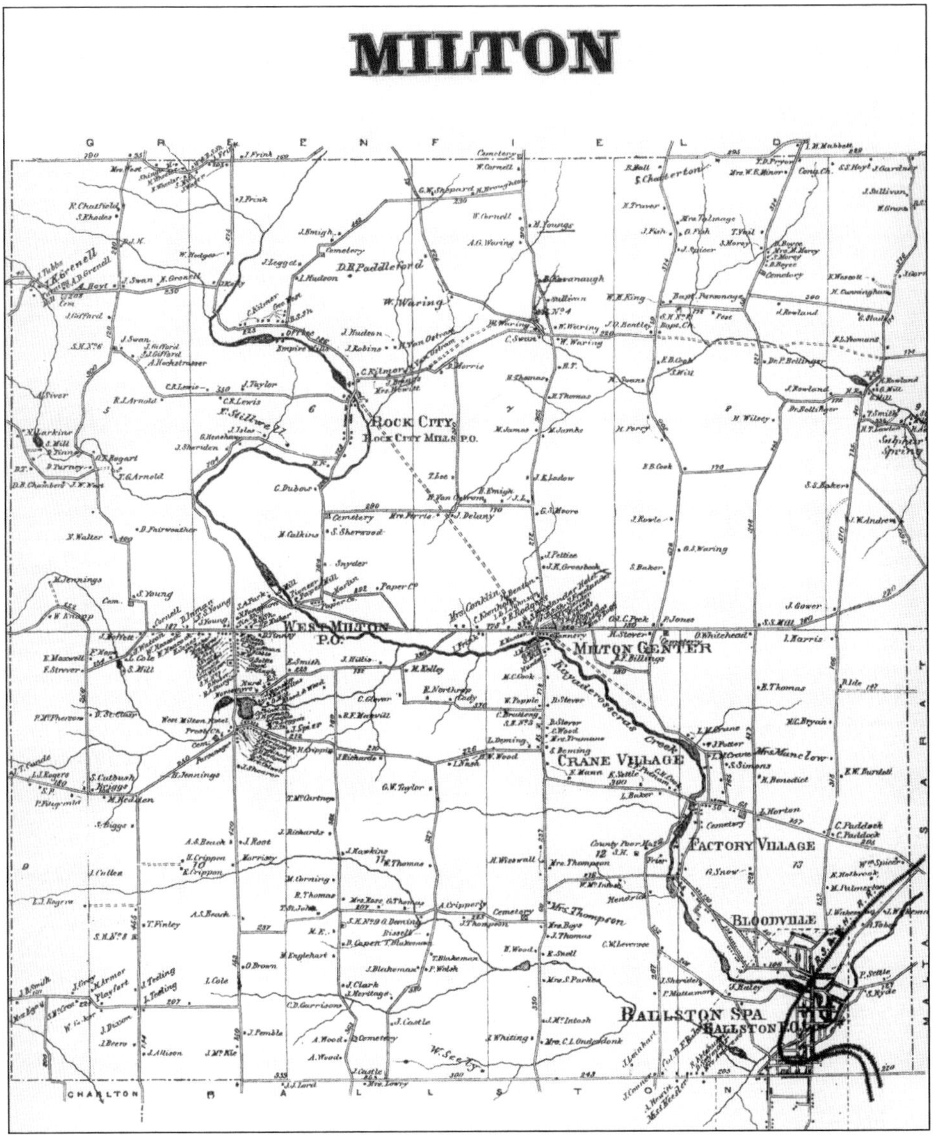

This S.N. & D.G. Beers and Associates map from the *New Topographical Atlas of Saratoga County, New York*, shows the town of Milton as it looked in 1866. By the middle of the century, the town had become heavily industrialized, as evidenced by the array of hamlets that were clustered around factory sites. Some of the largest—such as Bloodville, Factory Village, Milton Center, West Milton, and Rock City Falls—were along the Kayaderosseras Creek. Although only remnants of this industrial activity survive, these hamlets and the rest of the town have become part of a popular and fast-growing residential area. (Author's collection.)

On the Cover: Dennis Manogue operated a successful lumberyard and contracting business on Bath Street, next to the Bull's Head Tannery, throughout the late 1800s and early 1900s. One of the rails of the Ballston Terminal Railroad can be seen at the bottom of the photograph. This building has been remodeled and survives to this day, retaining its distinctive roofline. (Saratoga County Historical Society at Brookside Museum.)

IMAGES
of America

AROUND MILTON

Timothy Starr

ARCADIA
PUBLISHING

ISBN 978-1-4671-3392-0

Published by Arcadia Publishing
Charleston, South Carolina

Printed in the United States of America

Library of Congress Control Number: 2015934080

For all general information, please contact Arcadia Publishing:
Telephone 843-853-2070
Fax 843-853-0044
E-mail sales@arcadiapublishing.com
For customer service and orders:
Toll-Free 1-888-313-2665

Visit us on the Internet at www.arcadiapublishing.com

*Dedicated to the memory of Maurice "Chris" Morley,
who had a lifelong passion for the town of Milton*

Contents

Acknowledgments

Writing a book on the town of Milton, even one that consists mainly of photographs, was a daunting task given its long and accomplished history. In attempting such a project, one of the most difficult aspects was simply gathering the requisite number of historical images together, which could not have been done without having access to the collections listed below.

Most important was the collection of the Brookside Museum, home to the Saratoga County Historical Society. Volunteer Cassie Passinault spent hours sifting through the thousands of images in the Brookside collection to scan the ones that were needed. Former director Joy Houle and curators Linda Gorham and Kathleen Coleman also gave a great deal of support and time.

The late Maurice "Chris" Morley, a longtime collector and expert of Ballston Spa history, had an extensive photograph collection that focused on the industrial era of the village and the town of Milton. He was also able to fill in the gaps for captions of several obscure photographs. Ballston Spa resident Pat Streifert generously let me scan her postcard albums and photographs. Paul and Marilyn Pastore, who owned a pharmacy in Ballston Spa for 44 years, allowed the use of their Rock City Falls, West Milton, Milton Center, and Ballston Spa real-photo postcards and photographs from their large collection.

Thanks also to Saratoga County historian Lauren Roberts and Town of Milton historian Kim McCartney for their help in supplying historical photographs and to longtime attorney and historian John Cromie for editing the manuscript.

INTRODUCTION

The town of Milton has derived much of its past fame, wealth, and probably its name (a contraction of "mill town") from the vast array of industries that developed and flourished from before its establishment to the 1950s. Because these industries were so important to the town itself and Saratoga County as a whole, they are a featured component of this book. The almost complete loss of industry in the late 20th century is another reason for preserving its history within these pages.

Land now comprising the town of Milton was part of the Kayaderosseras Patent granted by the English crown in 1708. Settlement could not begin until claims of the Mohawks were settled in 1767 and the track was surveyed and divided among its owners. Originally part of the Ball's Town district of Albany County, Milton was not set out as a town by the state legislature until 1792. It is centrally located within Saratoga County, principally bounded by the towns of Greenfield, Ballston, and Galway and the city of Saratoga Springs. It contains 22,000 acres of moderately fertile farmland and forests in the southwest, gravelly hill country to the west and extreme north, and a giant sand plain in the remaining eastern portion.

Perhaps the most important factor in the initial settlement and subsequent growth of the town was the Kayaderosseras Creek, a Native American name meaning "land of the crooked stream." The Mohawks of the Iroquois Nation considered the Kayaderosseras valley an important hunting ground. The rapid fall in elevation of the creek within the town's borders created the perfect conditions for situating water wheels to power machinery. Other suitable streams for waterpower included the Gordon, Glowegee, and Rowland's Hollow Creeks.

The earliest settlers arrived in 1772 and purchased land along the Middle Line of Ballston's Five Mile Square (now Middle Line Road). However, local conflict with the British and their Native American allies prevented the growth of substantial communities until the Revolutionary War ended.

The town's only incorporated village, Ballston Spa, was first settled around 1787. One of the land speculators selling farm lots from his holdings retained 100 acres, including a rare mineral spring. Nicholas Low, a wealthy merchant from New York City, invested some of his fortune to develop a spa located near the Iron Railing Spring. His most prominent venture was the Sans Souci Hotel, considered one of the grandest of the era when it was built in 1804. Others erected hotels and boardinghouses, and for about 20 years the village was a popular tourist destination. Some of the most prominent people of the day traveled to Ballston to "take the waters" and be entertained.

The tourist industry turned out to be a fickle one. The springs of nearby Saratoga became fashionable, while those of Ballston declined. Some observers blamed overly aggressive spring owners who "couldn't leave well enough alone" and tubed the springs incorrectly. Others blamed the damming of the rivers for mills, which caused the weight of the water from the man-made ponds to seep deep underground and contaminate the fragile springs.

However, the same water source that may have led to the failure of the springs provided a means to develop industry. Mills at that time were not often located near urban centers; instead, they were situated near a water source to power the machinery. By the late 1800s, there were 10 paper mills, a large sash and blind complex, sawmills, and hard-edge tool factories operating along the banks of the Kayaderosseras and Gordon Creeks throughout Milton. Inside the village of Ballston Spa were additional sawmills, a large tannery, a paper collar mill, textile factories, and many other industries. These concerns provided jobs for thousands of people and generated millions of dollars for the economy.

The success of industry prompted residents to build a unique 12-mile railroad to serve the mills along the creek. It was unusual in that it was one of the only trolley railroads in the country primarily charged with moving carload freight. The town was also served by two other trolley lines that provided transit to nearby cities, including Saratoga Springs, Schenectady, and Mechanicville. More important, the Delaware and Hudson steam railroad operated through the center of Ballston Spa, giving its industries access to worldwide markets.

The combination of waterpower, an educated workforce, nearby raw materials, and a first-class transportation system led to the formation of significant communities in Milton, all clustered around industrial enterprises. Bloodville was best known for its hard-edge tool factories, Milton Center contained the county's largest tannery, and Factory Village and Rock City Falls hosted important paper mills. Thousands of residents prospered in factories that operated continuously for decades. Farms producing a variety of cash crops and animals filled the landscape around these industrial communities.

Technological advances in electricity brought change. Small, single-owner manufacturers located near water declined, beginning in the early 1900s, bringing to an end nearly all the industry along the Kayaderosseras Creek and within Ballston Spa. At first, they merely became consolidated into nationwide trusts or large collections of related factories. The American Axe & Tool Company absorbed the Ballston Axe & Scythe Works. The Union Bag & Paper Company purchased George West's paper mills, and the American Hide & Leather Company purchased the tannery. When it suited them, these large corporations had no hesitation in shutting down the long-standing local icons. The tannery in Ballston Spa lasted the longest, finally closing in 1961.

Milton was able to weather the Great Depression with the establishment of a successful chocolate factory and several textile mills. The massive plant of General Electric in Schenectady employed tens of thousands, some of whom commuted from Milton via one of the trolley lines. Local farms prospered by providing food for Schenectady and other cities.

During the two decades after World War II, the advancement of agrarian technology resulted in a rapid demise of the small family farm, and refrigerated trucking eliminated the need for a central cold-storage facility, such as the one in Ballston Spa. The town lost its role as a farming community, and its many farms seemed to evaporate, leaving a few sizable dairy operations, which themselves had gone out of business by the beginning of this century.

Yet the continued success of General Electric provided work for Milton's factory workers and farmers. The automobile allowed them to commute, and the population of the area was sustained even though it could no longer find much local employment. In addition, engineers and professionals found living in Milton well suited for raising their families. Much of the town became a bedroom community.

Another boost to the economy was the US Navy's decision to locate a nuclear propulsion–training program in West Milton, which has employed many residents and, over time, drawn thousands more from outside the area. Ballston Spa's designation as the county seat has also historically provided economic stability.

During the second half of the 20th century, Milton was transformed into a moderately populous residential, retail, and professional community. The town today is a thriving residential center, enjoying steady growth within one of the fastest-growing counties in New York State. In conjunction with this growth, efforts are being made to maintain the feel of small-town America, with planned growth, preservation of rural areas, and establishment of town parks and other recreational sites.

One

The Tourism Era

Naturally occurring mineral springs were a rare find, sought after by those seeking hydrotherapy for their health. When surveyors of the Kayaderosseras Patent came upon a mineral spring in 1771, it was soon known throughout the 13 colonies. However, conflict with Native Americans and the British delayed any meaningful settlement.

For about 20 years, travelers who frequented the spring were forced to stay in nearby homes. It was not until 1792 that Nicholas Low erected what later became known as the McMaster House, and Benajah Douglas, grandfather of Stephen A. Douglas, built the hotel now known as Brookside.

Low owned most of the buildable land, and he attempted in vain to sell sizable lots to visitors. By 1800, however, he had changed direction and began a complex plan of creating a spa where people would be accommodated and entertained while "taking the waters." He subdivided his land into smaller lots to rent to merchants and tradespeople, channeled the Gordon Creek, built bathing and gaming facilities that he rented to others to run, and established the Sans Souci Hotel with its half dozen or so ancillary structures. Low was determined to encourage the development of a complete village and donated land for churches and schools and, most important, for the construction of a county building. Thereafter, Ballston Spa has been the county seat of Saratoga County.

Ballston Spa continued to grow, becoming an incorporated village on March 21, 1807. Eminent scientists like Yale College's Prof. Benjamin Silliman pronounced the original spring (known as the Iron Railing Spring) was "surpassed by no mineral fountain in the world." Other mineral springs were discovered that proved to be as "medicinal" as the first. In 1818, it was estimated that the village's permanent population of 2,000 was increased by 2,500 visitors during the tourist season, 1,200 of whom were from states south of New York. Ballston Spa was known as "America's First Watering Place."

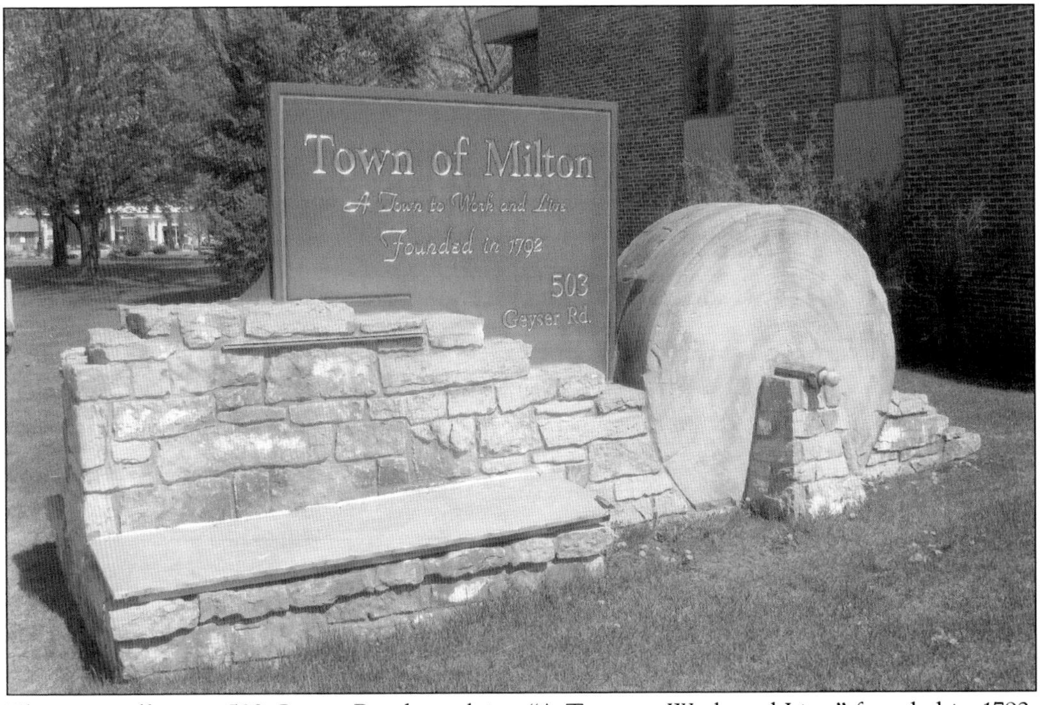

The town offices at 503 Geyser Road proclaim, "A Town to Work and Live," founded in 1792. The large sharpening stone embedded within the stonework represents the significant industrial endeavors during its formation. Several of these large stones still lie at rest, mostly forgotten, on the banks of the Kayaderosseras Creek in Bloodville. (Author's collection.)

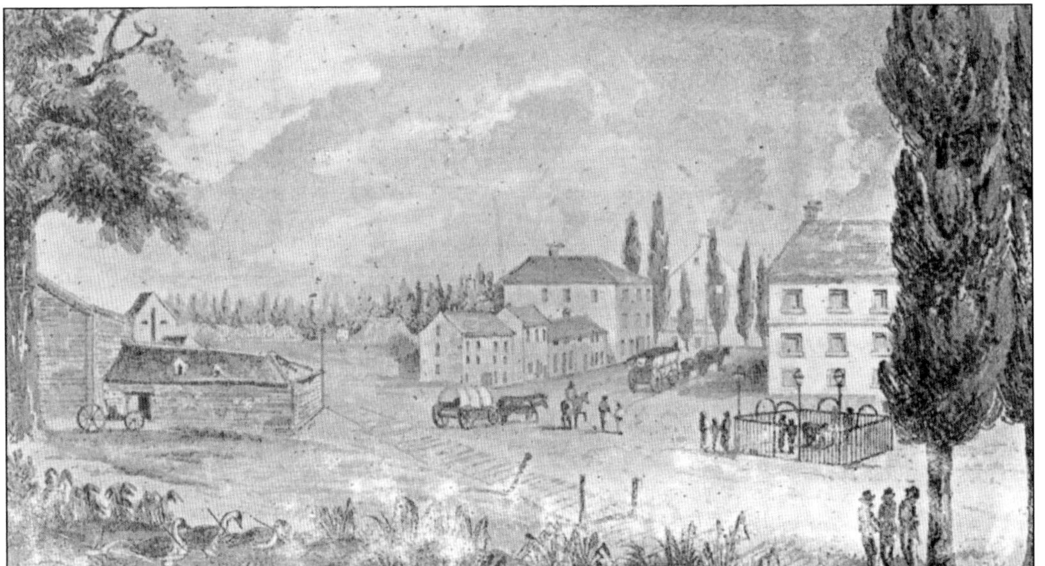

One of the only images of the original spring is seen in this 1817 drawing from the vantage point of Aldridge's (Brookside). Surrounded by an iron railing, the spring was located in the middle of Charlton Street. The McMaster House is on the right, while the large building on Front Street is probably an early version of the American Hotel. (Town of Milton Historian.)

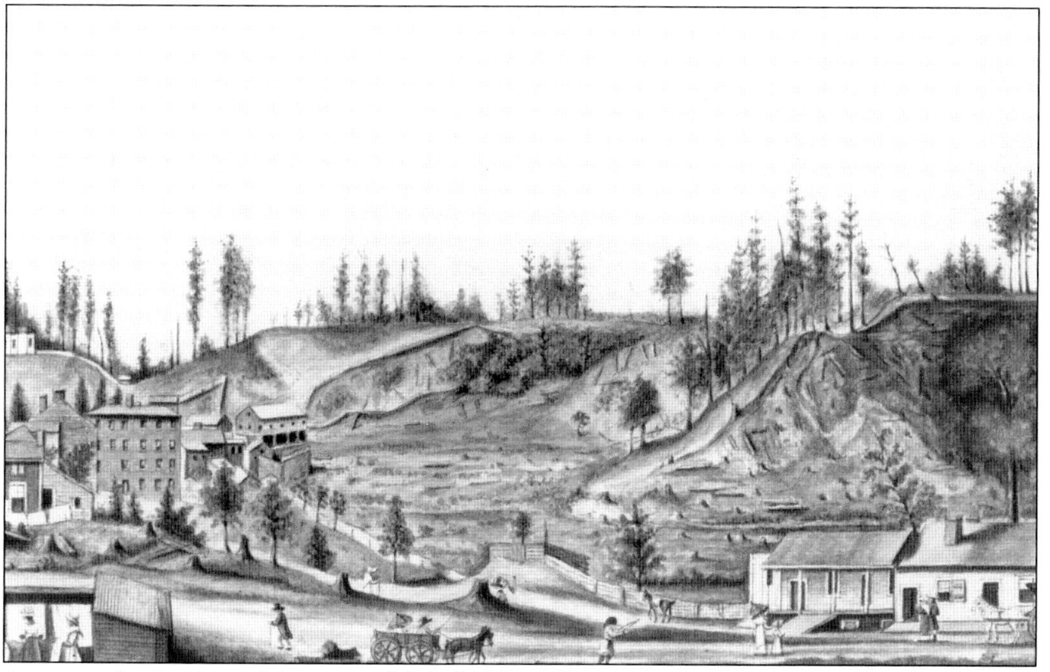

A watercolor by Anne Marguerite Hyde DeNeuville portrays Ballston Spa as it looked in the summer of 1807. It was probably painted from an upper-story room of the Sans Souci Hotel, with Front Street on the far left and the Pavilion (or garden temple) on the hill overlooking the Aldridge House. Recent logging of the hills around the settlement is apparent. (New York Historical Society.)

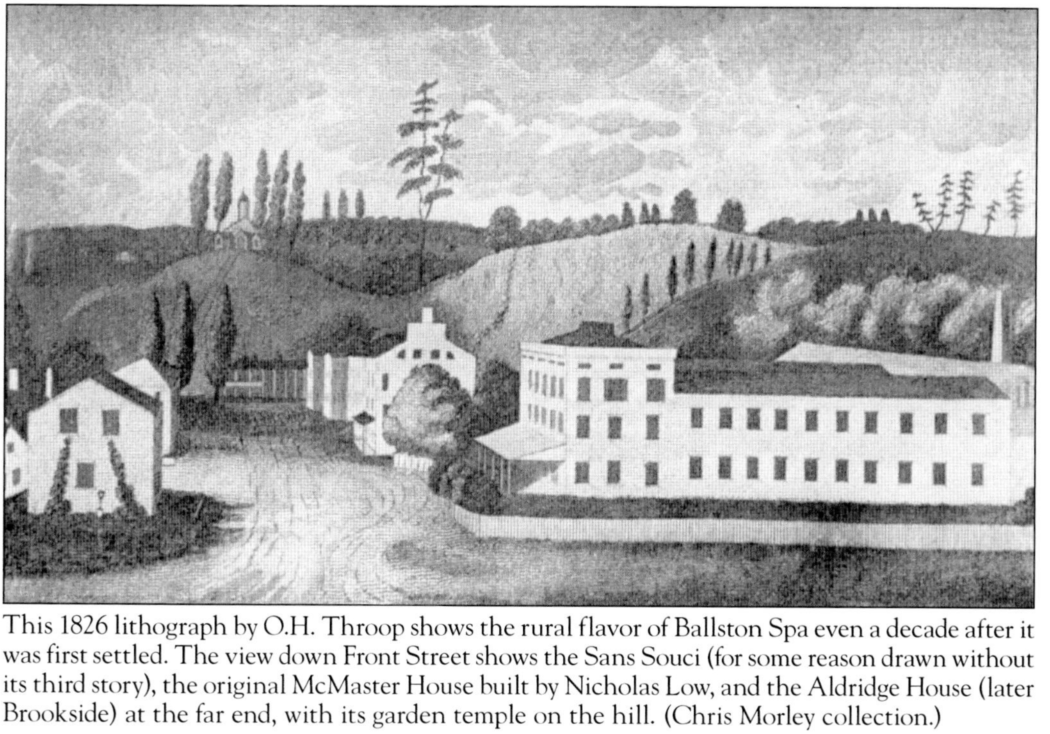

This 1826 lithograph by O.H. Throop shows the rural flavor of Ballston Spa even a decade after it was first settled. The view down Front Street shows the Sans Souci (for some reason drawn without its third story), the original McMaster House built by Nicholas Low, and the Aldridge House (later Brookside) at the far end, with its garden temple on the hill. (Chris Morley collection.)

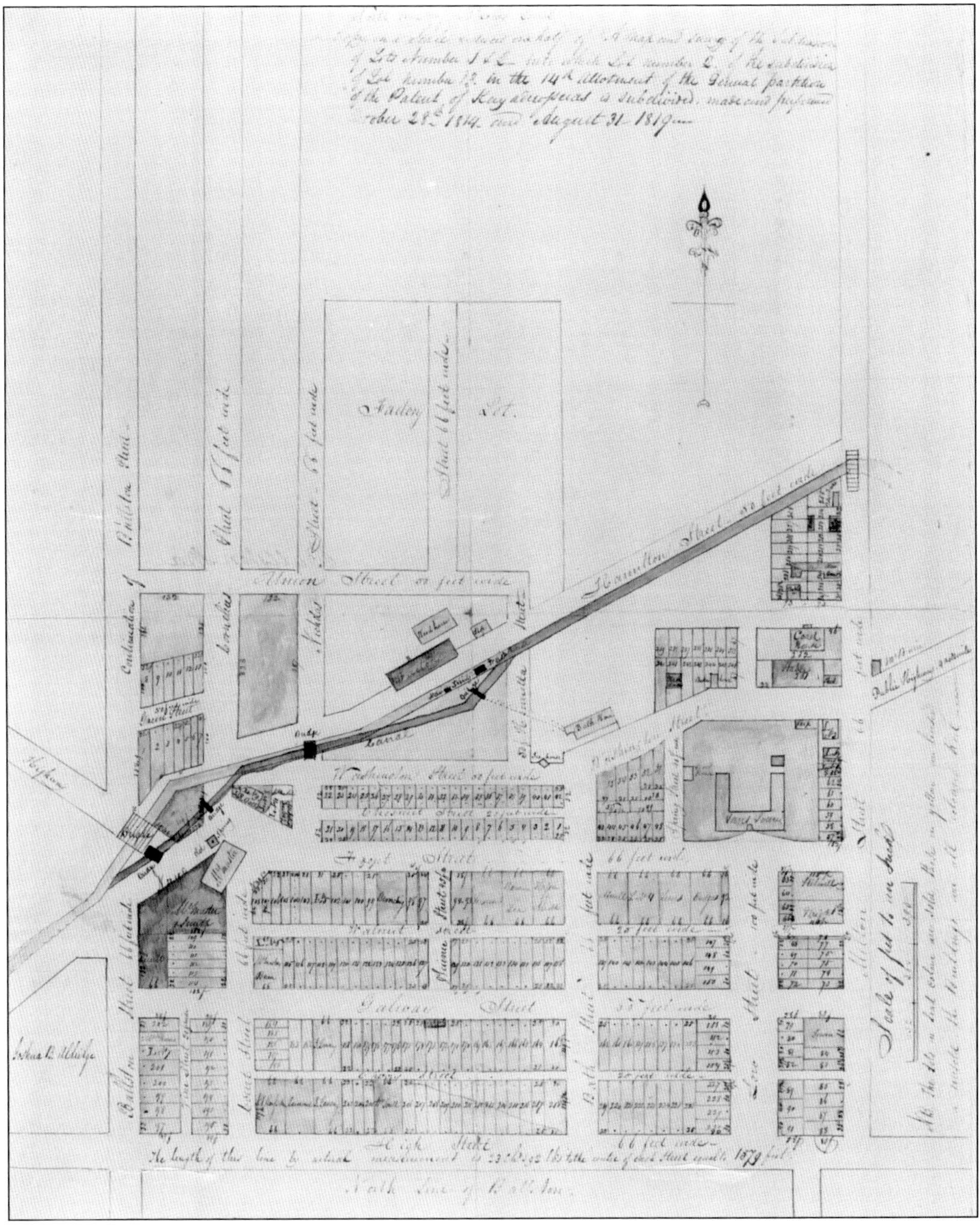

This 1819 map of Low's holdings in Ballston Spa shows the culmination of his plans over 25 years. Evident is the large Sans Souci complex and his woolen factory, built on Gordon Creek in 1812. After barely a month's operation, the walking beam broke and the enterprise was abandoned. It was later used as an oilcloth factory and, finally, the Bull's Head Tannery. (Paul and Marilyn Pastore collection.)

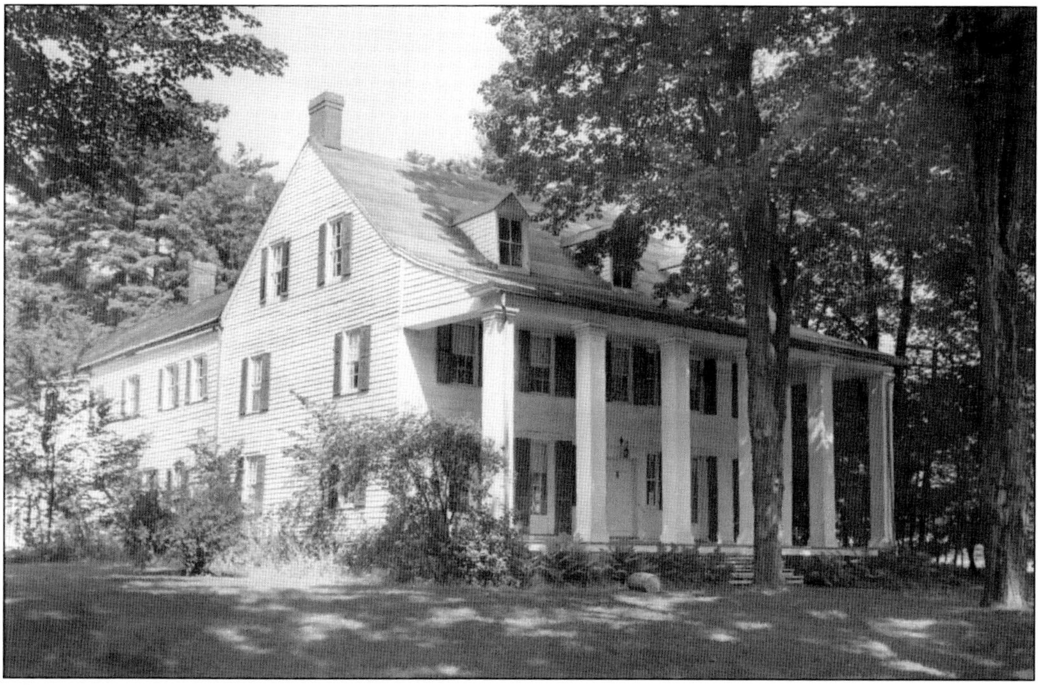

The structure now known as Brookside is the oldest building in Ballston Spa. It was first built by Benajah Douglas in 1792 and considerably enlarged by Joshua Aldridge in 1804. In the proceeding years, it became, respectively, a private residence, boarding school, sanitarium, apartments, and finally a museum. It was listed in the National Register of Historic Places in 1975. (Saratoga County Historian.)

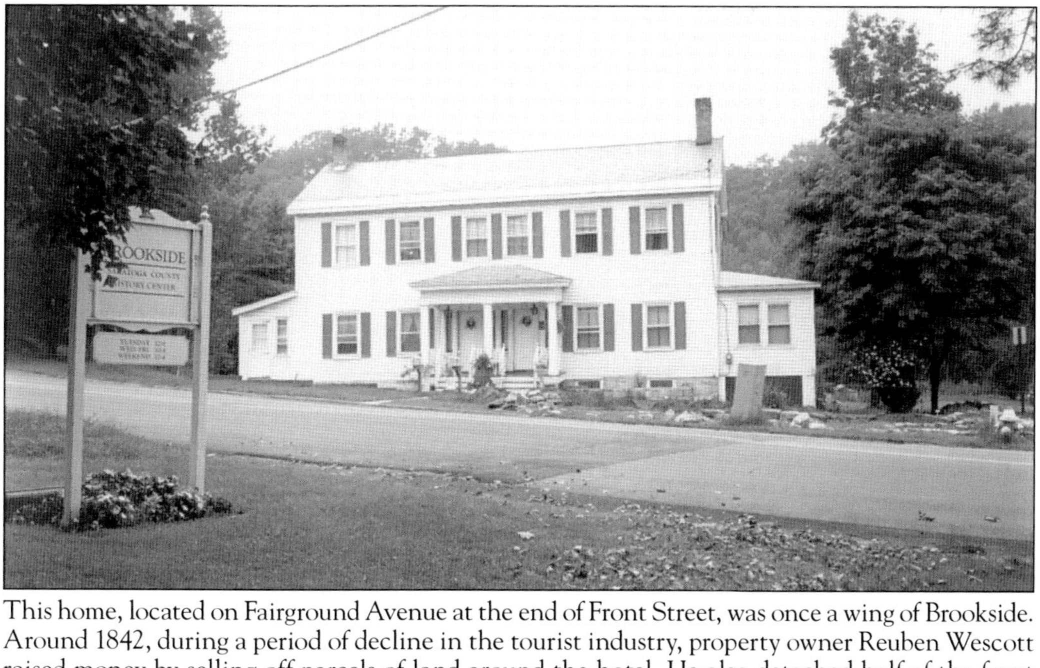

This home, located on Fairground Avenue at the end of Front Street, was once a wing of Brookside. Around 1842, during a period of decline in the tourist industry, property owner Reuben Wescott raised money by selling off parcels of land around the hotel. He also detached half of the front section and had it moved across the street to sell as a residence. (Chris Morley collection.)

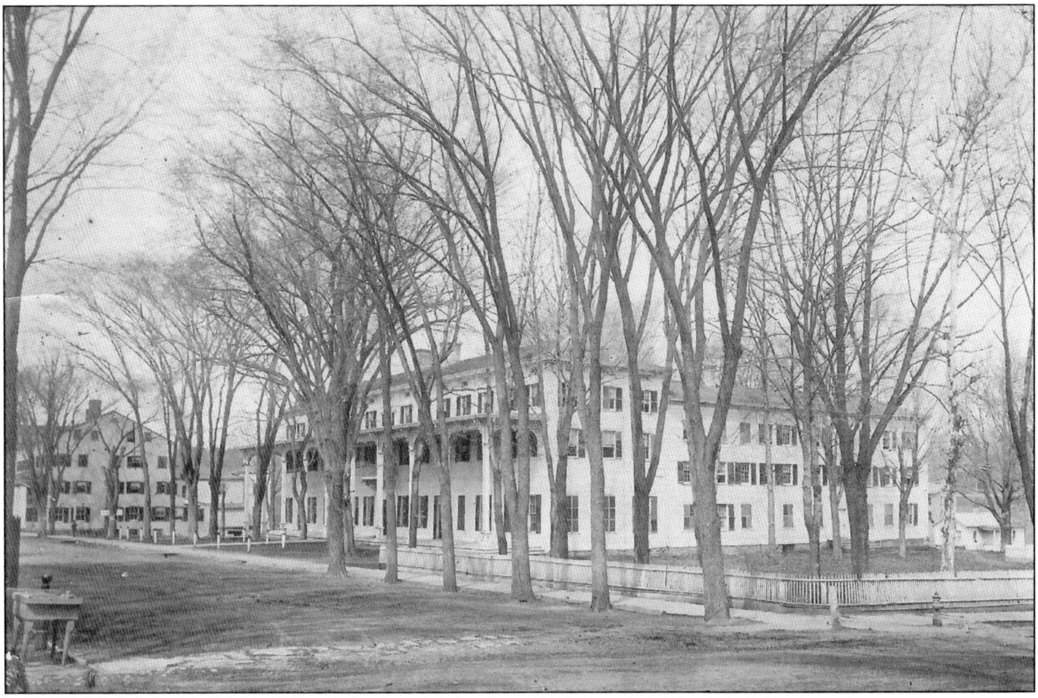

In 1803, Nicholas Low commissioned the construction of the Sans Souci Hotel, the largest of its kind in the United States with a capacity of 150 guests. The facade was 160 feet long, and the wings extended 153 feet back from each end. Other associated buildings included a washhouse, tavern, workshop, icehouse, coach house, and stables. (Saratoga County Historical Society at Brookside Museum.)

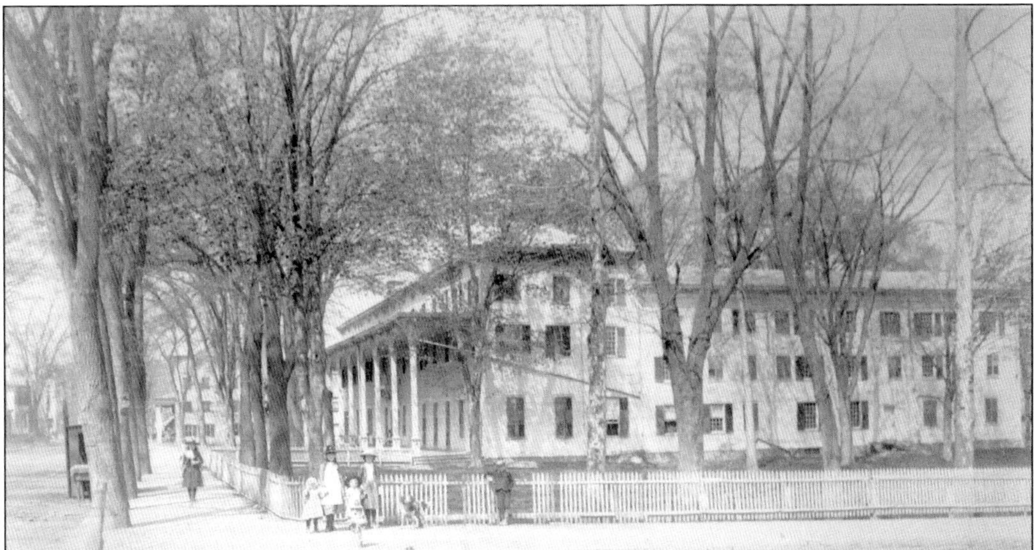

Famous guests of the Sans Souci Hotel included Martin Van Buren, James Fenimore Cooper, Andrew Jackson, Stephen Douglas, William Seward, Washington Irving, and Joseph Bonaparte, the ex-king of Spain who stayed for several months in the summer of 1821. (Paul and Marilyn Pastore collection.)

Although Nicholas Low tubed several springs in the early 1800s, they either dried up or fell to disuse. In 1870, George Smith purchased the Sans Souci and renovated it as the tourist trade began to reappear. He contracted with Jesse Button to drill a new spring behind the hotel. Carbonation from the spring waters was used to make flavored sodas until around 1970. (Chris Morley collection.)

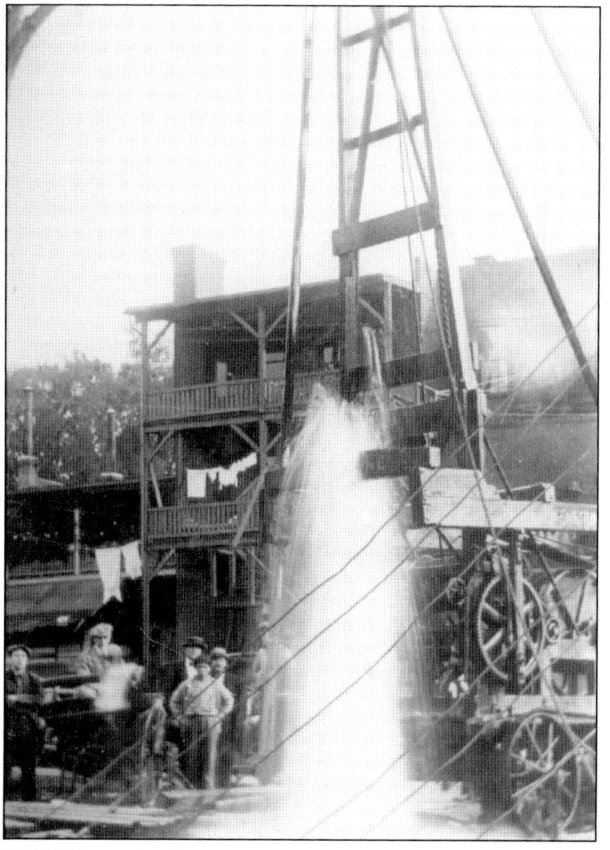

British artist William Henry Bartlett created this engraving of Front Street in 1835 as part of a travelogue of the United States. The Village Hotel (later known as the Medbery) is on the left. The Sans Souci Hotel is blocked by the trees. Facing the viewer is the second church edifice of the village's Baptist congregation. (Author's collection.)

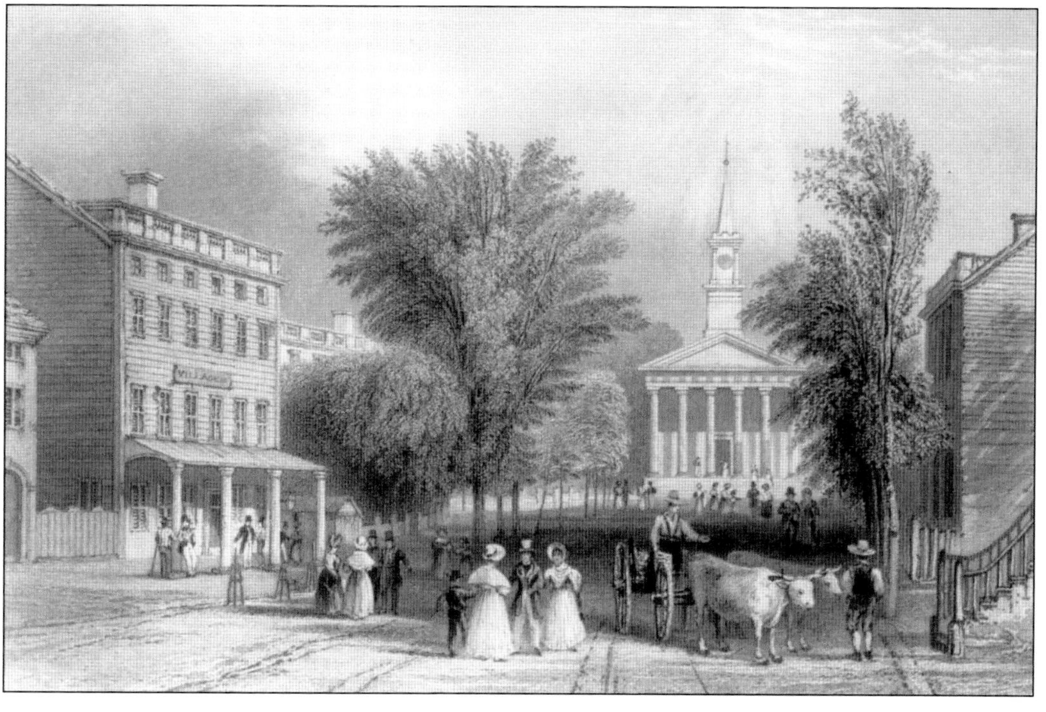

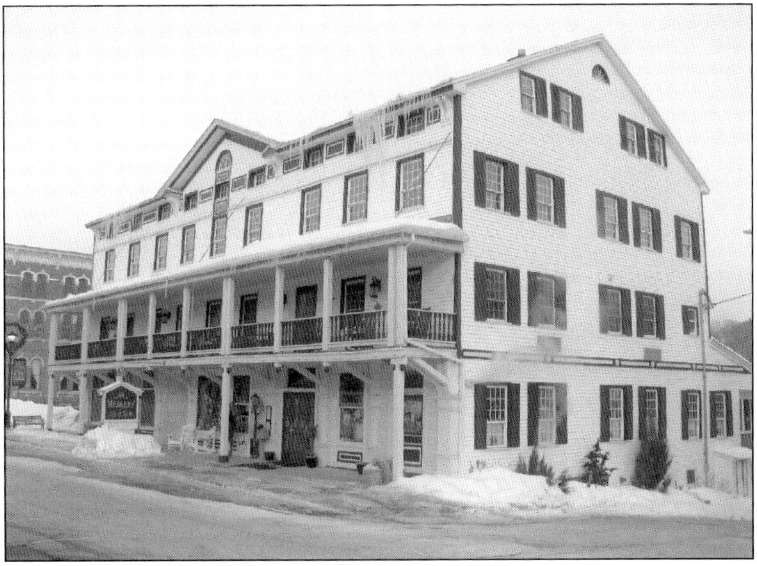

The Medbery on Front Street was one of the first hotels built in the village. In 1804, it was known as the Village Hotel and measured only 25 feet wide, but William Clark added another 25 feet on the left side of the building in 1824. Clark's son built an addition that brought it to its present size before selling it to Stephen Medbery in 1851. (Dorothy Kelliher collection.)

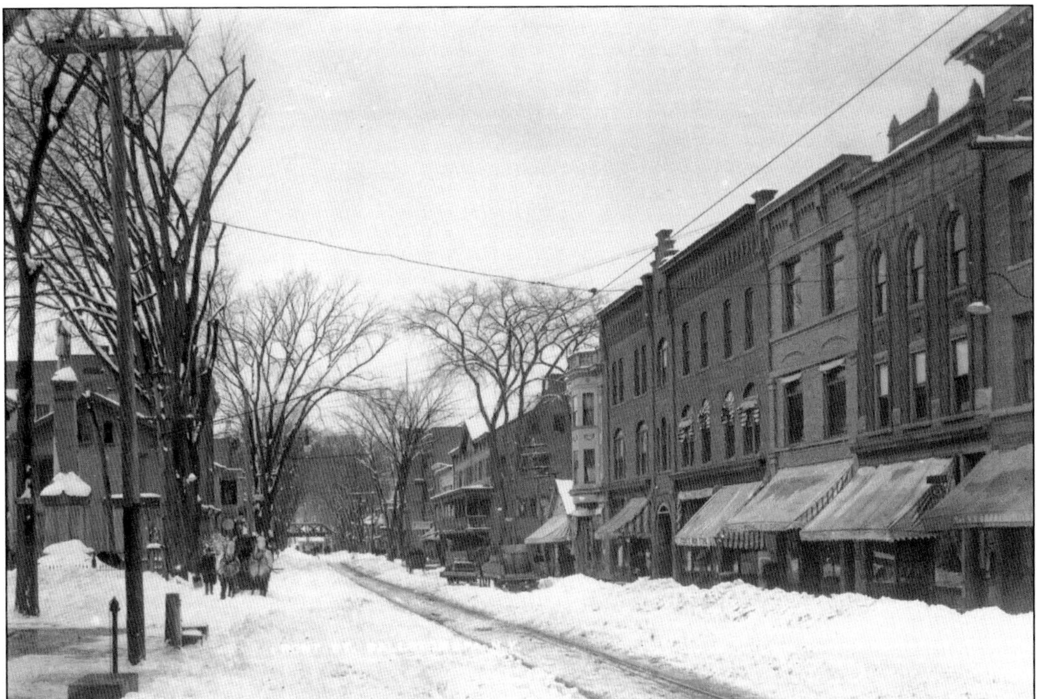

This view of the Front Street business block shows the venerable Medbery Hotel in the center. The Medbery has served as a hotel and boardinghouse for over 200 years and continues to do so today as the last of its kind. The tracks of the Schenectady Railway lead toward Brookside, sitting just beyond the Delaware and Hudson Railway bridge in the distance. (Saratoga County Historian.)

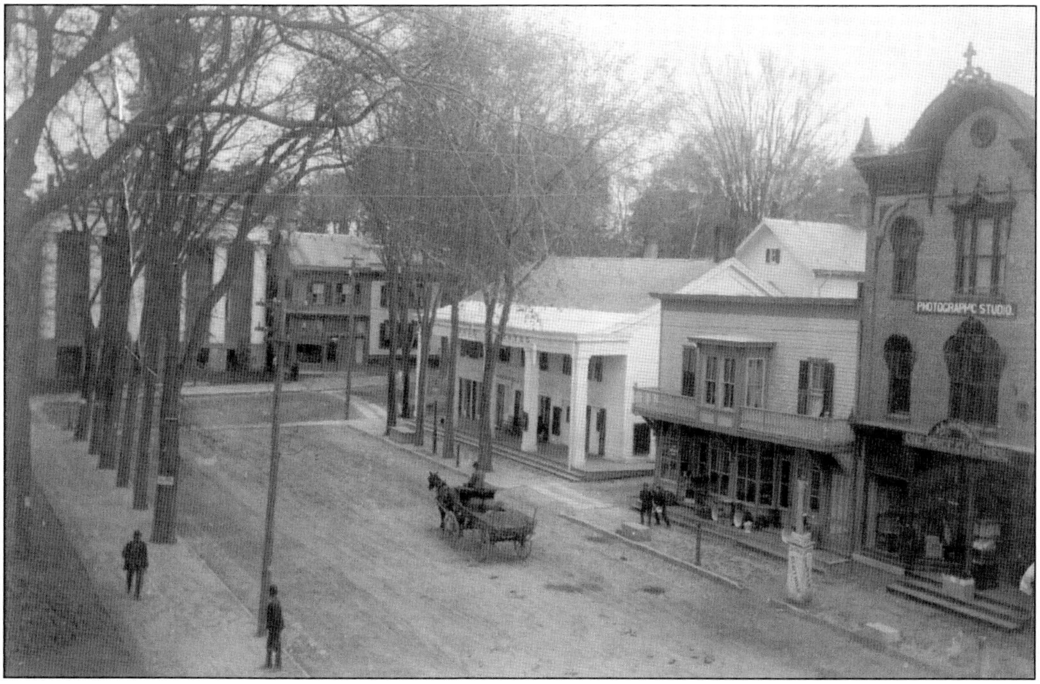

This view of Front Street looking toward Milton Avenue from the balcony of the Medbery Hotel shows the Baptist church (left), Eagle Hotel, J.J. Jacob's "One Price" Clothier, and Jesse Wooley's photographic studio. (Saratoga County Historical Society at Brookside Museum.)

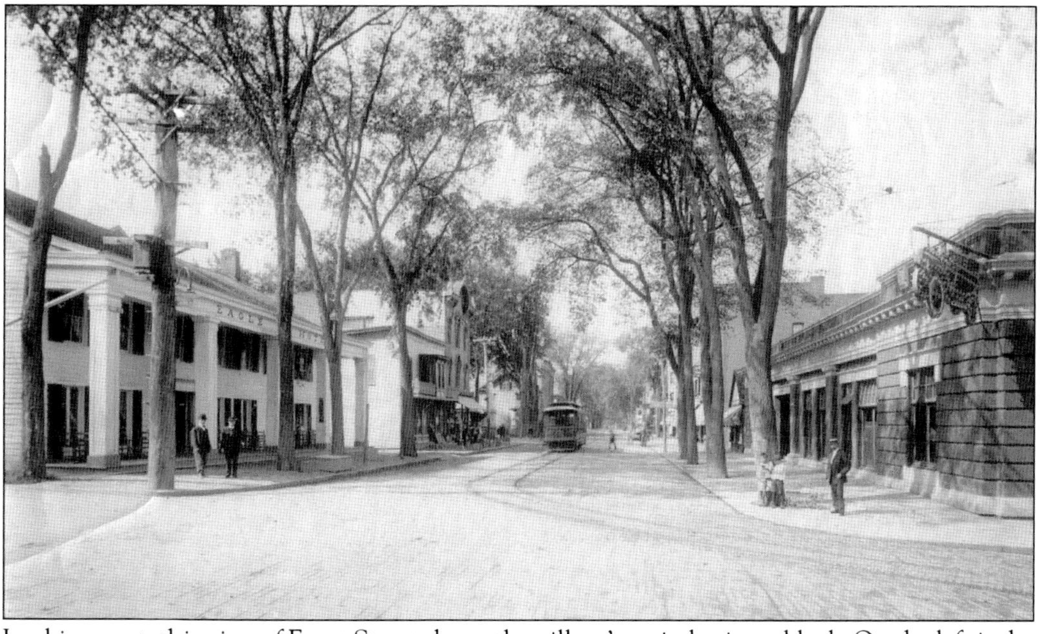
Looking west, this view of Front Street shows the village's main business block. On the left is the Eagle Hotel. On the right is the George West Jr. Garage, one of the earliest automobile shops. Today, the village post office is located where the Eagle Hotel once stood, and a pharmacy occupies the former garage. A Schenectady Railway trolley car is visible at center. (Saratoga County Historical Society at Brookside Museum.)

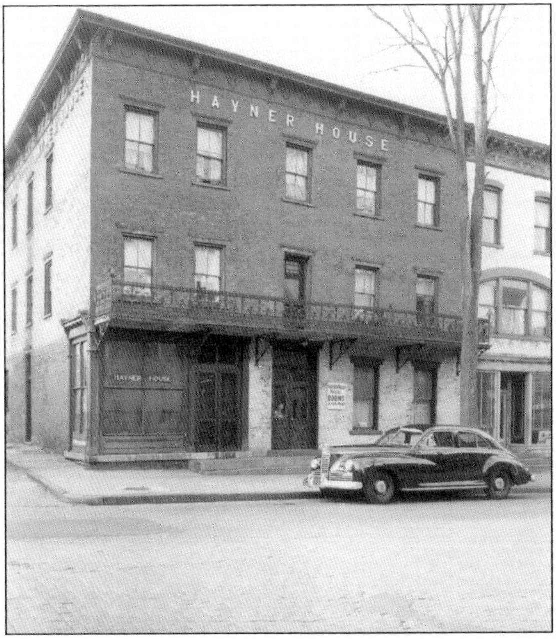

The Hayner House was originally located on the corner of Milton and Malta Avenues, but Sherman Hayner relocated it to a new building on Bath Street in 1884. It operated as a hotel until about 1950. The building was acquired by the Ballston Spa National Bank in 1985 and used as an operations center before passing to other owners. (Chris Morley collection.)

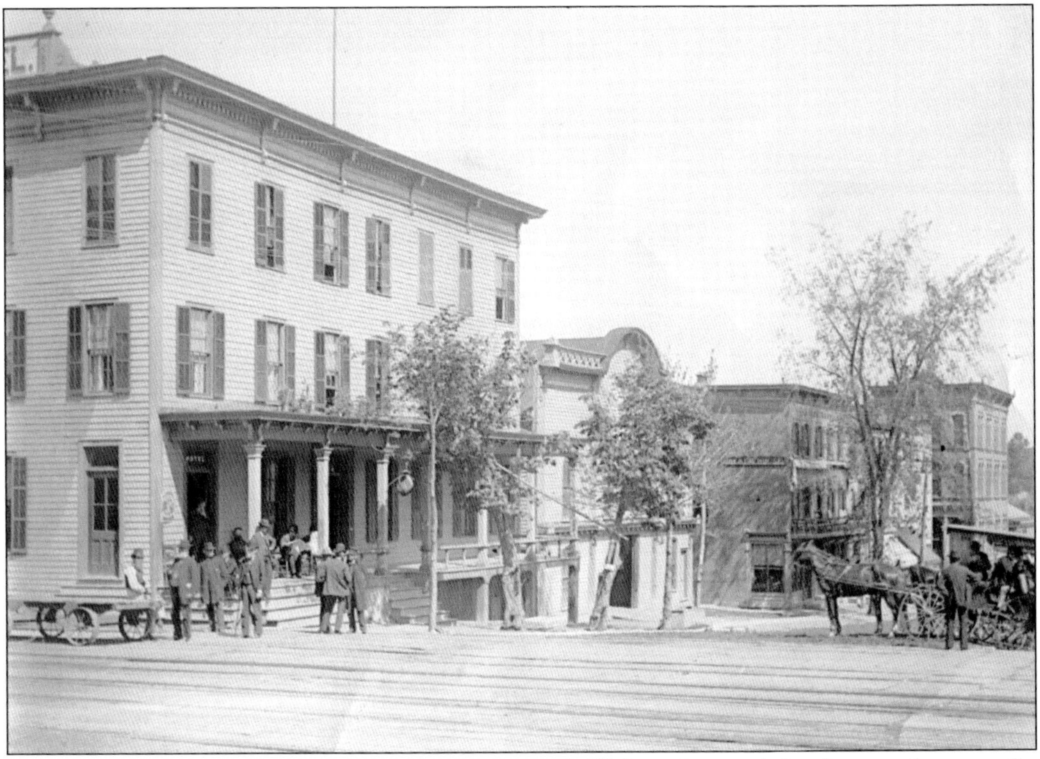

This hotel on Bath Street, near the intersection with Walnut Street, did a thriving business for many years, as it was located opposite the passenger depot. The first hotel on that site was built in 1835 and known as Railroad House. Henry Harrison built the hotel pictured in 1866. It was later known as the Peek, Commercial, American, and finally the Plaza Hotel, which burned down in 1893. (Saratoga County Historical Society at Brookside Museum.)

The site of the Eagle Hotel on the corner of Front Street and Milton Avenue (opposite the Sans Souci) was first occupied by furniture maker William Stillwell and later by a blacksmith shop. It was then converted to a trading post by Solomon Dake and Ezekial Chatfield. A few years later, the store burned, and the Eagle Hotel was built in its place. James Ladow was the first proprietor. (Saratoga County Historical Society at Brookside Museum.)

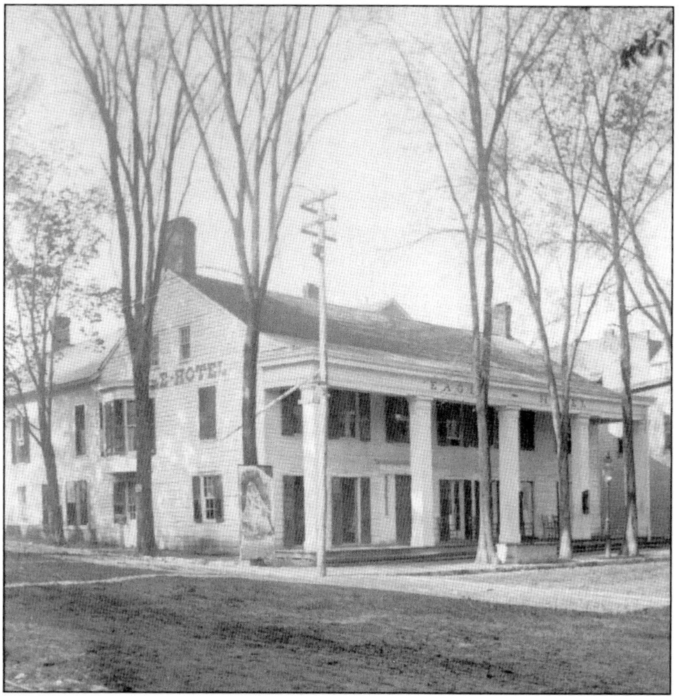

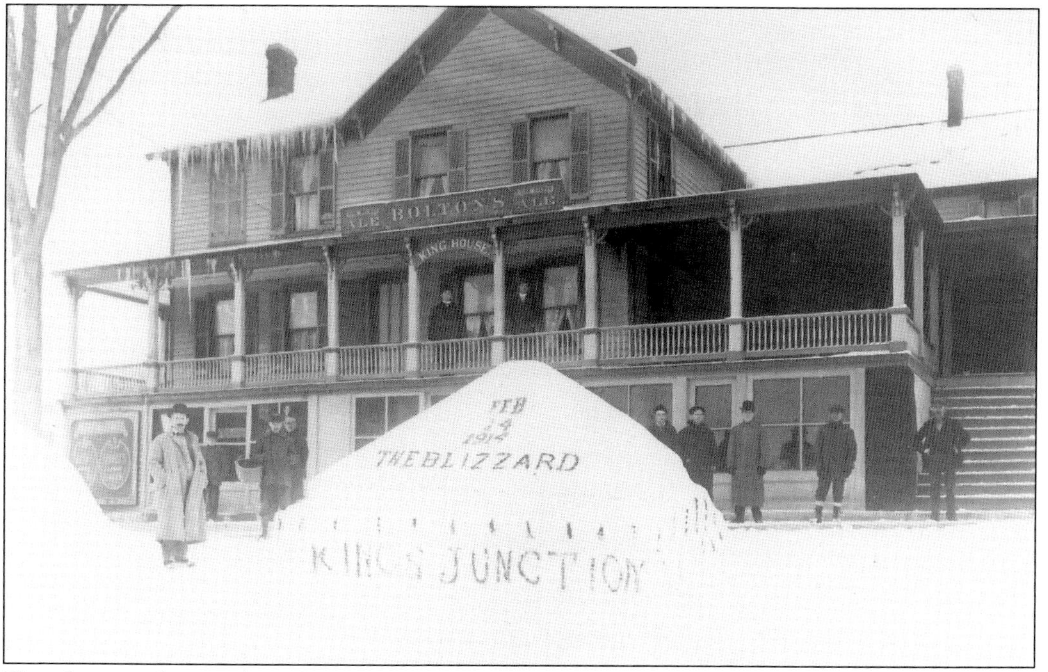

This photograph was taken of Lacy King's King House hotel soon after the blizzard of February 14, 1914. It was located at 50 West North Street, near the border with Bloodville. Although it catered mostly to boarders, the hotel was open to the public year-round and was "located on high ground, giving a fine view of Ballston," had an attached barn and livery, and operated a "first-class pavilion for private parties," according to an advertisement in *The Ballston Journal*. (Saratoga County Historical Society at Brookside Museum.)

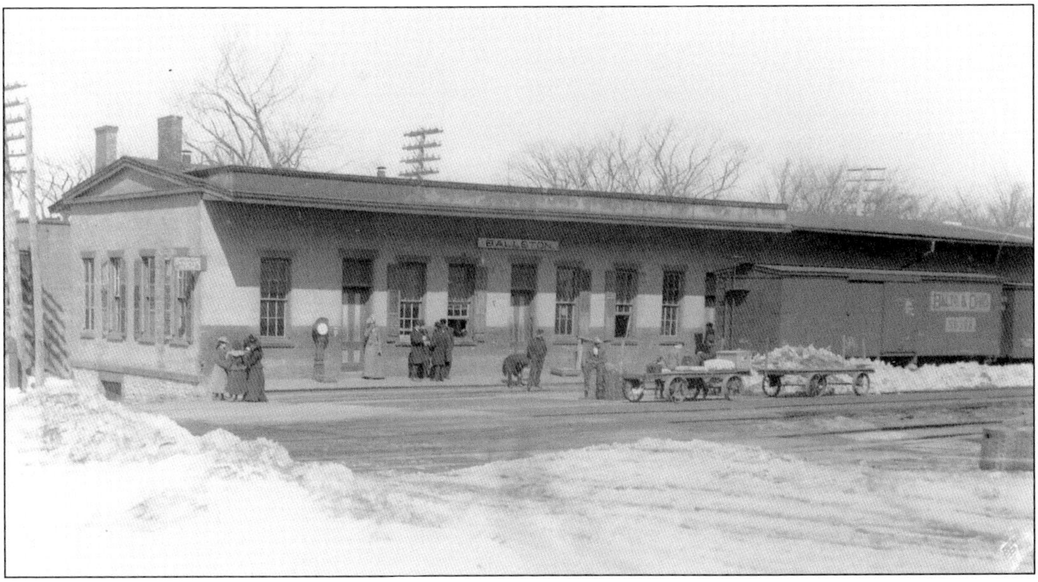

The construction of the Saratoga and Schenectady Railroad from Schenectady to Ballston Spa in 1832 was one of the most significant events in the history of Milton. A new worldwide market for finished goods was opened to the town's many industries, while tourists were able to visit in record numbers. This station, located on Bath Street, was built in 1849 and served the village for 50 years. (Chris Morley collection.)

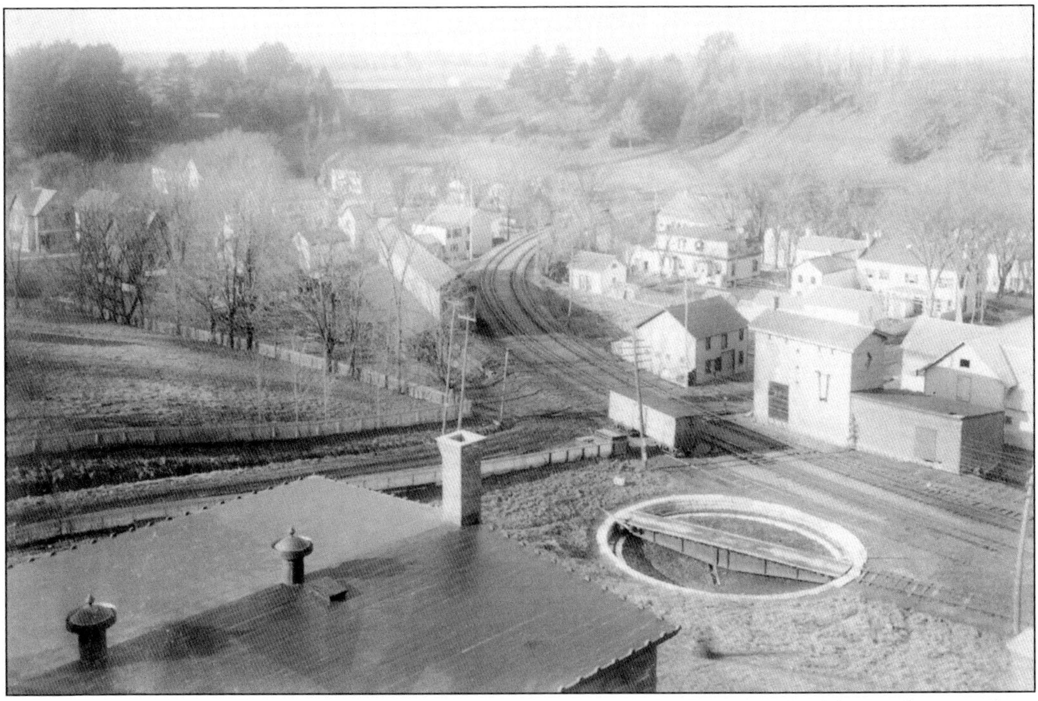

This bird's-eye view of the Delaware and Hudson Railway shows the double-track main line snaking its way through the center of Ballston Spa as it did from 1832 to 1950, when it was relocated outside village limits. The street running from the left is Science Street. Several hotels and boardinghouses were historically located near the main line. (Chris Morley collection.)

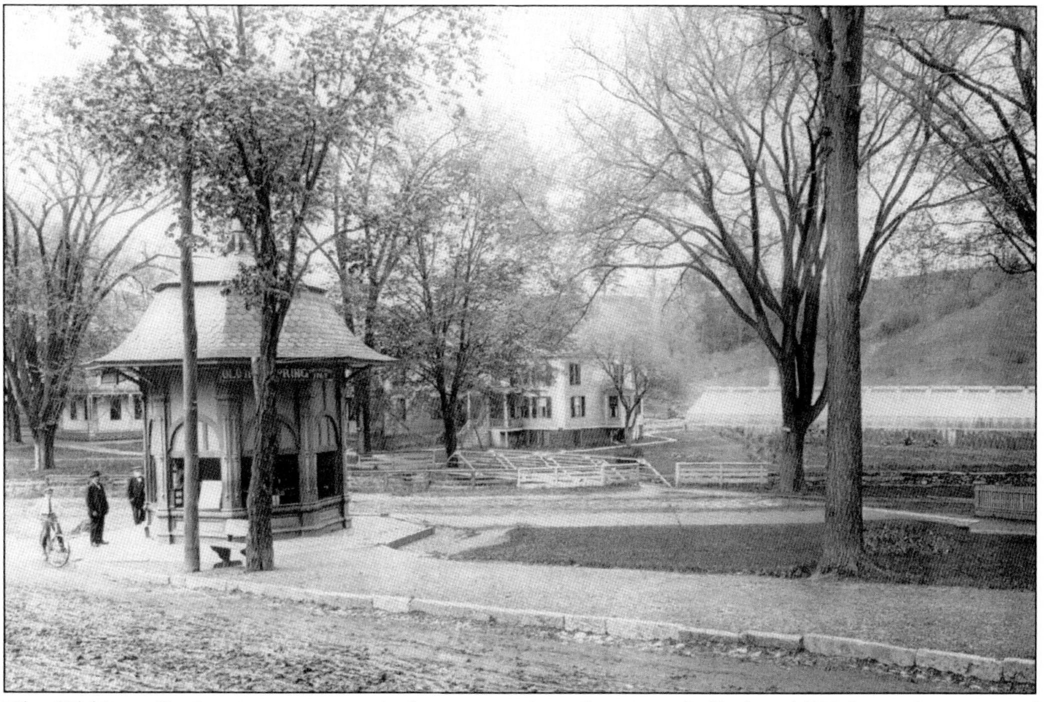

The Old Iron Spring is a comparatively newer mineral spring, drilled in 1874, long after most of the first village springs had stopped flowing. The first spring was called the Iron Railing Spring and located just 50 feet away from this one. Owned and maintained by the village, the Old Iron Spring is the only one still accessible today. (Town of Milton Historian.)

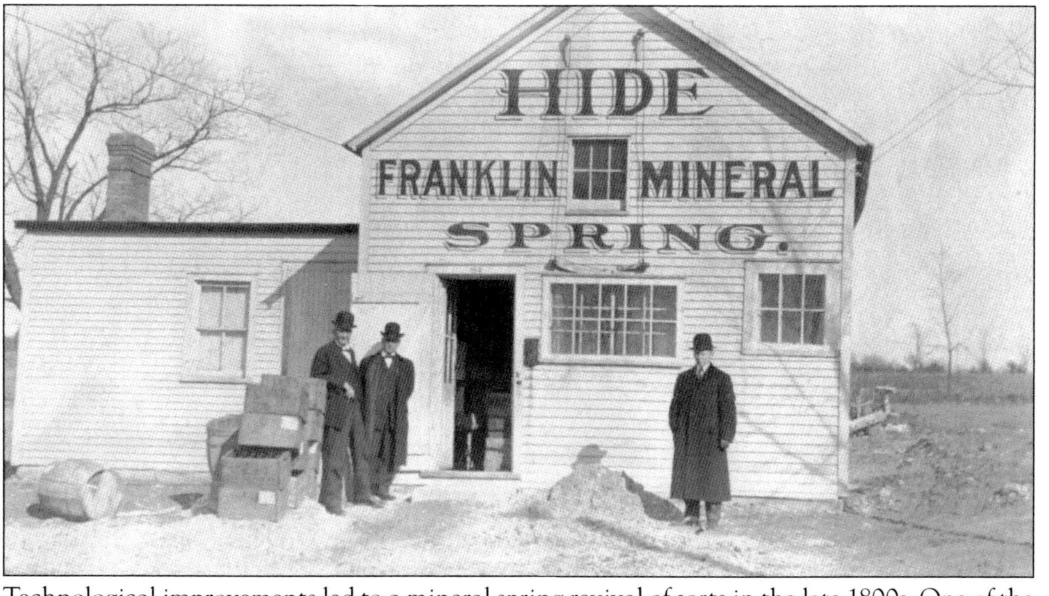

Technological improvements led to a mineral spring revival of sorts in the late 1800s. One of the most successful was Hide's Franklin Mineral Spring. In 1868, Samuel Hide claimed that Benjamin Franklin's spirit instructed him to drill a well on his Malta Avenue property. Hides dutifully hired the Artesian Well Company to start drilling. Water began gushing forth when the drill reached a depth of 715 feet. (Saratoga County Historical Society at Brookside Museum.)

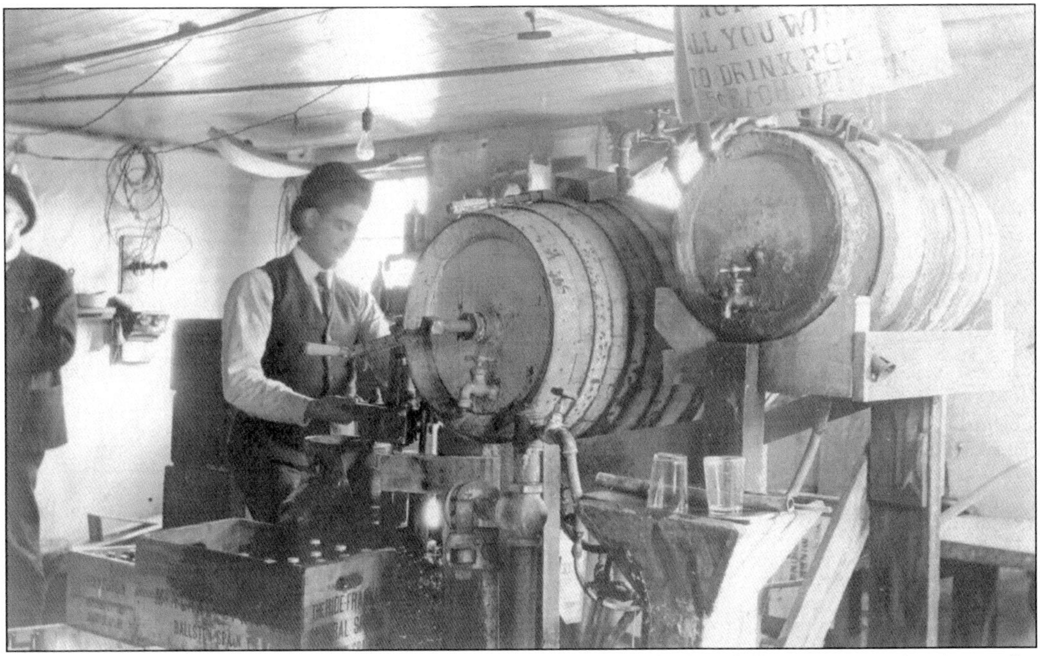

Hide's Franklin Mineral Spring operated for about 20 years before falling to sporadic disuse for a time, but it was later "rediscovered" and bottled for several decades. Hide's son-in-law Abijah Comstock was a longtime proprietor of the company and renamed it the Comstock Spring in 1897. (Saratoga County Historical Society at Brookside Museum.)

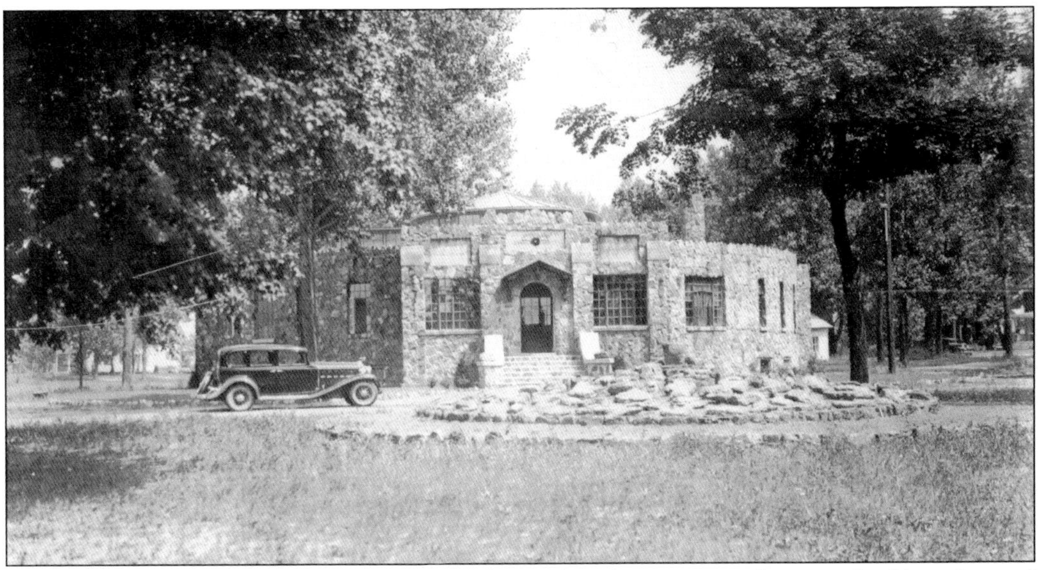

The Streever Lumber Company constructed this 75-foot-diameter circular stone building, located on Malta Avenue near the intersection with Ralph Street, for Hide's Franklin Mineral Spring to replace a smaller wooden one. After almost a century of operation, the spring company closed in 1950. Having been neglected for a few years, the beautiful building was torn down by a developer to make way for apartments. (Saratoga County Historical Society at Brookside Museum.)

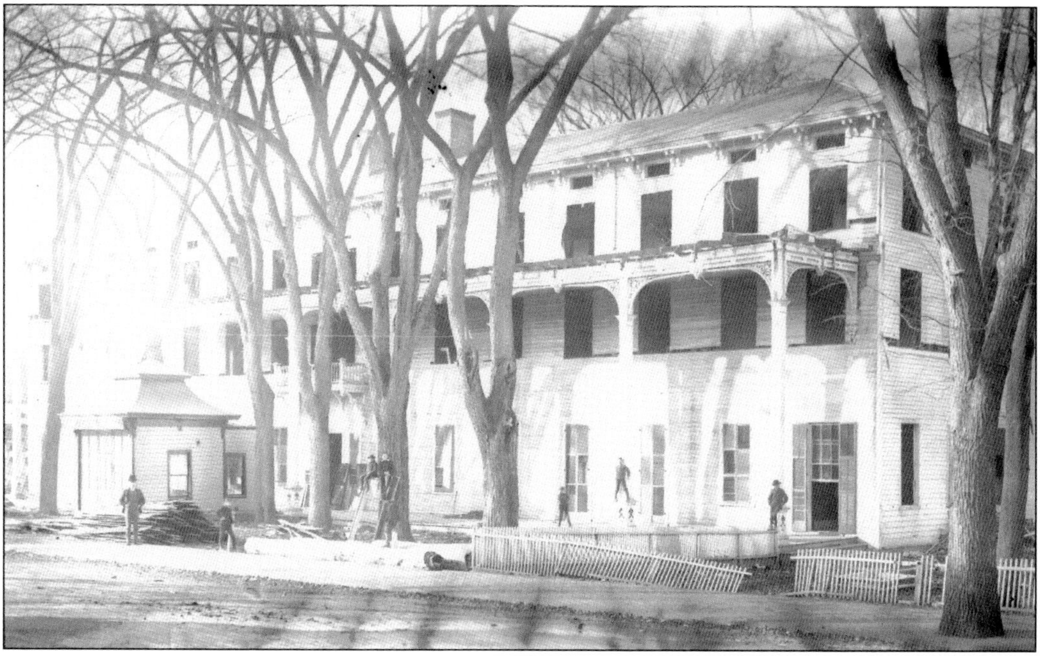

The Sans Souci was used as a boarding school before returning to its roots as a hotel in the 1870s. The hotel was too big to sustain itself, however, and the once proud landmark was finally torn down in 1887. (Saratoga County Historical Society at Brookside Museum.)

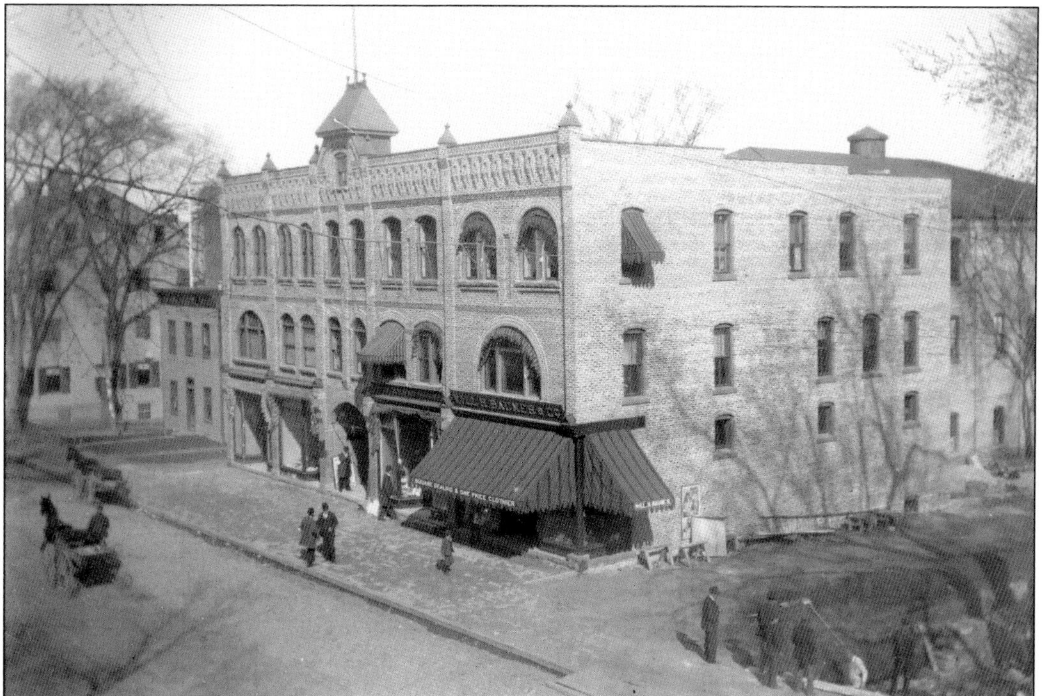

After the Sans Souci Hotel was demolished, an opera house was constructed in its place. The building on the left was known as the Schaffer Building. Both were destroyed by fire in the spring of 1900. The Medbery Hotel is on the far left. (Chris Morley collection.)

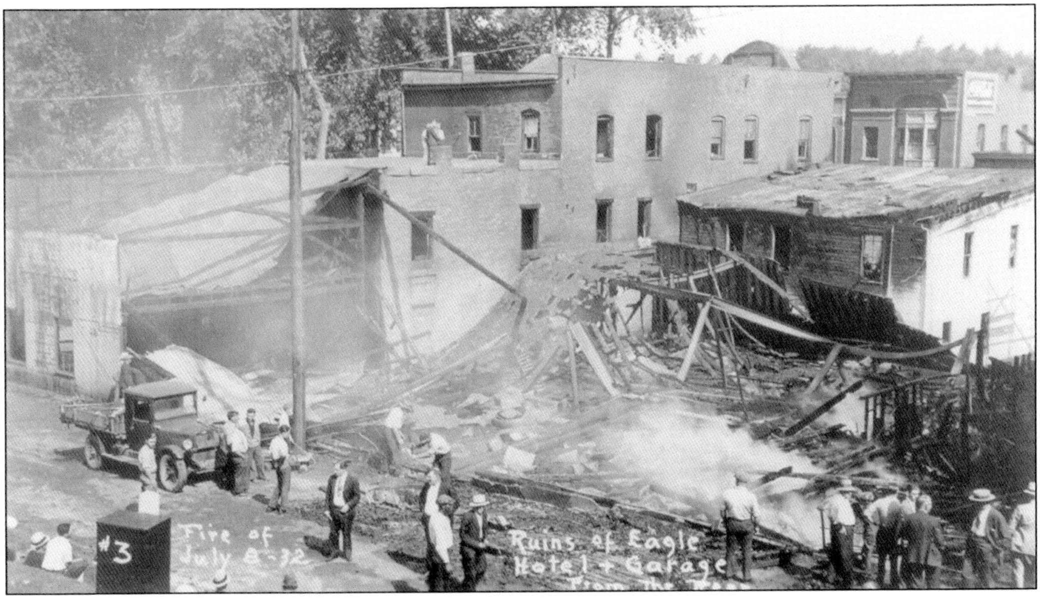

The Eagle Hotel advertised furnace heating, electric lights, bells, telephone connections, and "special rates to commercial men and theatrical troupes." It was one of the longest-lived hotels in Ballston Spa, operating into the Great Depression. However, tragedy struck on July 8, 1932, when a destructive fire consumed the hotel and damaged several nearby buildings. It was never rebuilt. Today, the village post office occupies the site. (Both, Chris Morley collection.)

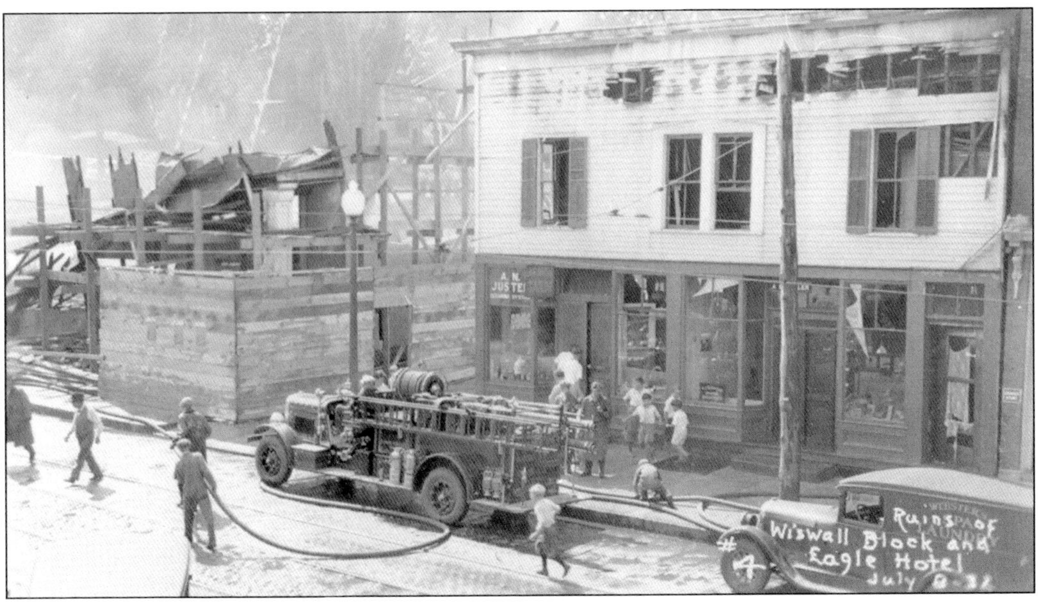

Two

The Kayaderosseras

The Kayaderosseras Creek is the largest stream whose whole course lies completely within the boundaries of Saratoga County. Commencing in the Kayaderosseras mountain range of Greenfield, the creek follows a winding course south through a wooded valley in the town of Milton. Upon reaching Ballston Spa, it heads east, emptying into Saratoga Lake. Fish Creek then takes the waters to the Hudson River.

Prior to the arrival of European colonists, the valley had been a favorite hunting ground and summer retreat for the tribes of the Iroquois Six Nations, primarily the Mohawks, who occupied the northeastern corner of New York State. It is said that the saline waters of the Kayaderosseras Valley attracted wild animals in such numbers that several of the tribes, including the Oneidas and the Onondagas, would make the long journey each summer to hunt and fish.

Kayaderosseras Creek was ideally suited for harnessing waterpower. The waters were more robust prior to 1850 than they are today, and several areas had significant drops in elevation, as well as many twists and turns, that provided locations for constructing dams and flumes. In fact, at the height of mill activity in the late 1800s, the creek resembled a series of lakes rather than a river, since huge bodies of water were formed behind the dams of the mills.

Nearly all of the large factories in Milton were located on the banks of the Kayaderosseras Creek prior to 1900. These included a large tannery, the famous hard-edge tool works of Isaiah Blood, and the paper mill empire of George West. The output of these industries prompted investors to construct an electric trolley railroad to serve them. The 12-mile line closely followed the Kayaderosseras, from the Delaware and Hudson interchange in Ballston Spa through Milton. For over a century, the Kayaderosseras was the hub of industrial activity.

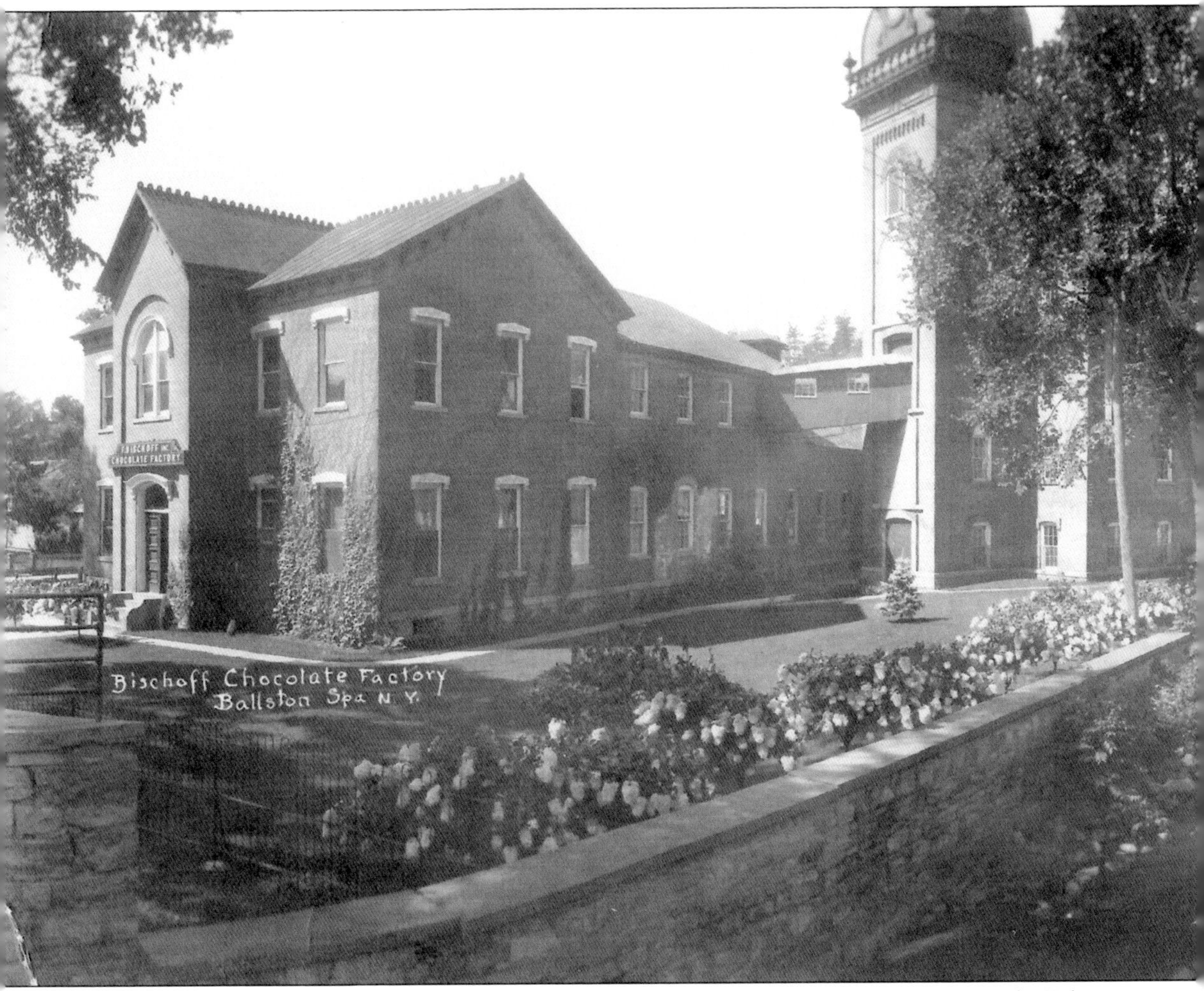

This panoramic photograph is perhaps the most iconic view of Kayaderosseras Creek. Taken in the 1920s, it shows the Bischoff Chocolate Factory on the left and the Blue Mill Dam with its well-known waterfall on the right, spanned by the trolley bridge. Bischoff's Park is just out of view to the right. This scene would have been familiar to nearly all county residents, as it was

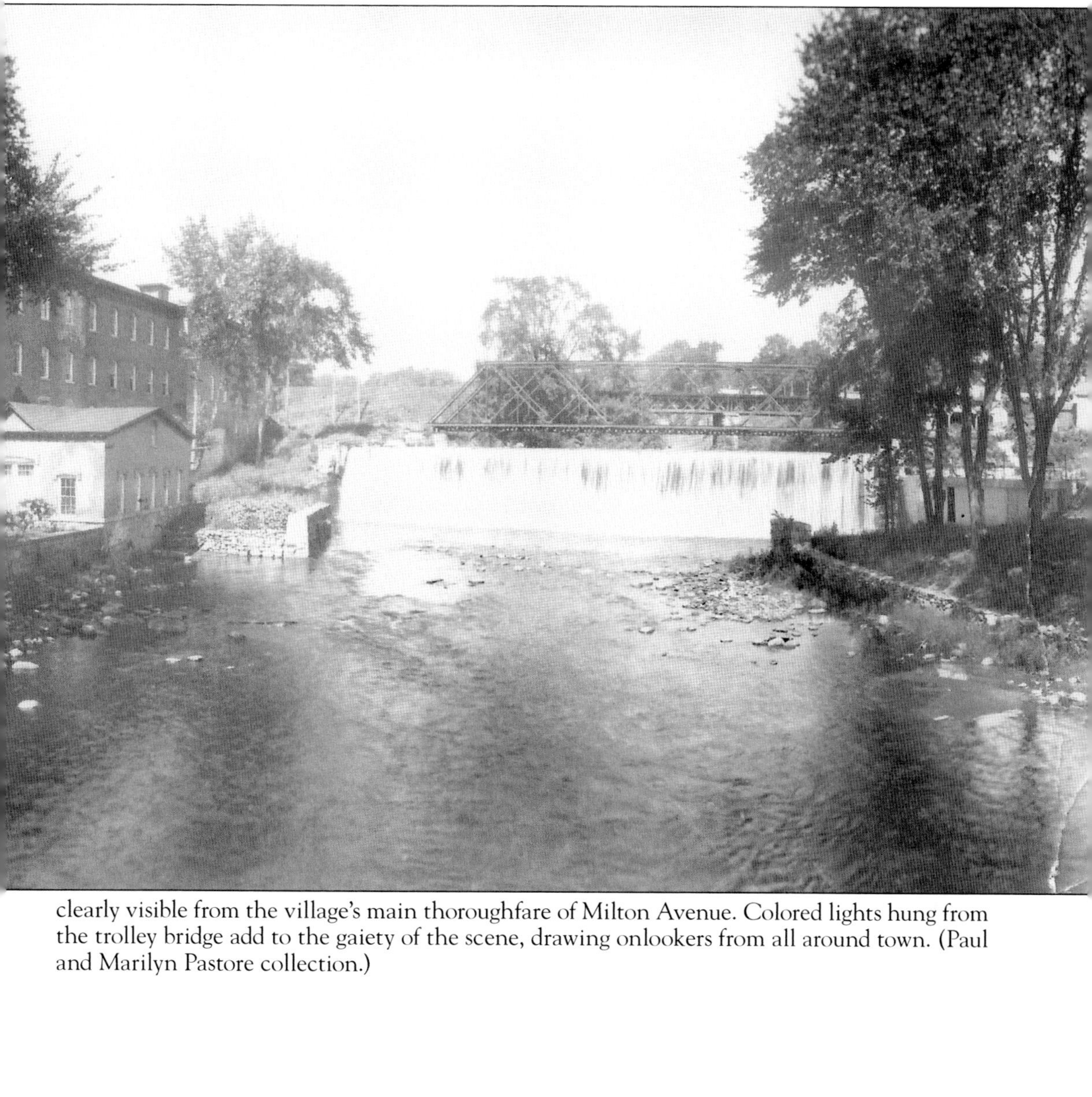

clearly visible from the village's main thoroughfare of Milton Avenue. Colored lights hung from the trolley bridge add to the gaiety of the scene, drawing onlookers from all around town. (Paul and Marilyn Pastore collection.)

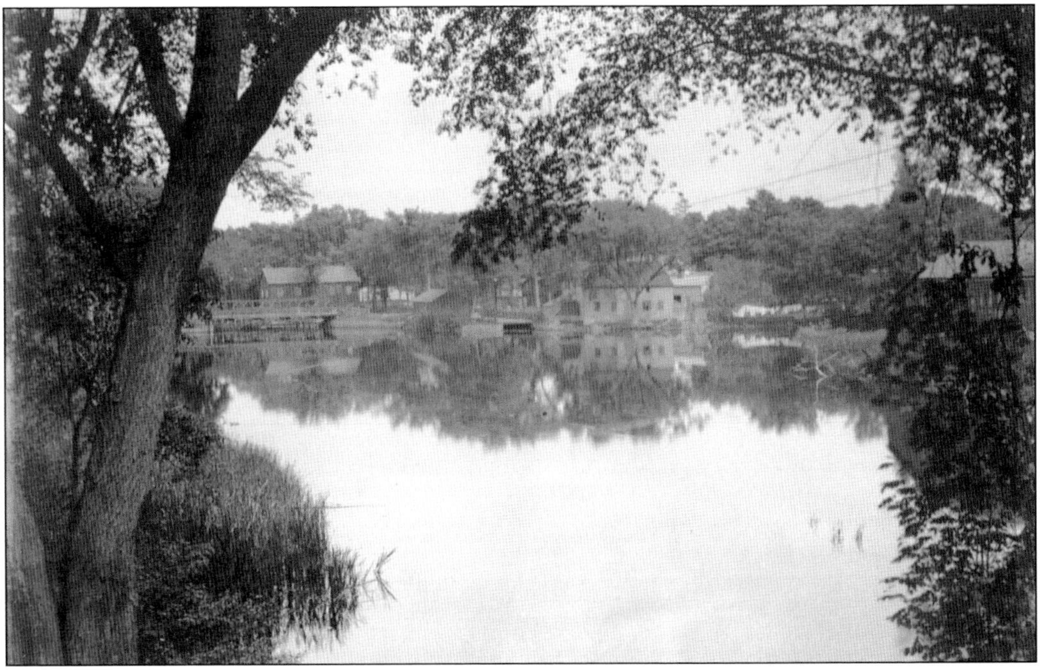

Island Mill was the southernmost mill to utilize the Kayaderosseras for power. Island Pond was formed by damming the creek near Mechanic Street. For almost a decade, it was called Hovey's Pond after Jonas Hovey, who owned nearly all the Ballston Spa mills until his death in 1873. (Saratoga County Historical Society at Brookside Museum.)

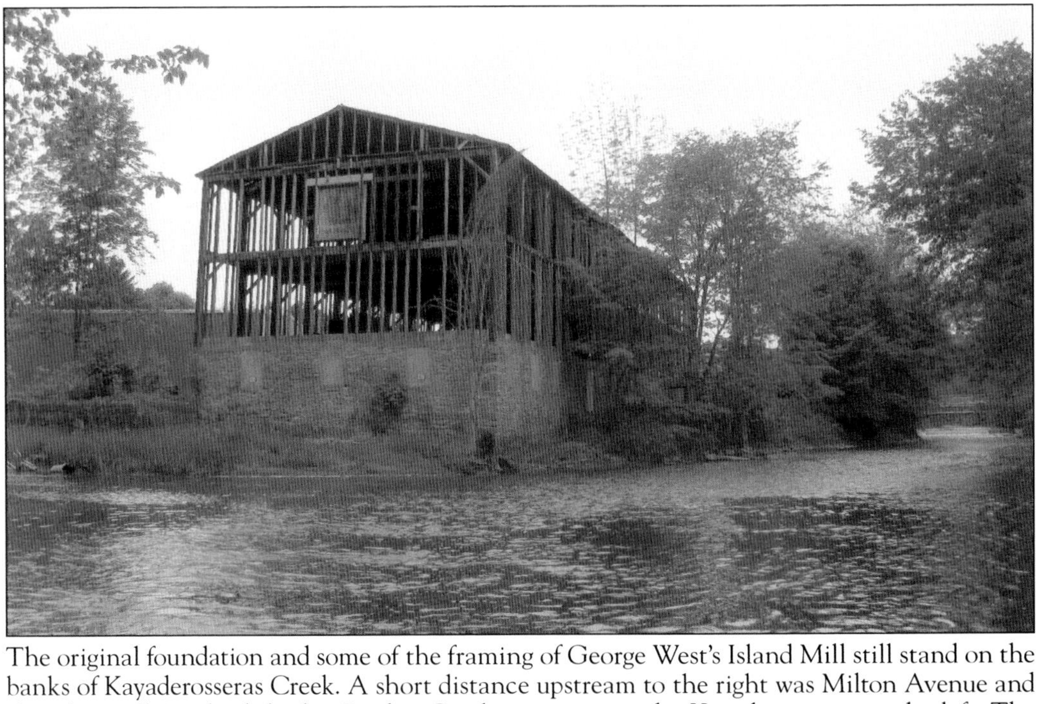

The original foundation and some of the framing of George West's Island Mill still stand on the banks of Kayaderosseras Creek. A short distance upstream to the right was Milton Avenue and the Blue Mill Pond, while the Gordon Creek empties into the Kayaderosseras on the left. The building has since been renovated. (Author's collection.)

For almost 10 years, the Blue Mill was occupied by the Glen Paper Collar Company, which manufactured millions of paper collars and cuffs. Proprietors Horace Medbery and Henry Mann Jr. took advantage of the new clothing fad and attained great success within a few short years. The Milton Avenue bridge is in the center, while the Delaware and Hudson embankment can be seen in the distance. (Paul and Marilyn Pastore collection.)

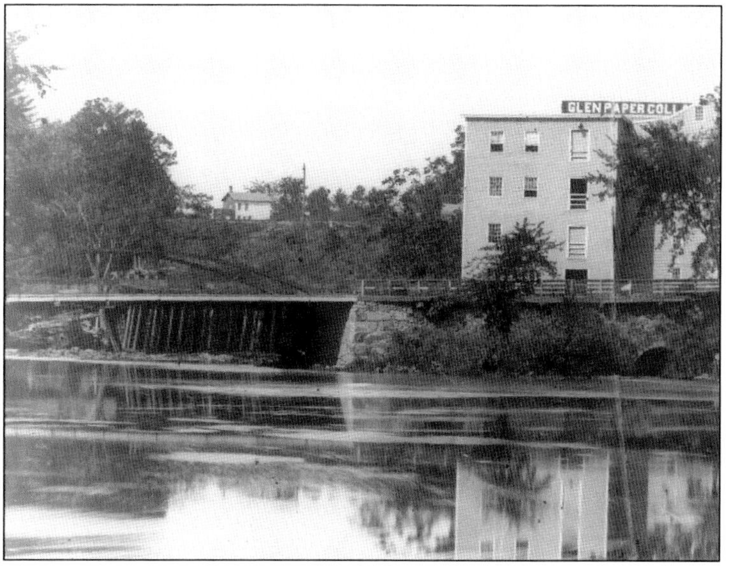

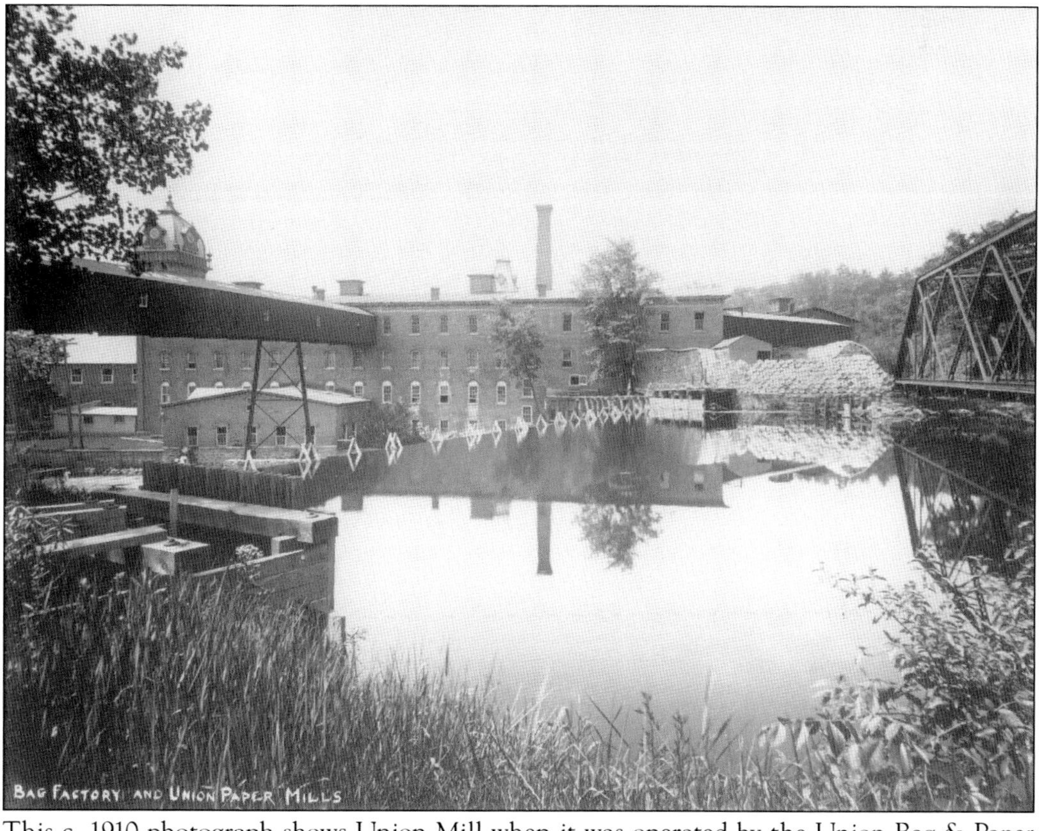

This c. 1910 photograph shows Union Mill when it was operated by the Union Bag & Paper Company. Ready to be processed, rolls of paper pulp are stacked next to the Ballston Terminal Railroad bridge. The walkway over the Blue Mill Dam led to the Blue Mill, which at the time was used as storage. (Chris Morley collection.)

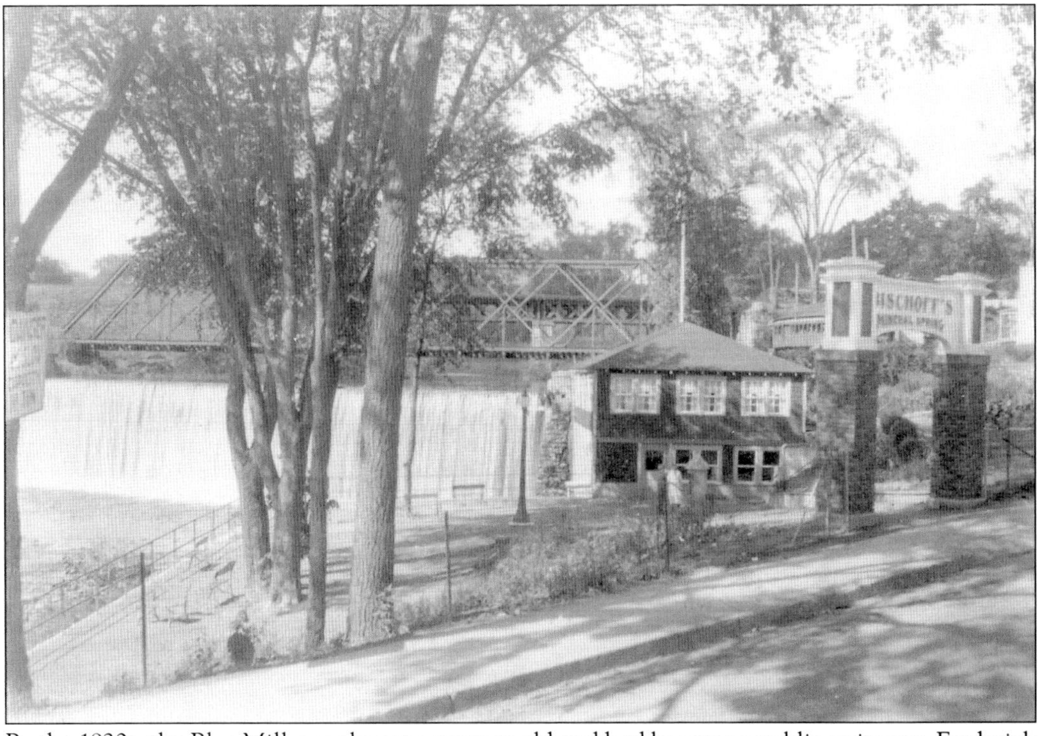

By the 1920s, the Blue Mill was almost a century old and had become a public nuisance. Frederick Bischoff, who owned the Bischoff Chocolate Factory next door, decided to tear it down to indulge his passion for nature. He commissioned the boring of a new mineral spring (the last in Ballston Spa), erected a tearoom, and planted beautiful gardens in what became known as Bischoff's Park. (Chris Morley collection.)

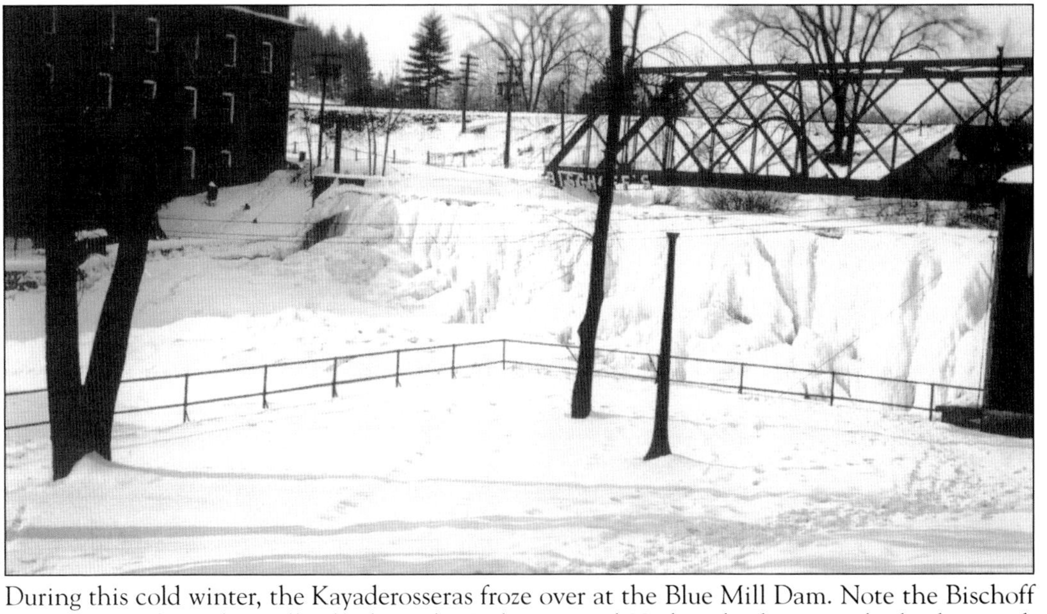

During this cold winter, the Kayaderosseras froze over at the Blue Mill Dam. Note the Bischoff sign hanging from the trolley bridge. The Delaware and Hudson bridge is in the background. (Saratoga County Historical Society at Brookside Museum.)

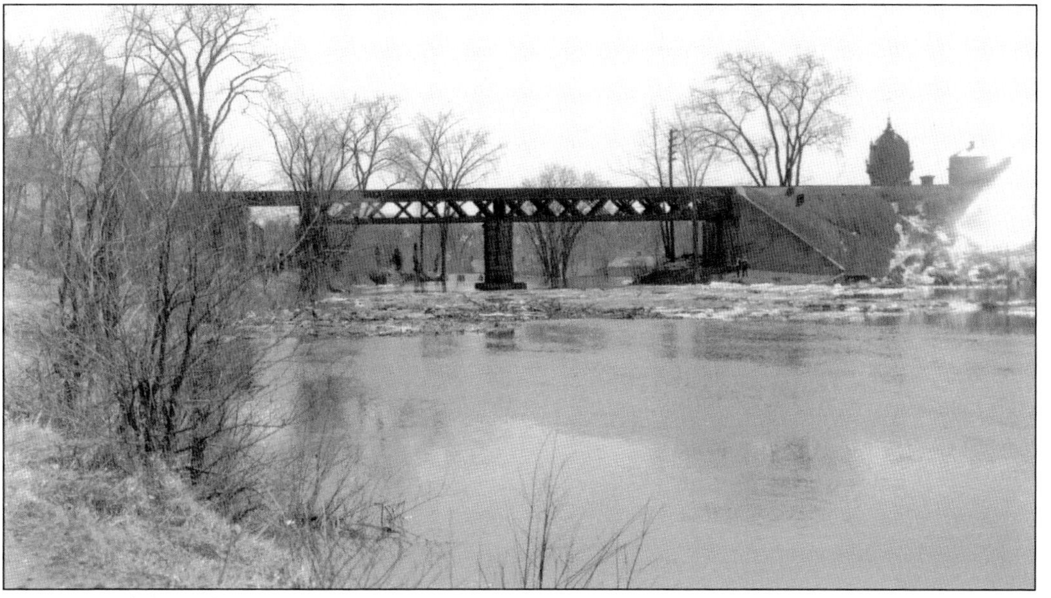

This view of the Delaware and Hudson Railway bridge over the Kayaderosseras looks downstream toward Milton Avenue. The clearance for the Ballston Terminal Railroad trolley can just be made out under the left side. The tower for the Union Mill peaks over the embankment on the right. (Saratoga County Historical Society at Brookside Museum.)

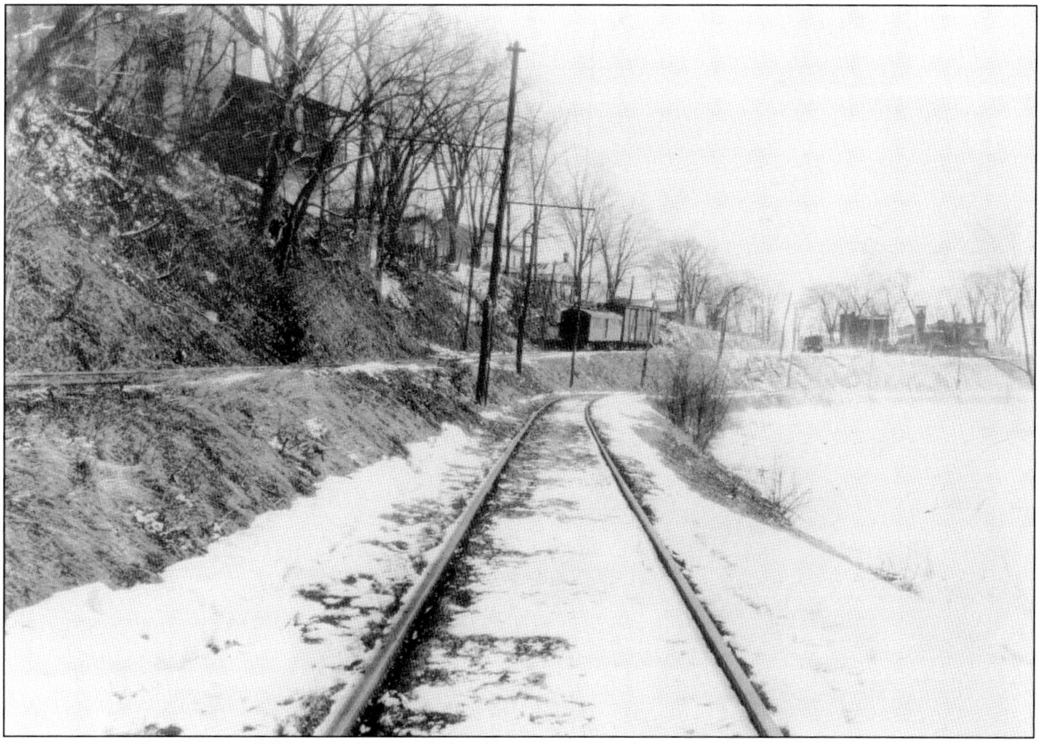

Here is another view of Blue Mill Pond, looking south. The *George West* trolley car is pushing a boxcar up the steep incline toward the interchange with the Delaware and Hudson Railway. (Chris Morley collection.)

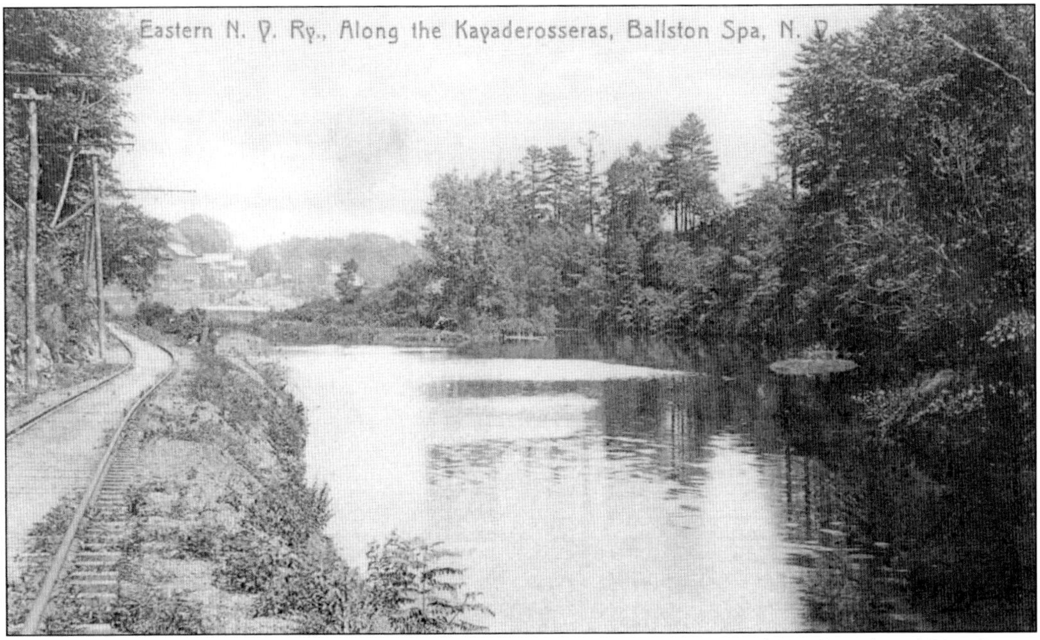

The Ballston Terminal Railroad (later known as the Eastern New York Railroad and Kaydeross Railroad) served the industries located along the Kayaderosseras and therefore was forced to follow the bank rather closely at some points. This led to sporadic flooding problems during the spring months, especially here in Bloodville, where the tracks were only a few feet from the water's edge. (Chris Morley collection.)

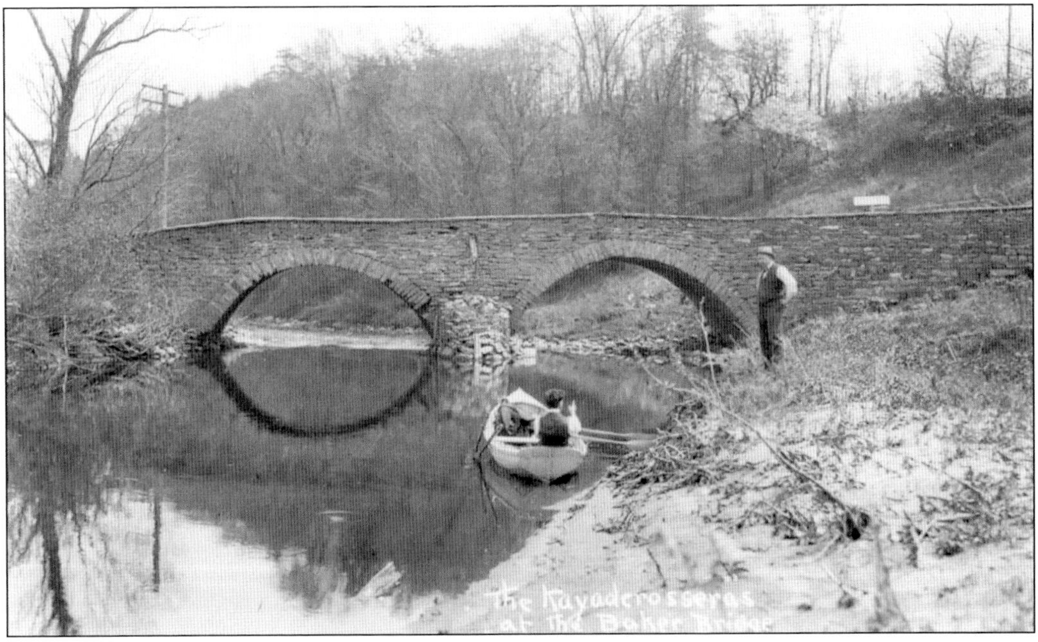

Benjamin Baker was a prominent farmer and member of the New York State Legislature. This stone bridge, named in his honor, crossed the Kayaderosseras near the site of the Eagle Wood and Iron Works, just north of Ballston Spa. Baker partnered with Benjamin Barber in the successful sawmill and foundry until Barber's death in 1877. (Chris Morley collection.)

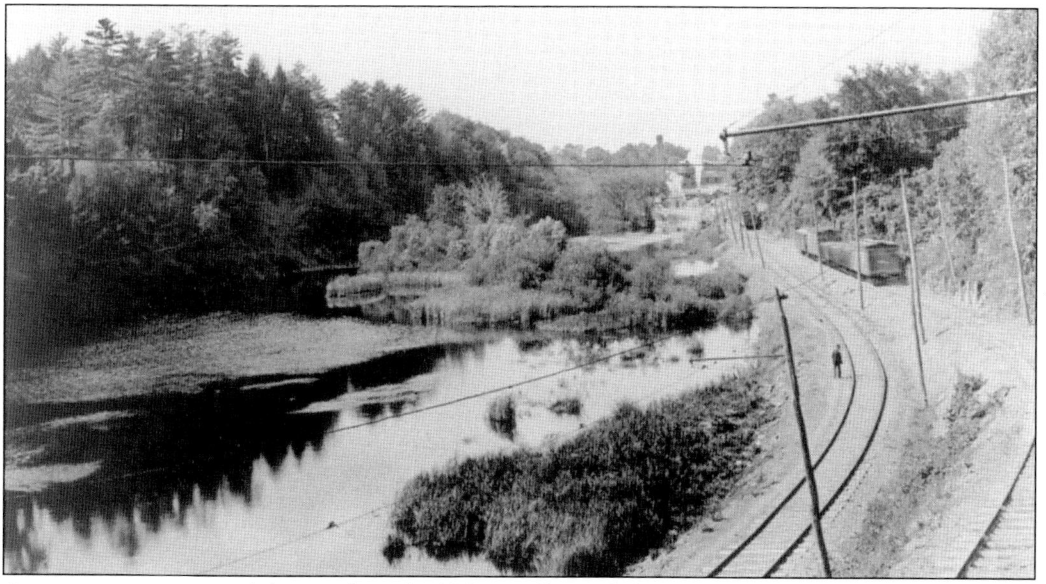

A summertime view of the north end of Blue Mill Pond shows the Ballston Terminal Railroad main line along the bank of the creek and the incline that led to the Delaware and Hudson interchange (far right). The smokestack and structure of the Glen Mill is in the background. (Saratoga County Historical Society at Brookside Museum.)

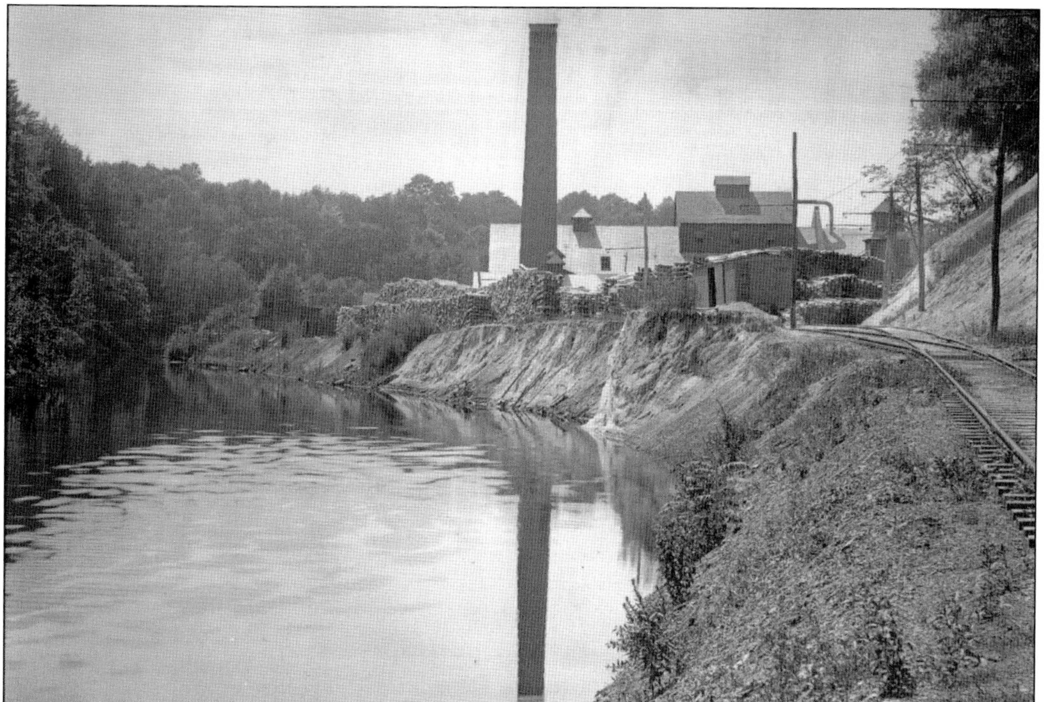

This view of the Glen Mill from the south shows the Ballston Terminal Railroad main line and spur track that served the mill directly, with an empty boxcar ready to be loaded. Also visible are the massive piles of lumber needed to sustain operations. (Saratoga County Historical Society at Brookside Museum.)

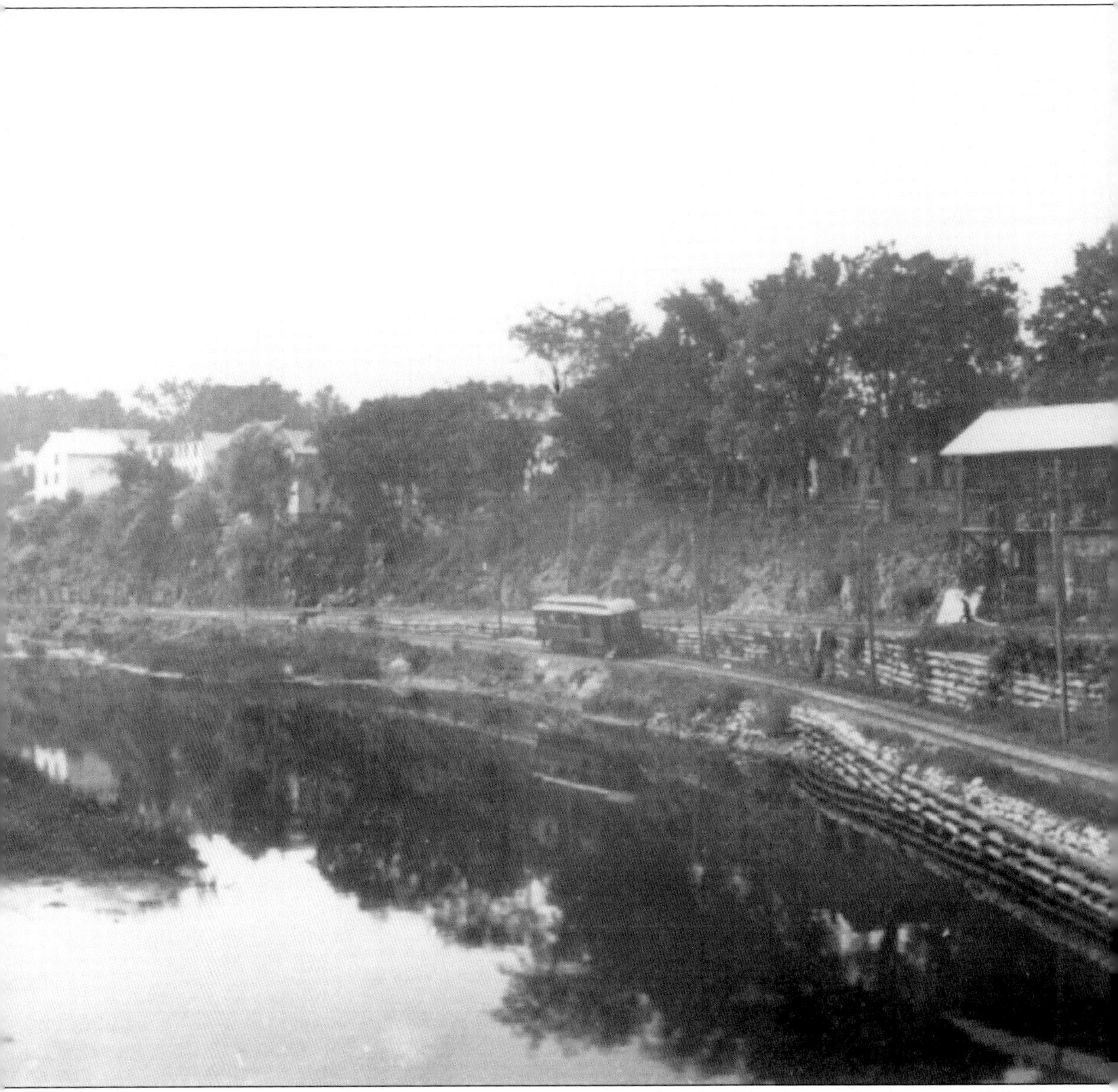

David Thompson's extensive finishing mill carried "all kinds of lumber, sash, doors, and blinds, with plans furnished and estimates given on all kinds of buildings." It was located at 9 Middlebrook Avenue and had customers throughout Saratoga County and northeastern New York during the

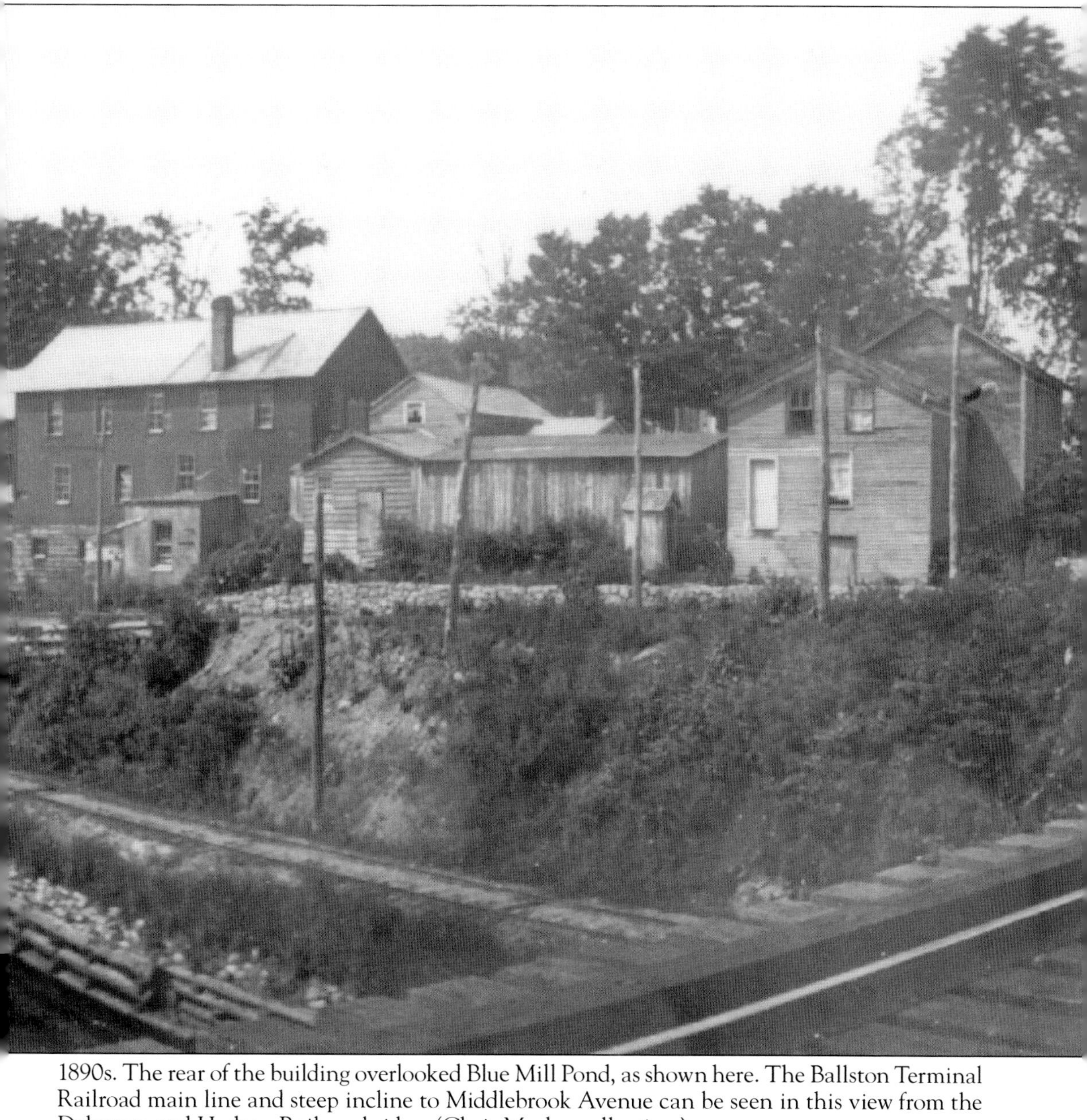

1890s. The rear of the building overlooked Blue Mill Pond, as shown here. The Ballston Terminal Railroad main line and steep incline to Middlebrook Avenue can be seen in this view from the Delaware and Hudson Railway bridge. (Chris Morley collection.)

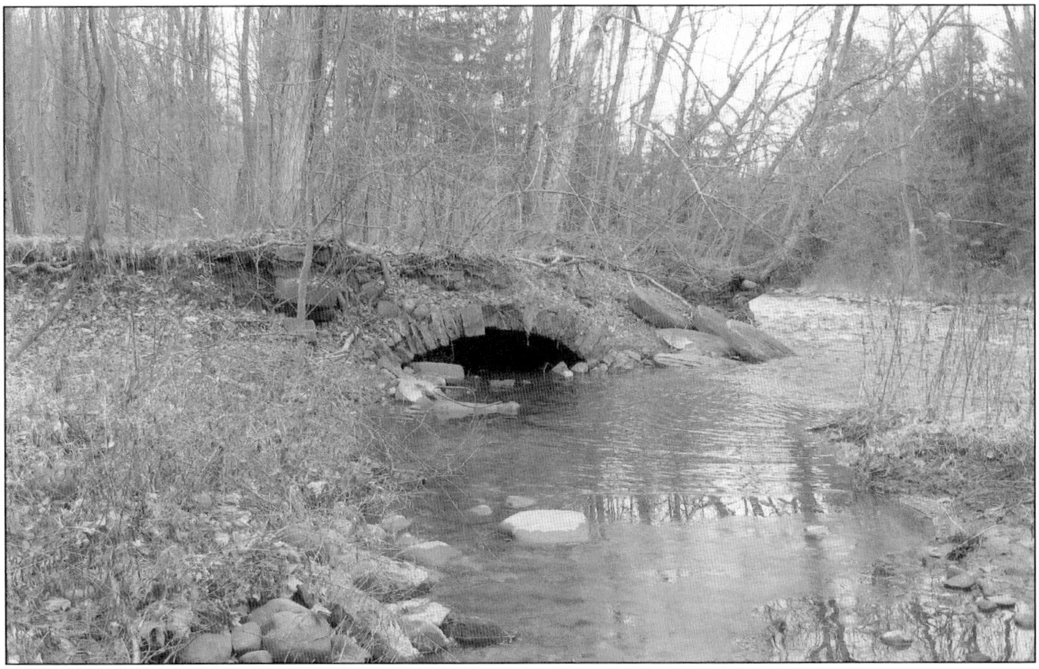

Today, Kayaderosseras Creek is somewhat smaller than it was in the early 1800s. Through farming, thousands of trees were removed from its watershed, which increased runoff and caused seasonal creek levels to drop. In several areas, however, indications of former industrial activity can still be seen, such as this bridge foundation and nearby sharpening stones at the site of the former Isaiah Blood Scythe Works in Bloodville. (Author's collection.)

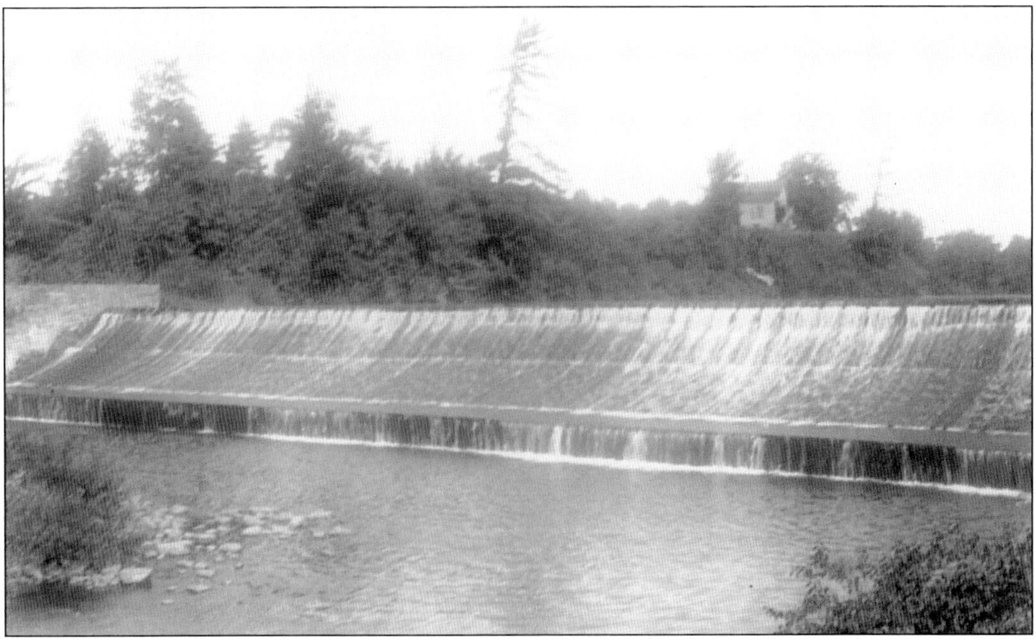

It may seem hard to believe, but dams like this one at the National Mill once existed at several locations. Remnants of the stone wall at far left still remain along the creek bed near Factory Village. (Paul Pastore collection.)

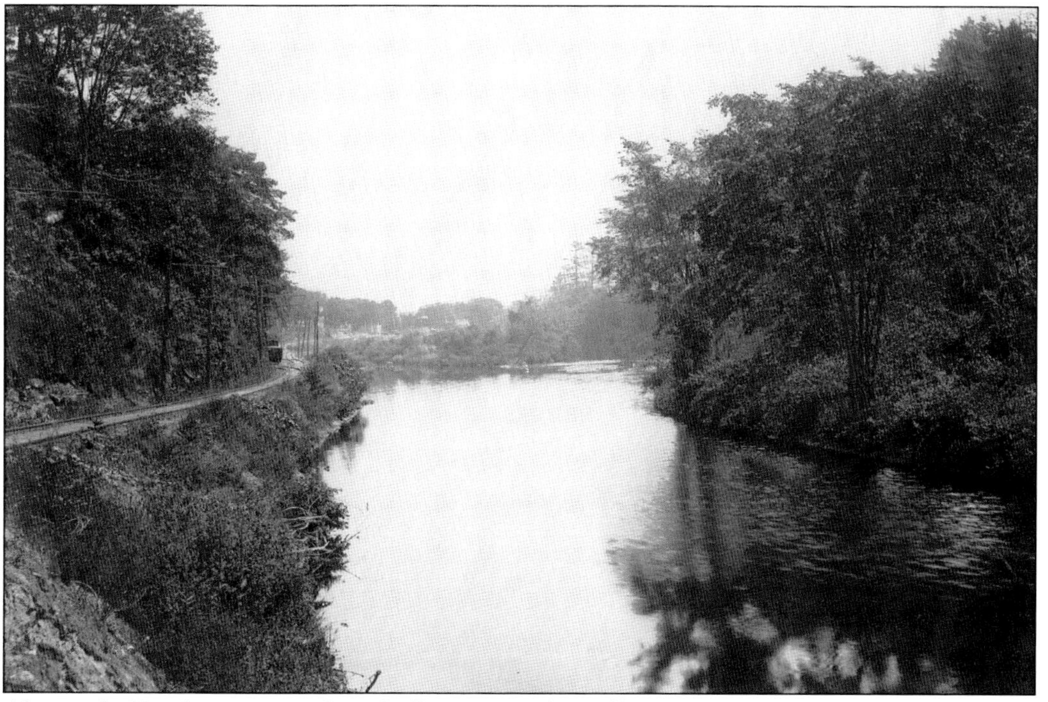

About a half mile upstream from Ballston Spa, the Ballston Terminal Railroad continued to closely follow the bank of the Kayaderosseras. It ascended to street level in Factory Village, near the powerhouse and carbarn. (Saratoga County Historical Society at Brookside Museum.)

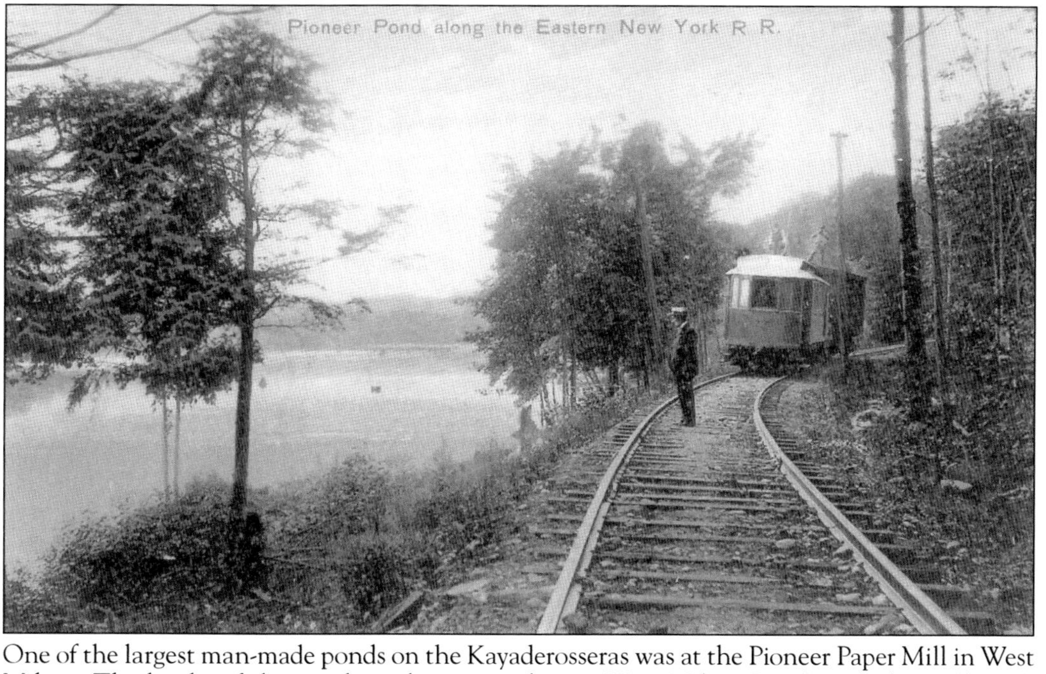

One of the largest man-made ponds on the Kayaderosseras was at the Pioneer Paper Mill in West Milton. The banks of the pond can be seen today on West Milton Road, near the Mill Rock restaurant. The trolley line (then known as the Eastern New York Railroad) operated nearby. (Pat Streiffert collection.)

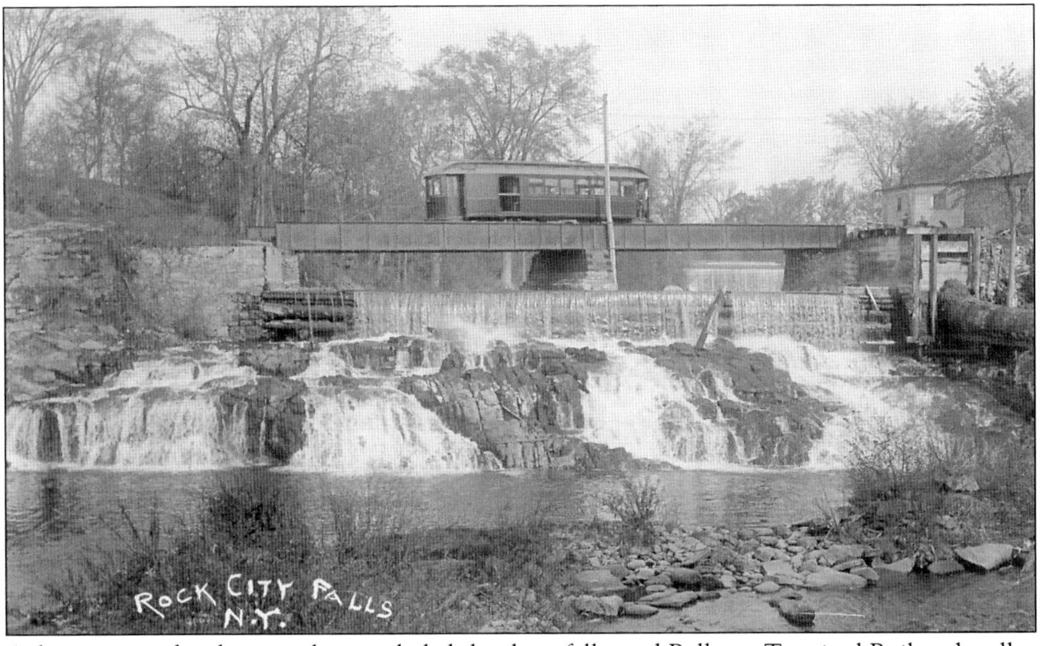

A favorite spot for photographers included the dam, falls, and Ballston Terminal Railroad trolley bridge at the Kilmer Stone Paper Mill. Rock City Falls derived its name from "the Big Falls" shown here, as well as the rock quarry just out of view to the left. (Paul and Marilyn Pastore collection.)

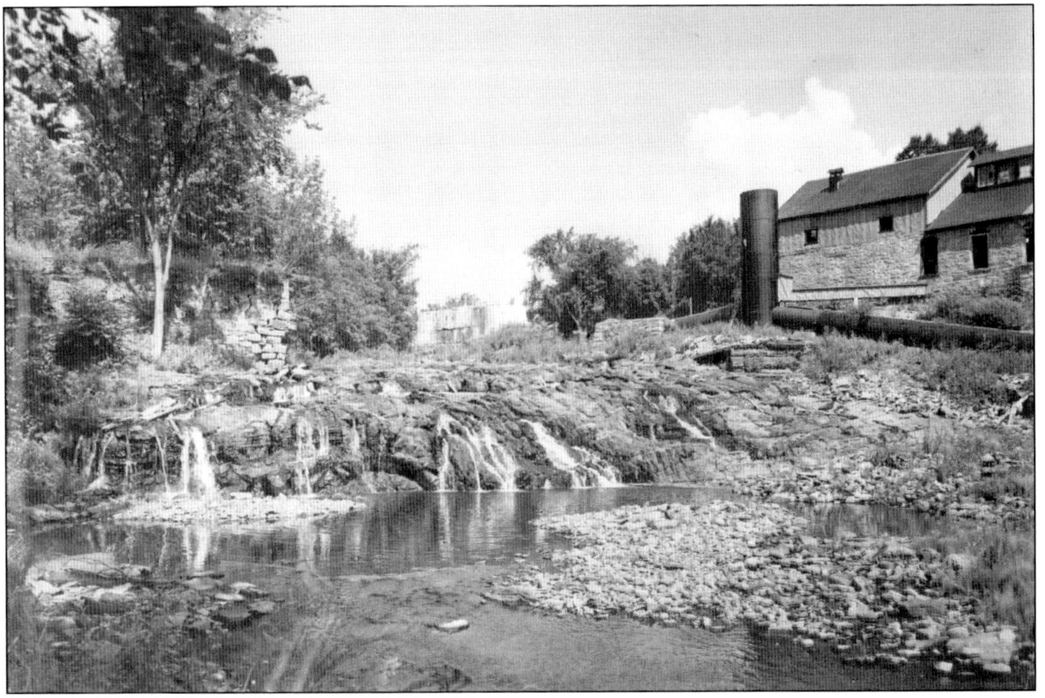

The water-powered mills sometimes had to shut down during periods of low water levels. Here, at the Cottrell Paper Mill (formerly Kilmer's Mill) in Rock City Falls, the water has slowed to a trickle. This photograph was taken after the Ballston Terminal Railroad trolley bridge was removed in 1929. (Saratoga County Historian.)

Three

BALLSTON SPA

Despite the wealth and activity of several settlements throughout Milton in years past, the only incorporated village in town is Ballston Spa. It first rose to fame as a tourist attraction on the strength of its rare mineral springs in the early 1800s. Saratoga County's first newspaper was published nearby on Middle Line Road in 1798. At first, it was called the *Saratoga Register* or *Farmers' Journal* but was later changed to the *Ballston Journal.*

As the county seat, the village could also count on the dependable incomes of county attorneys, the most prominent of whom made their homes in Ballston Spa. The educational system was unusually robust in relation to the population, as several boarding schools operated within town limits. A bank was formed as early as 1838, which was also unusual for the time. It was only the second bank to be established within Saratoga County. Front Street was a hub of activity, home to storekeepers and tradesmen, such as bookstores, cabinetmakers, tailors, silversmiths, and dry goods dealers.

Ballston Spa's industrial endeavors expanded rapidly during the 1800s. The first large industry consisted of four cotton mills within the village that employed hundreds during the 1840s and 1850s, many of them women and girls. Samuel Haight relocated his tannery to the old oilcloth factory on Bath Street. George West purchased a large tract of property at the north end of the village and opened two paper mills, a bag factory, and a pulp mill. The Glen Paper Collar Company shipped millions of paper collars a year. The Ballston Axe & Scythe Works manufactured thousands of scythes, axes, and other hard-edge tools of all types. A wide variety of other industrial enterprises began operation during the 19th and 20th centuries, including a soap factory, chocolate factory, refrigerated storage company, three carriage makers, and several textile mills. Meanwhile, farmers from nearby towns brought their goods to Ballston Spa for storage or shipment elsewhere, making it the area's primary marketplace and commercial center.

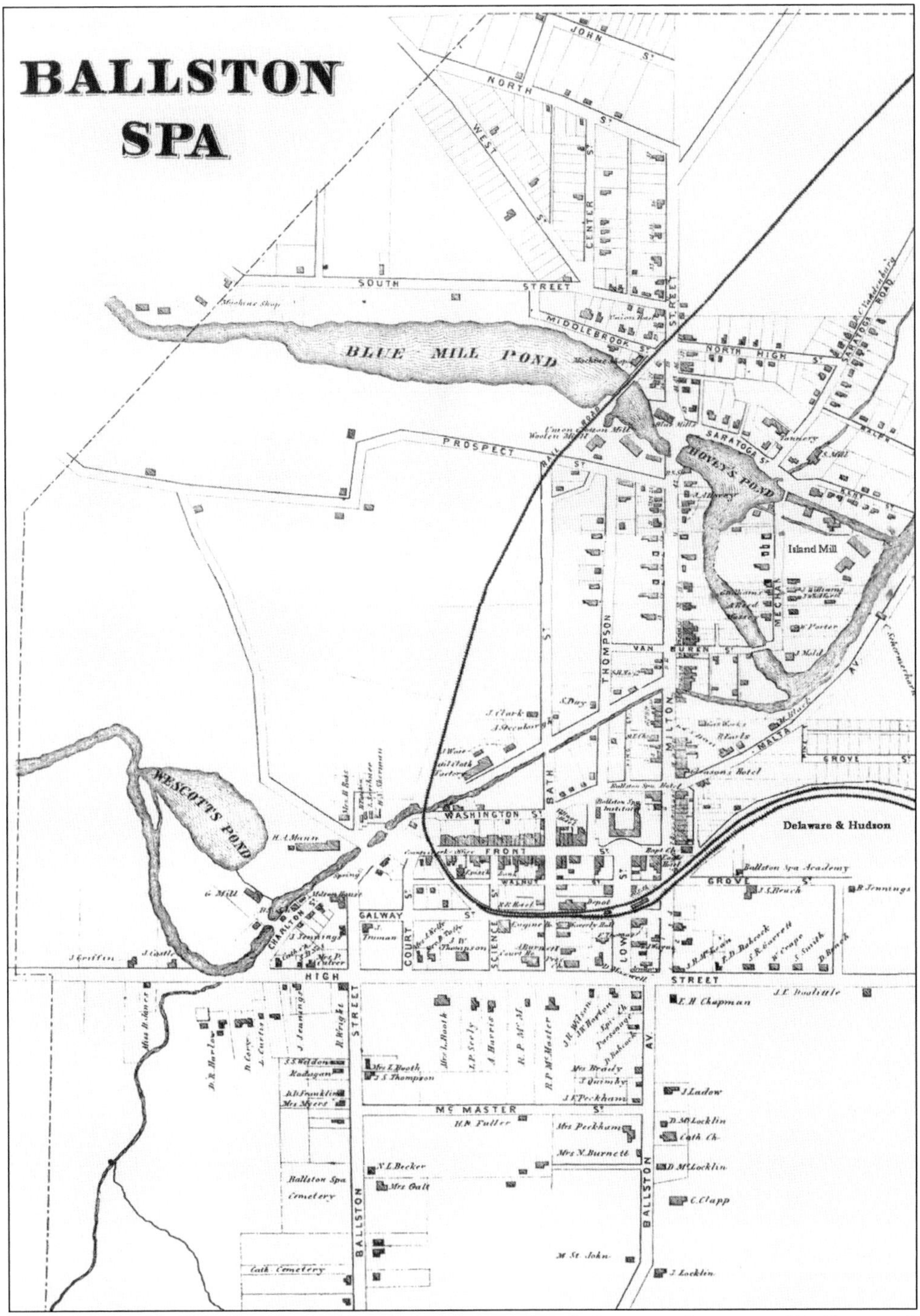

The village of Ballston Spa borders two towns. South of High Street is the town of Ballston, while north of that boundary is the town of Milton, where the majority of the population and industry is located. This 1866 Beer's map highlights landmarks that no longer exist: the S-shaped curve of the Delaware and Hudson (since rerouted), the Blue Mill and Hovey Ponds, and a variety of mills and industrial sites. (Author's collection.)

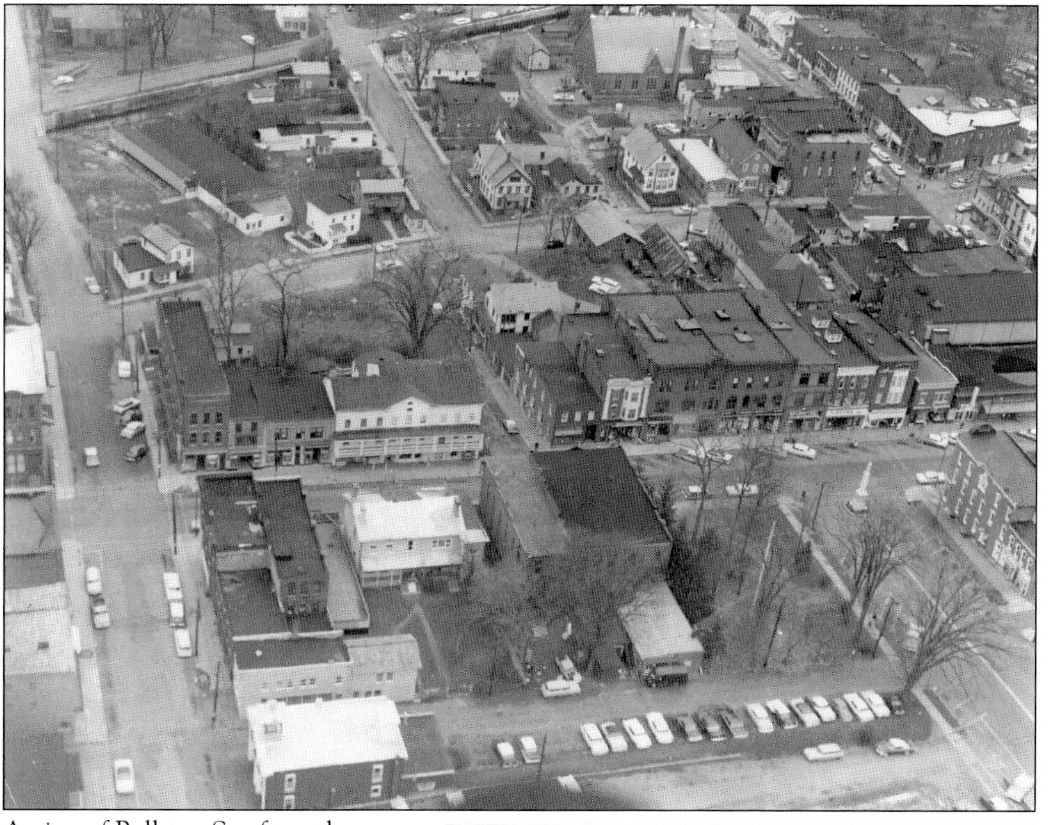

A view of Ballston Spa from the air shows Front Street (center), flanked by Bath Street (left) and Low Street (right). Above Front Street is Washington Street, bisected by Spring and Fenwick Streets. The small stream following Hamilton Street at the top is Gordon Creek. Since some of the major landmarks like the Sans Souci and Eagle Hotels were taken down or burned, downtown has changed little over the past century. (Chris Morley collection.)

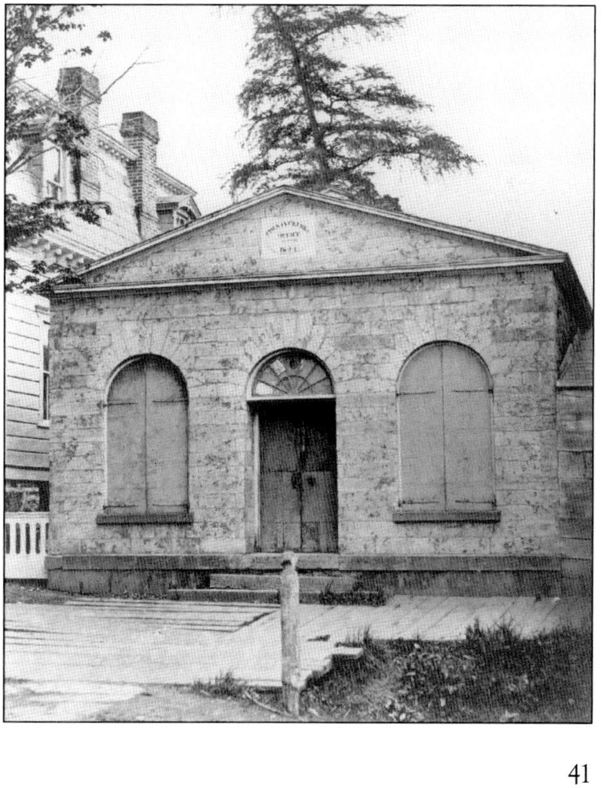

County records were kept in the homes of various town clerks until 1824, when this stone building was erected on Front Street at a cost of $10,000. It proved to be too small, however, and in 1866 a new one was built on High Street. (Saratoga County Historian.)

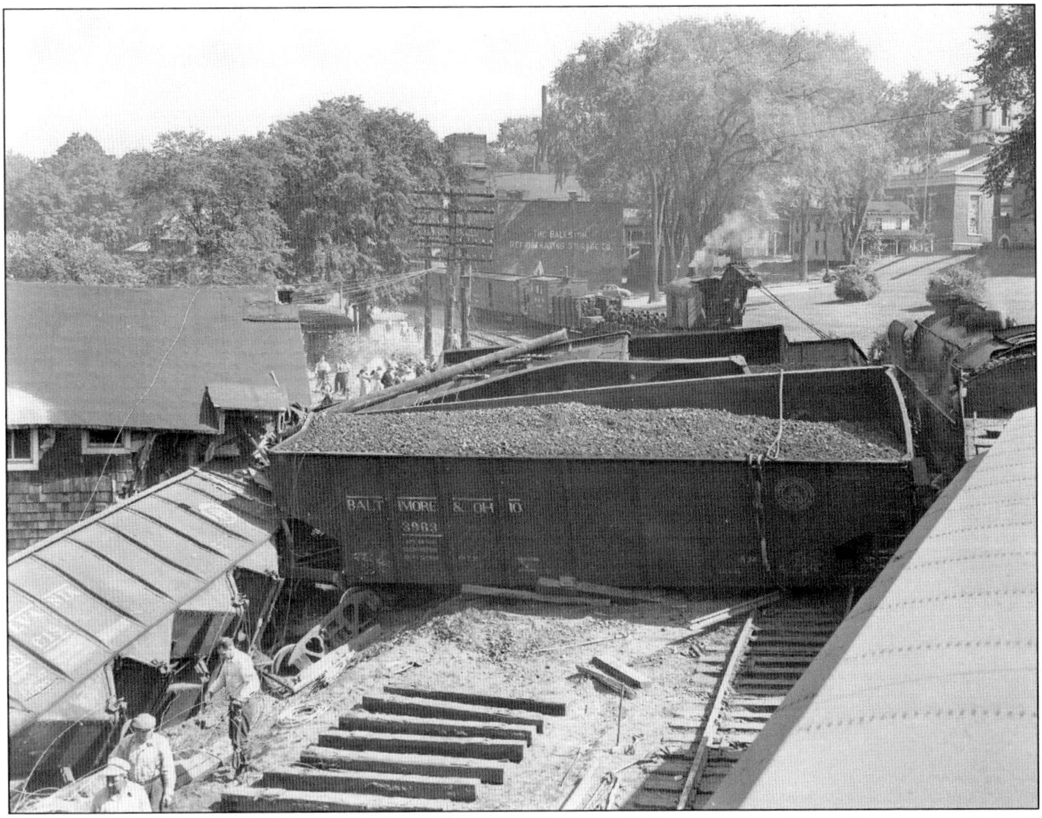

Dealing with long trains running through the village and the occasional accident was a fact of life in Ballston Spa. This view of a Delaware and Hudson Railway derailment shows the Ballston Refrigerating Storage Company building in the background. When commercial refrigeration was no longer needed, the business slowly shut down. Tufflite Plastics then occupied the large building from 1950 to 1997. (Dorothy Kelliher collection.)

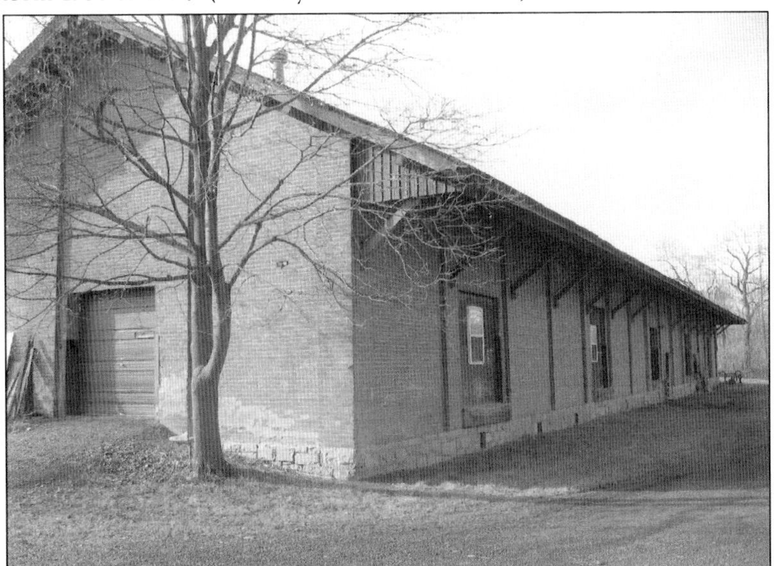

This freight house off Grove Street continued to serve the Delaware and Hudson Railway on a spur track well into the mid-1900s, even after the main line through the village was relocated. The last train station was built on the Columbia Avenue Extension. Today, the railroads do not stop in Ballston Spa. (Author's collection.)

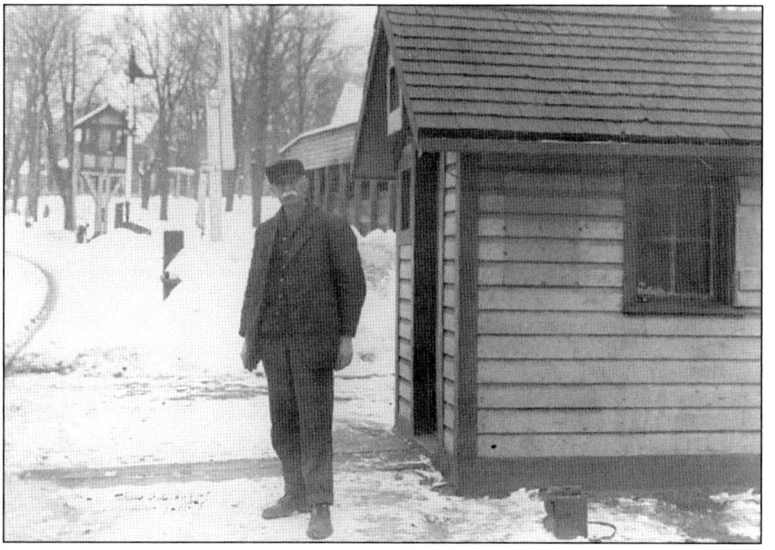

The Delaware and Hudson Railway made its way through Ballston Spa in an S-shaped curve that resulted in over a dozen street crossings. This flagman's shanty was located at the Low Street crossing. In the background is the C.W. Eede Coal Yard, established near the site of the present village library in 1894. (Chris Morley collection.)

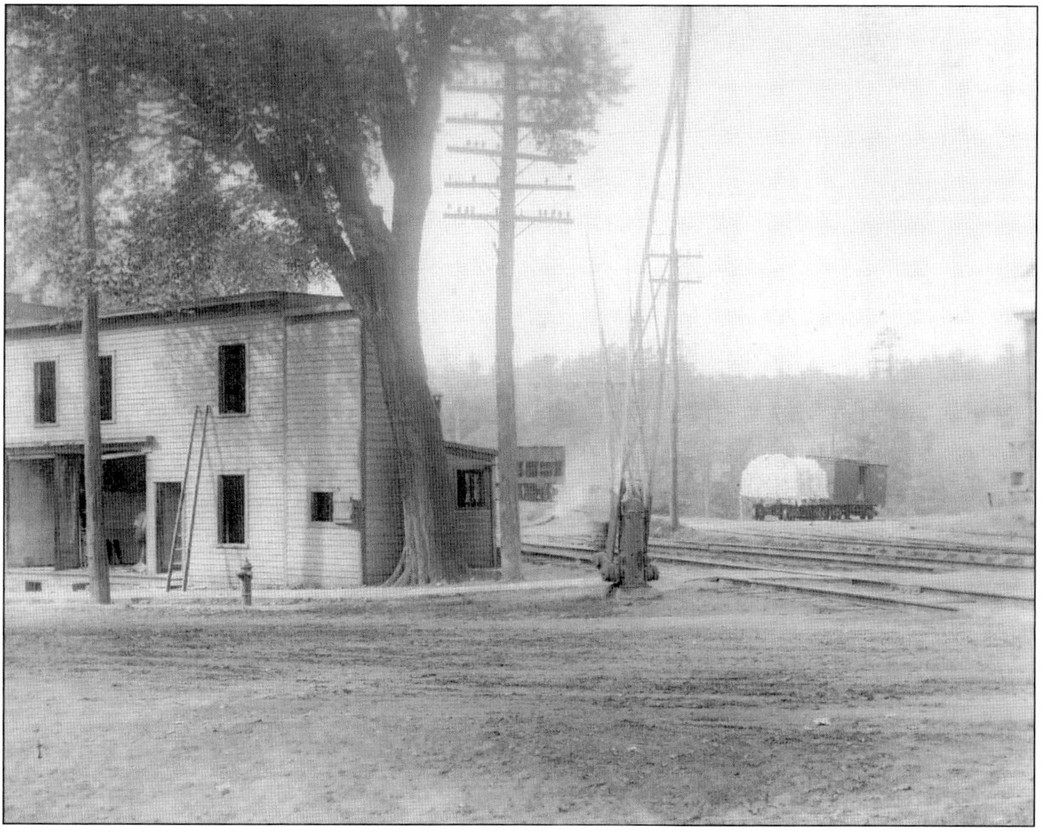

Here, on Middlebrook Avenue, the Delaware and Hudson Railway main line exited the village and began its run toward Saratoga Springs along present-day Route 50. The two cars on the right are at the top of the incline that led to the Ballston Terminal Railroad trolley tracks on the banks of Blue Mill Pond. (Chris Morley collection.)

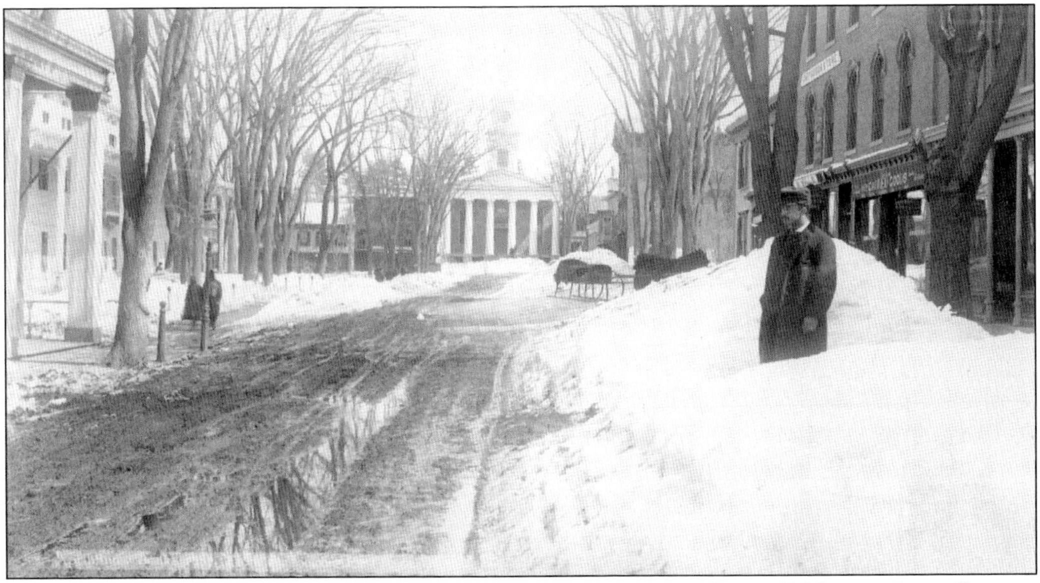

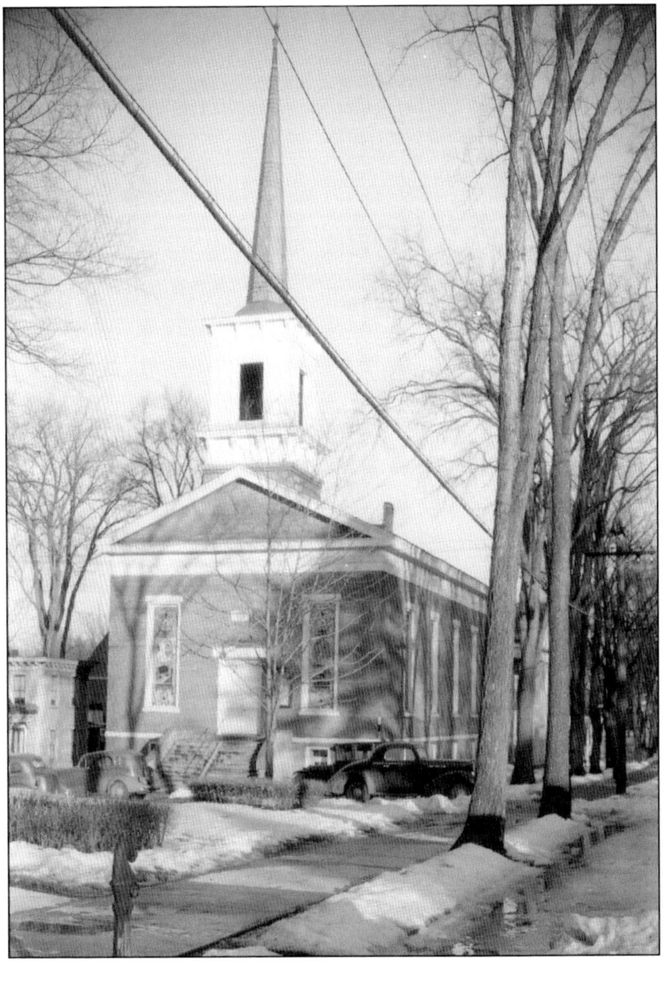

This c. 1880 view down Front Street shows the location of the Baptist church. The Sans Souci Hotel is just visible on the left. Unfortunately, the Delaware and Hudson main line was built a little too close to the church, causing it to sustain some damage. Therefore, the church was moved to a new location farther north on Milton Avenue in the 1890s. (Chris Morley collection.)

The First Presbyterian Church on the corner of High and Bath Streets is the oldest church building standing in the village today, dating back to 1835. Rev. Samuel Irenaeus Prime was installed as the first minister. (Library of Congress.)

The Methodist Episcopal Society first met at "the Academy" on Galway Street, later purchasing the building and moving it to the corner of West High and Charlton Streets. In 1845, a new property was acquired on Milton Avenue, where the church pictured here was built and used for almost 50 years before being torn down to make way for the present-day church. (Chris Morley collection.)

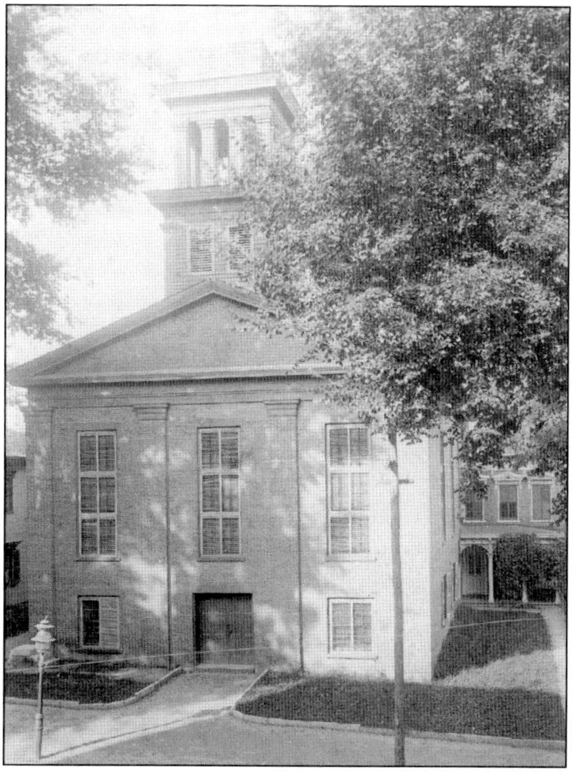

For many years, Abner Doubleday (1819–1893) was considered the creator of baseball after the Mills Commission named him as such in 1908. Although his baseball legacy has largely been disproved, he was a prominent Union general who fired the first return shot of the Civil War in defense of Fort Sumter, South Carolina. The house where his family once lived still stands on the corner of Washington and Fenwick Streets. (Saratoga County Historian.)

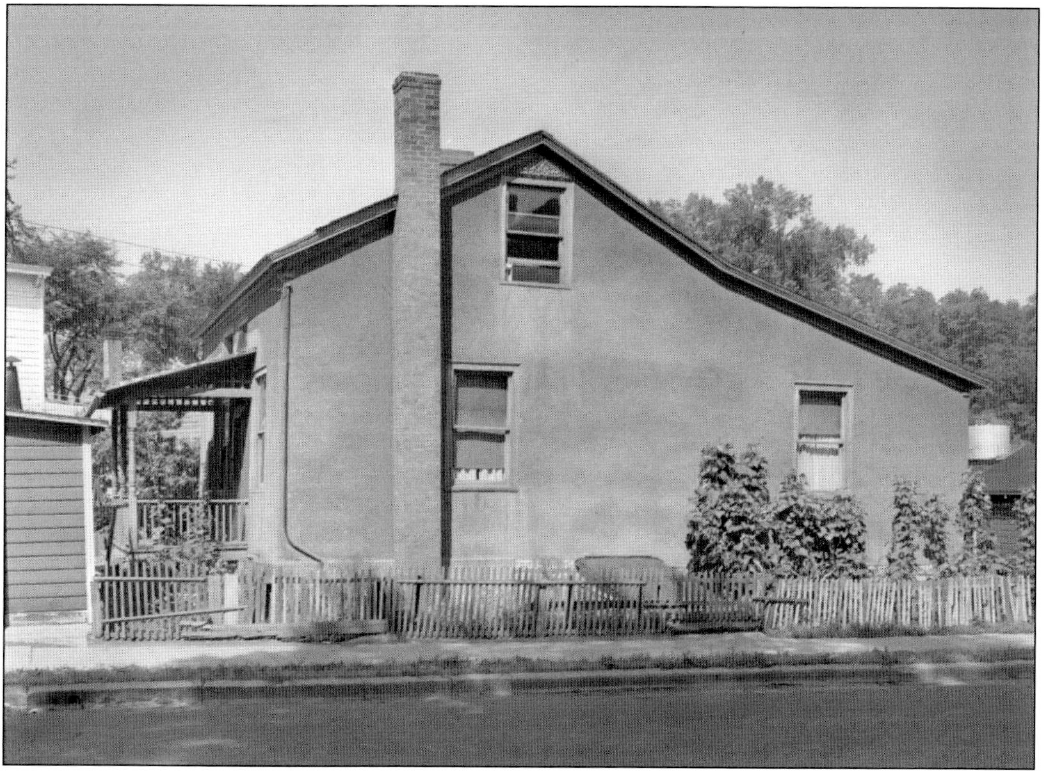

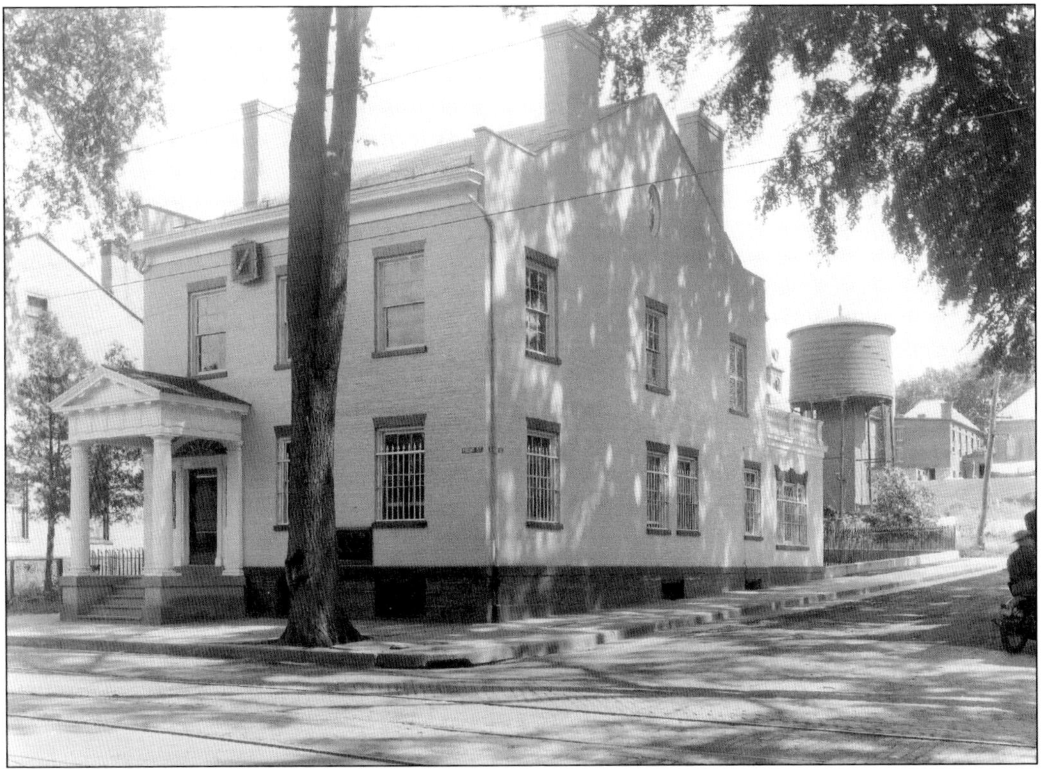

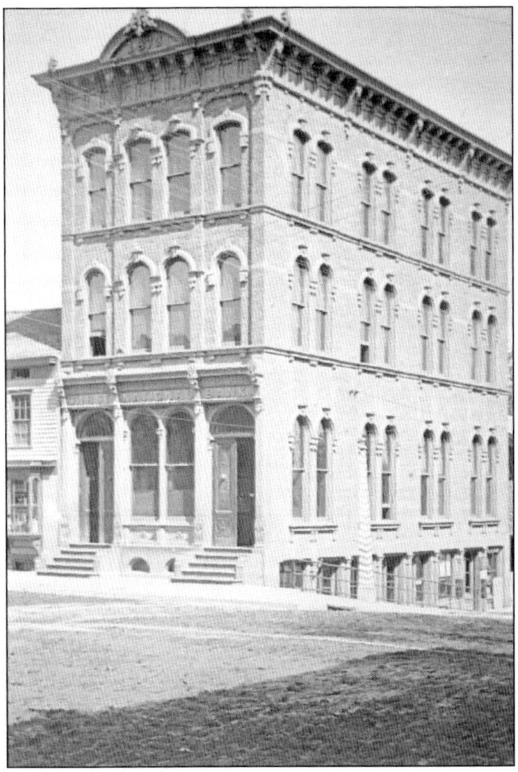

Established in 1838, Ballston Spa National Bank is the oldest continuously operating bank in Saratoga County. It had a prime location on the Front Street Business Block, near the Delaware and Hudson Railway main line (at the rear of the property). The home office pictured here has not changed much since it was built. The tracks are those of the Schenectady Railway. (Chris Morley collection.)

The First National Bank was established in 1865, but this Front Street building was not constructed until 1873. James McKinney Iron Works of Albany fabricated the front of the structure. Lawyers occupied the top floors, while the Town of Milton offices, a telephone operator, and a printer shared the lower level (right). (Chris Morley collection.)

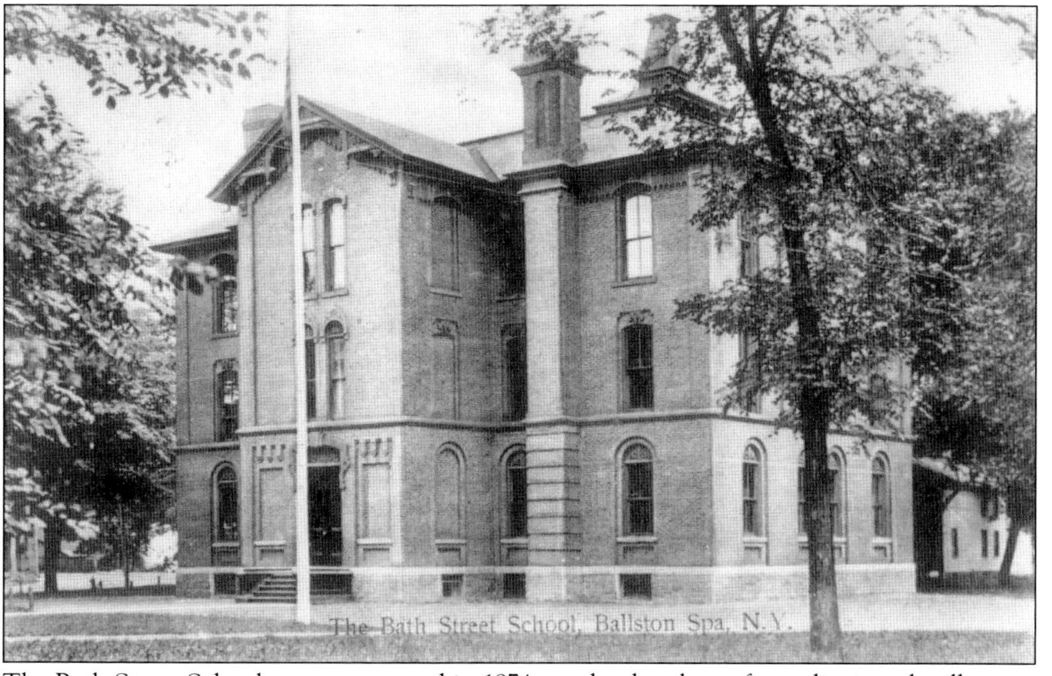

The Bath Street School was constructed in 1874 to take the place of two district schoolhouses. For about 25 years, it served all grades until the high school on Malta Avenue was built in 1900. It then served as a grammar school. (Chris Morley collection.)

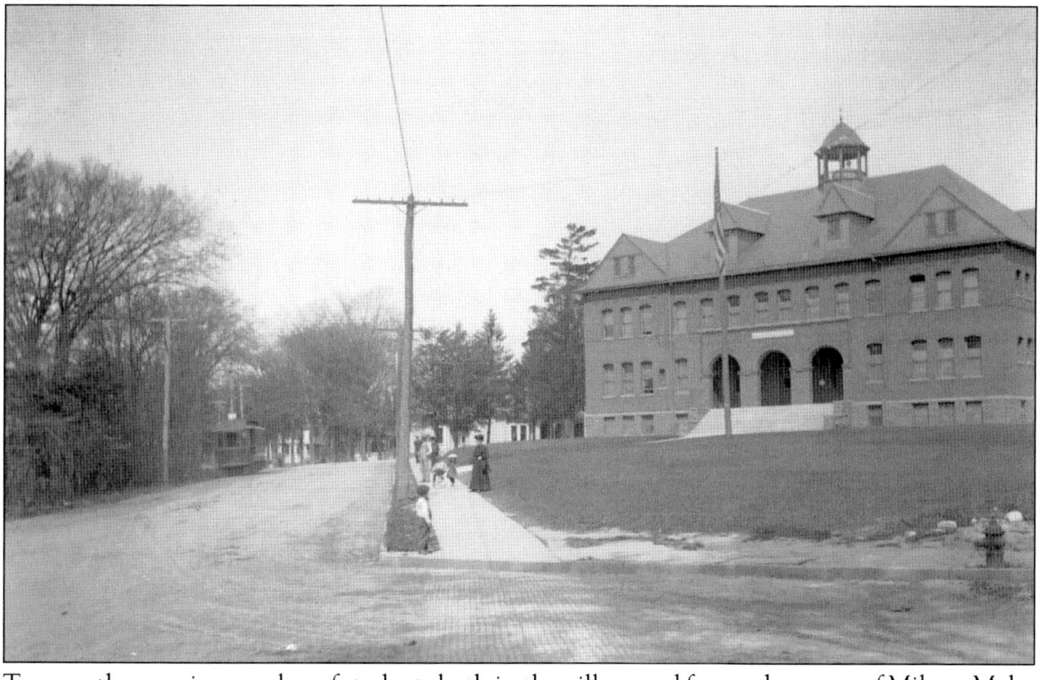

To serve the growing number of students both in the village and from other parts of Milton, Malta Avenue High School was built at a cost of about $36,000 in 1900. Children from as far away as Rock City Falls rode the Ballston Terminal Railroad trolley to the high school every day, as it was the only high school in Milton. (Saratoga County Historical Society at Brookside Museum.)

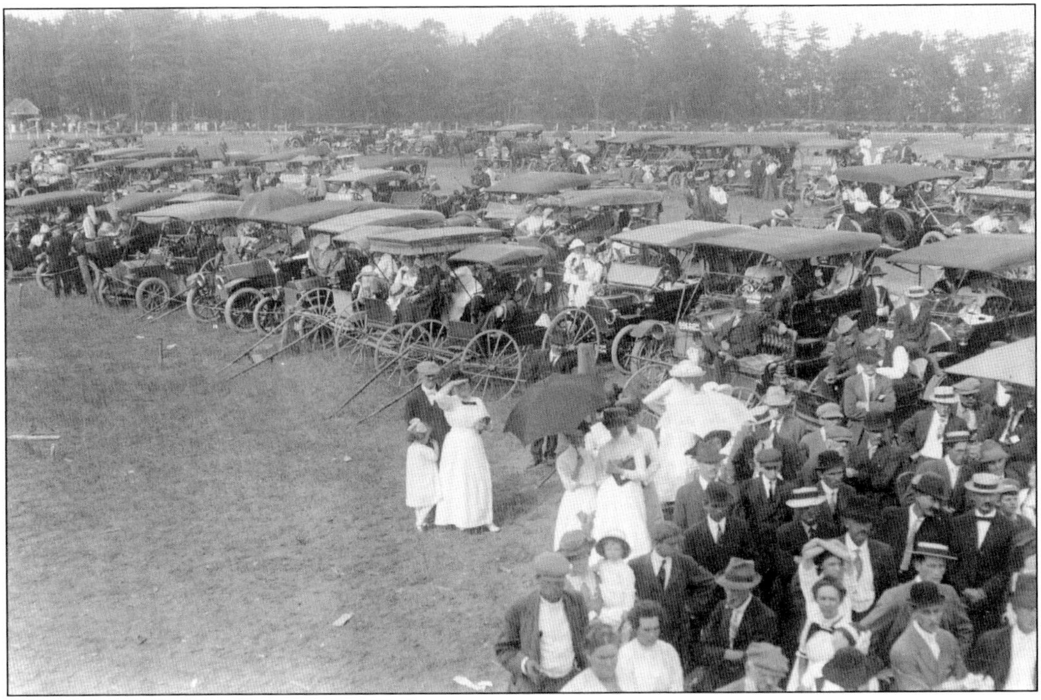

The first county fair was organized at the courthouse in 1819 and held there for a number of years. For a decade, the fairs were then held in Mechanicville until the Agricultural Society moved them to Saratoga Springs. Finally, the Union Fair Association voted to hold the annual fairs at the county fairgrounds in Ballston Spa, where they have been located ever since. (Both, Chris Morley collection.)

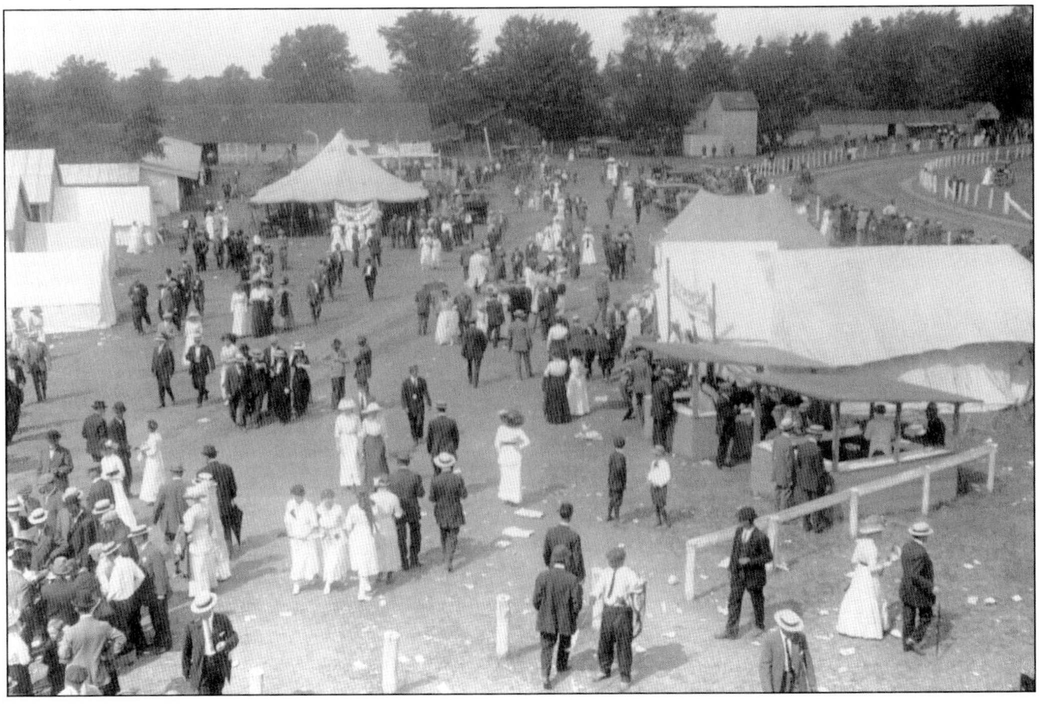

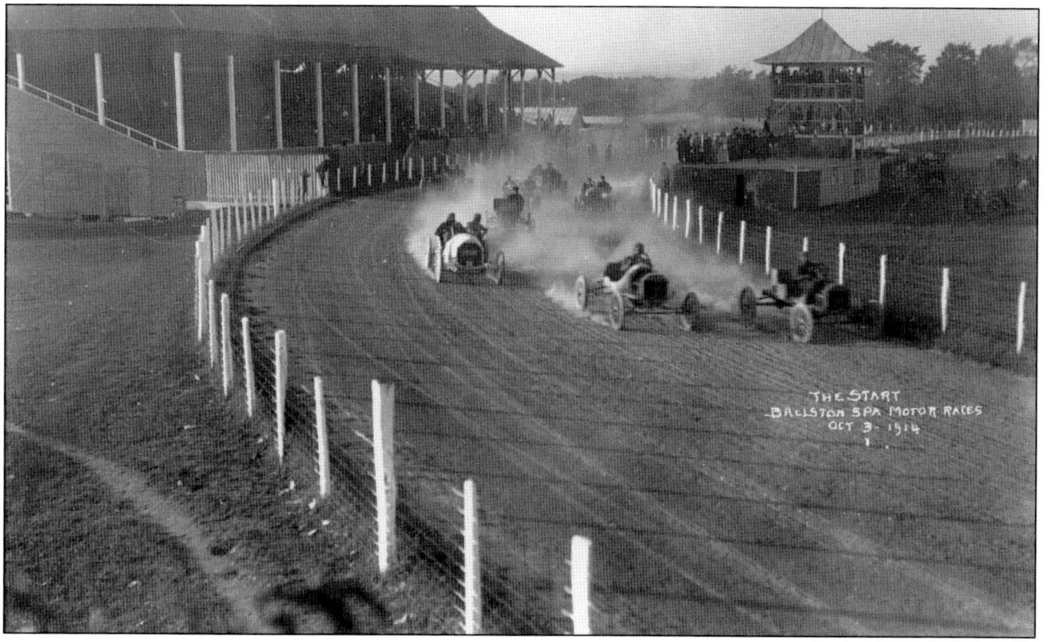

The Saratoga County Fair's covered grandstand holds 1,500 people and has hosted a variety of popular races. There are also five covered pavilions, seven buildings, and four barns contained within its 30 acres. (Chris Morley collection.)

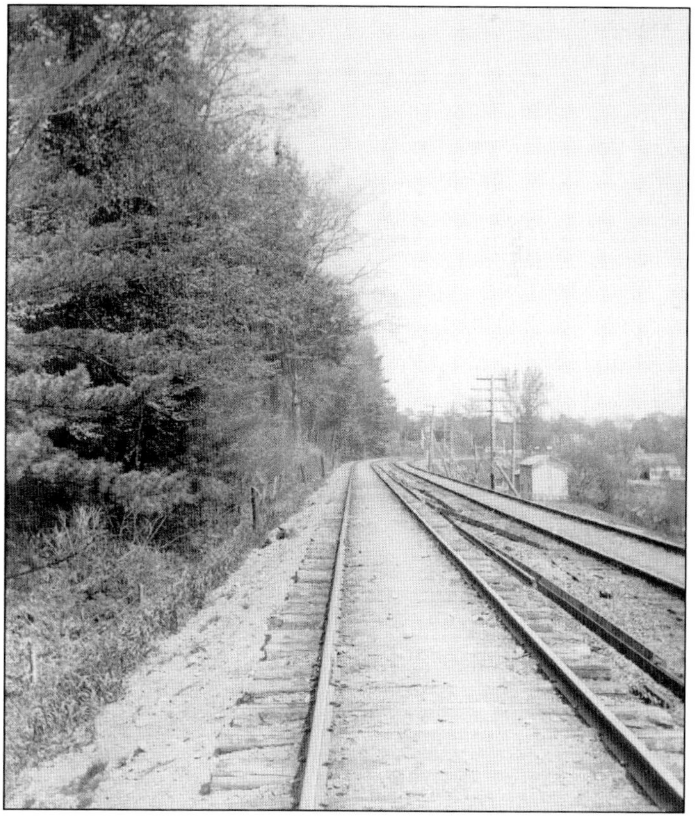

Pictured is the Delaware and Hudson Railway main line on Fairground Hill looking north. These tracks continued to be used as a spur to the tannery for several years after the village bypass was constructed in 1950 but later were torn up to make a walking trail. (Saratoga County Historical Society at Brookside Museum.)

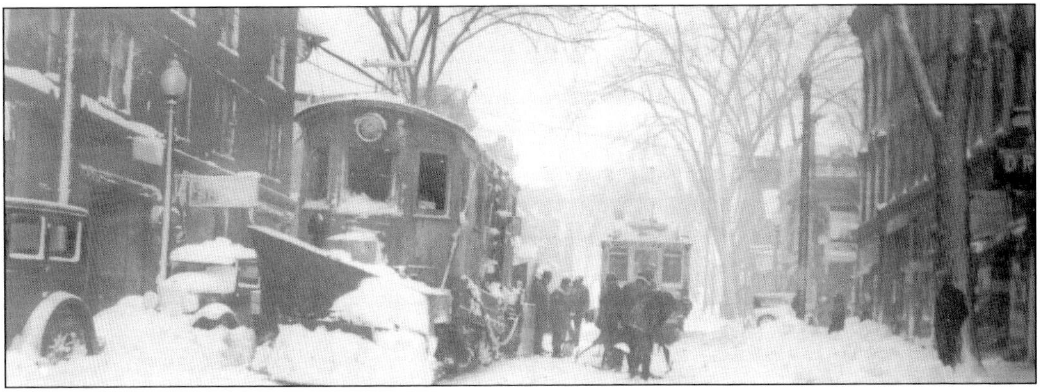

Winters often presented hardships for Milton residents in the days before truck-mounted snowplows came into use. Roads had to be shoveled out by hand. The construction of the trolley lines on Milton Avenue and Front Street in Ballston Spa in the late 1800s allowed the trolleys to plow at least the main business corridors. (Saratoga County Historical Society at Brookside Museum.)

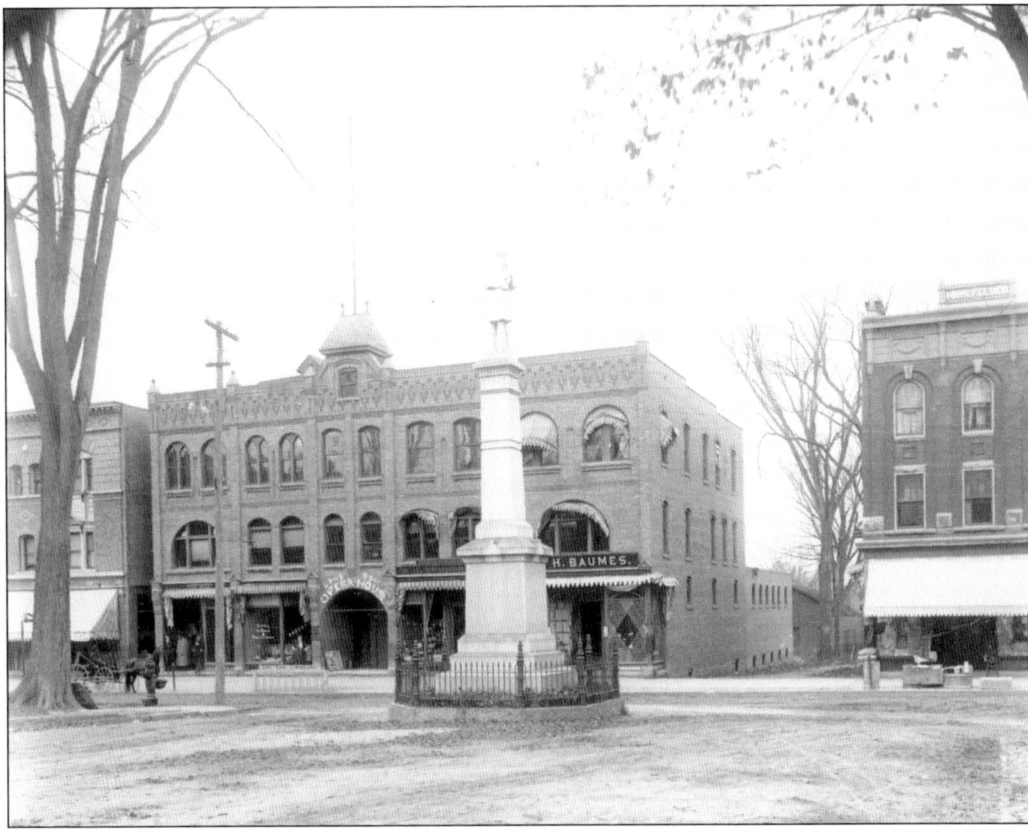

With seating for 800 patrons, the Sans Souci Opera House was built on the site of the former hotel of the same name at the bottom of Low Street in 1890. Some of the most famous vaudeville acts in the country performed there each week. The 1888 Soldiers Monument and the stores of William Baumes, Muhfelder, and W.J. Redmond are also visible. (Saratoga County Historical Society at Brookside Museum.)

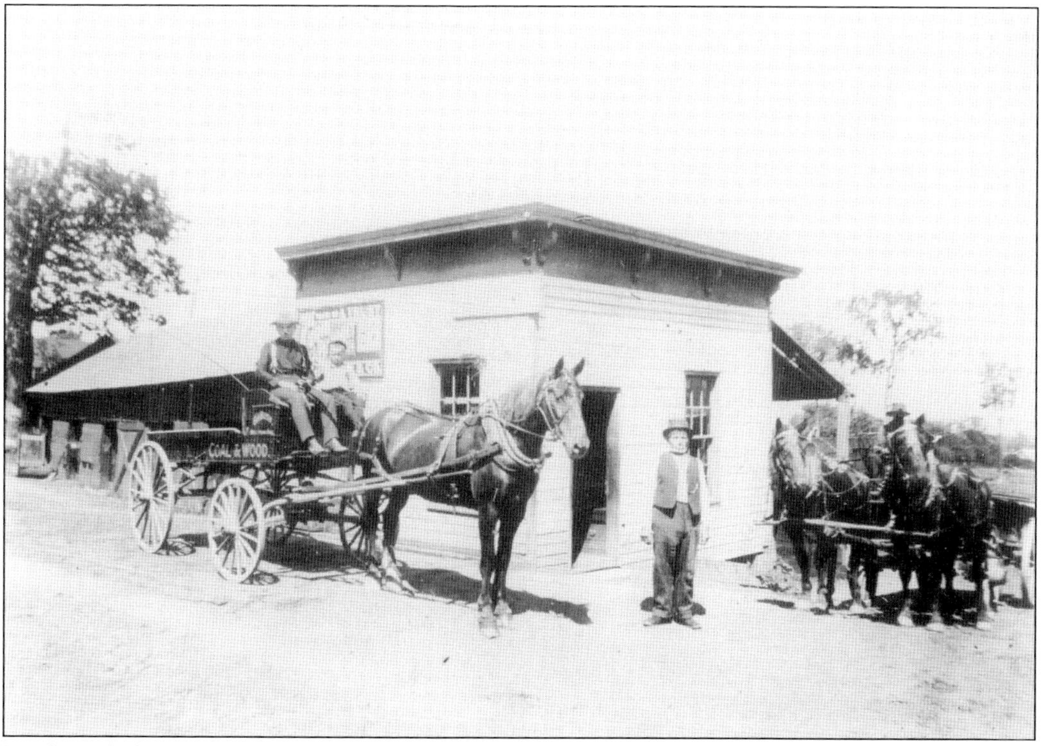

Jacob Bush (standing) established the Bush Coal and Wood Company at the north end of Milton Avenue with his son George (seated on the coal rig). His grandson J. Edward (seated next to George) moved the coal yard to South Street after his father passed away. He went on to become a village trustee and mayor before passing away in 1937. (Saratoga County Historical Society at Brookside Museum.)

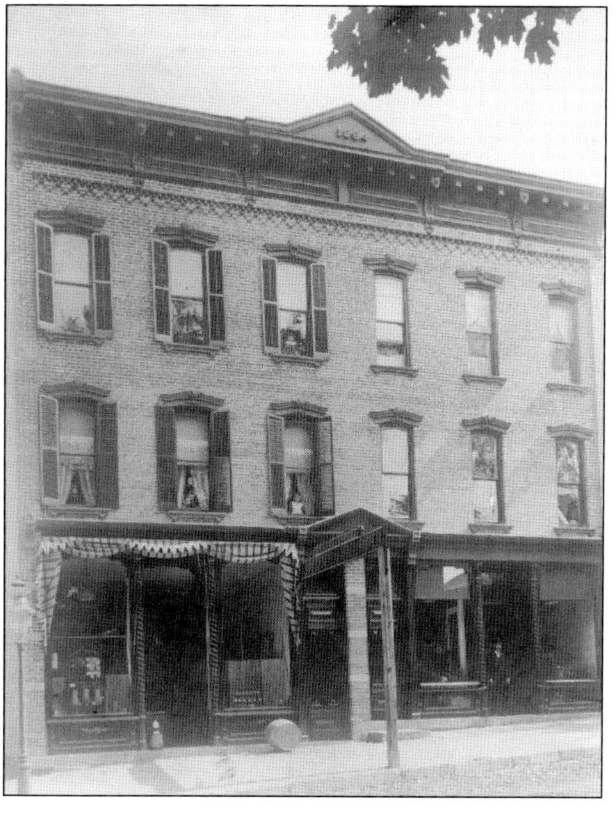

In the early 1890s, the building located at 76–78 Milton Avenue contained William Clements's store (left, at No. 78) and Rush Young. Clements sold paint, oil, and wallpaper, while Young acted as an embalmer, undertaker, and funeral director. Tracy Hardware later occupied No. 76. (Saratoga County Historical Society at Brookside Museum collection.)

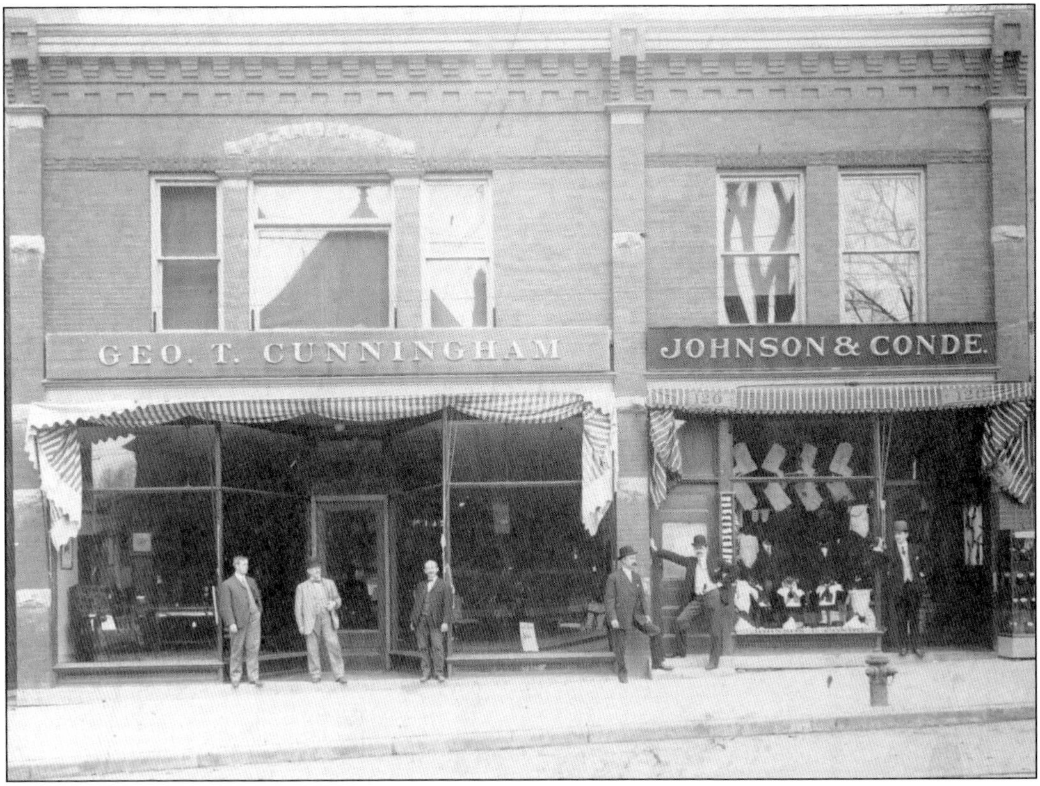

The Milton Avenue business block contained George T. Cunningham's furniture store and Johnson & Conde, advertised as "Ballston's biggest clothing store." Edward Morley, a clerk at Johnson's as well as father of the late Ballston Spa historian Chris Morley, is standing on the far right. Collars and cuffs made at the nearby Glen Paper Collar Company are displayed in the window. (Saratoga County Historical Society at Brookside Museum.)

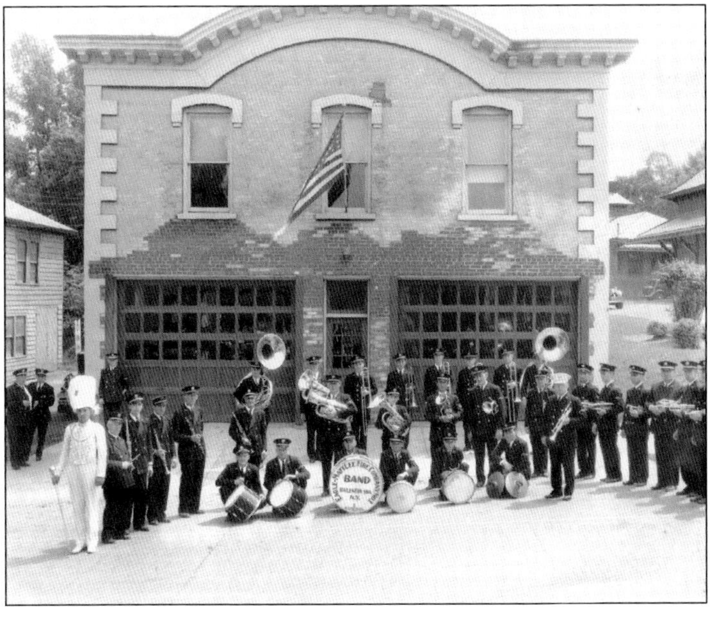

The first fire company, called Fire Engine Company No. 1, was formed in 1815. In 1843, it became known as the Eagle Fire Company. The J.A. Hovey Hook and Ladder Company became the Matt Lee Hook and Ladder Company in 1887. The two companies were consolidated in 1933 to become the Eagle–Matt Lee Fire Company, located near the corner of Bath and Walnut Streets. (Saratoga County Historical Society at Brookside Museum.)

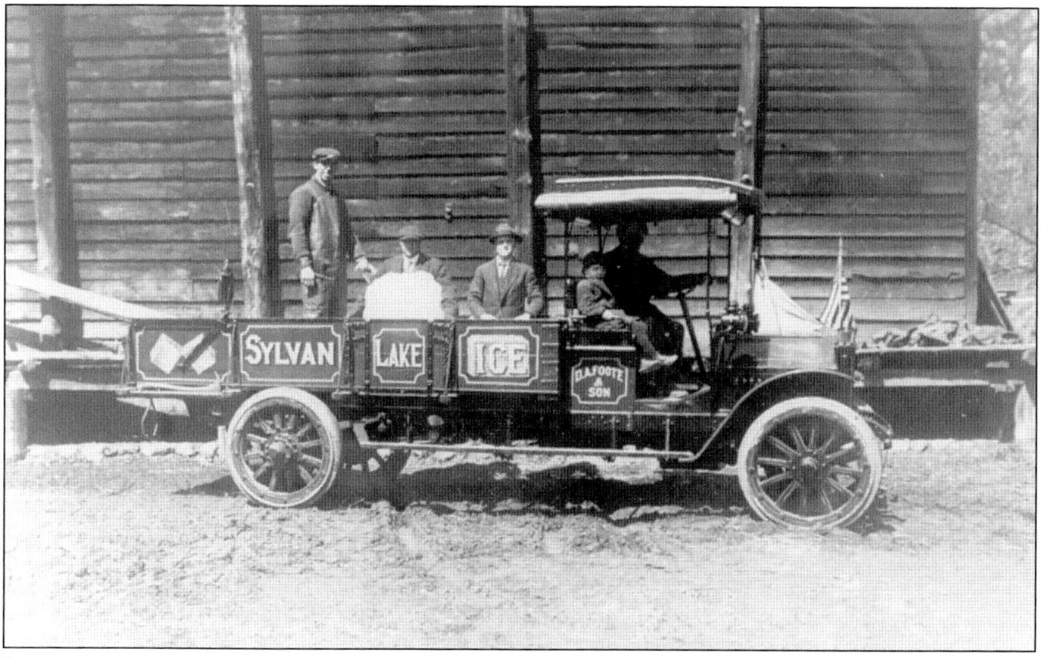

Beginning in 1887, D.A. Foote and Son operated an ice-cutting business for several decades. Foote renamed the pond on top of the hill above the Brookside Museum as Sylvan Lake. During winter, the ice would be stored in sheds near the pond. In the summer, Foote would deliver it to stores and residences around town. (Chris Morley collection.)

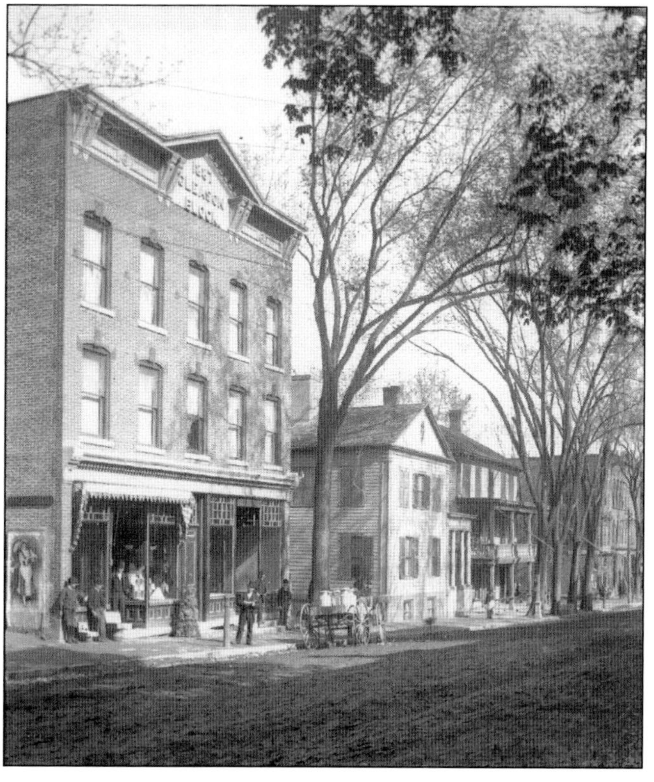

The Gleason Block on Milton Avenue, between Front and Washington Streets, was first developed by village founder Nicholas Low. The Ballston Spa House catered to tourists during the off-season, while another building was reserved as a residence for the Sans Souci manager. Later, photographer Jesse Wooley, the F.E. Mitchell Pharmacy, and the Carter and Spoor Funeral Home occupied these buildings, which were all torn down in 1965 and replaced by a gas station. (Chris Morley collection.)

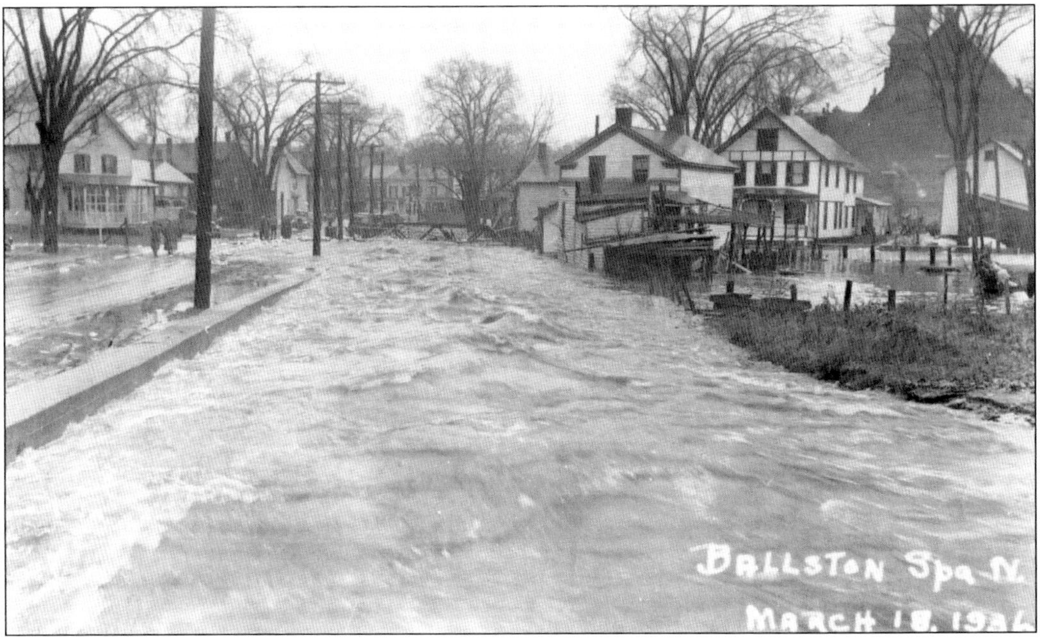

The flood of 1936 wreaked havoc throughout the village. Even the normally placid Gordon Creek overflowed its banks and inundated dozens of residences and businesses. The back of the Methodist church can be seen on the right. The house in the center of the photograph must have been built well, as it still stands today. Milton Avenue is in the background. (Saratoga County Historical Society at Brookside Museum.)

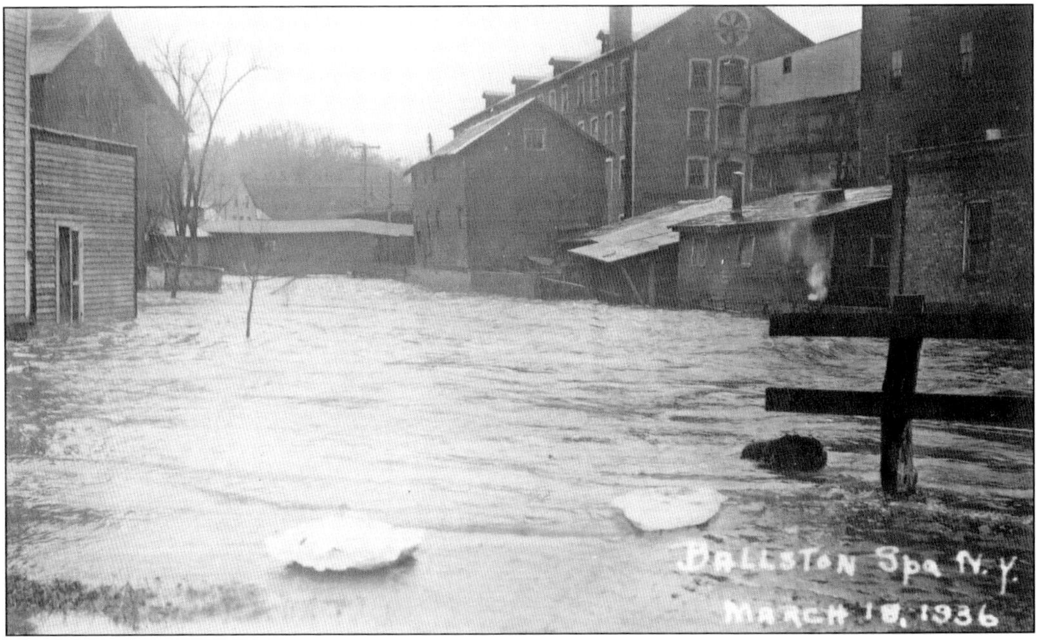

Several buildings of the American Hide & Leather Company tannery (formerly the Bull's Head Tannery) on Bath Street were inundated during the flood of 1936. The company's close proximity to the Gordon Creek resulted in several flooding events over the years. (Saratoga County Historical Society at Brookside Museum.)

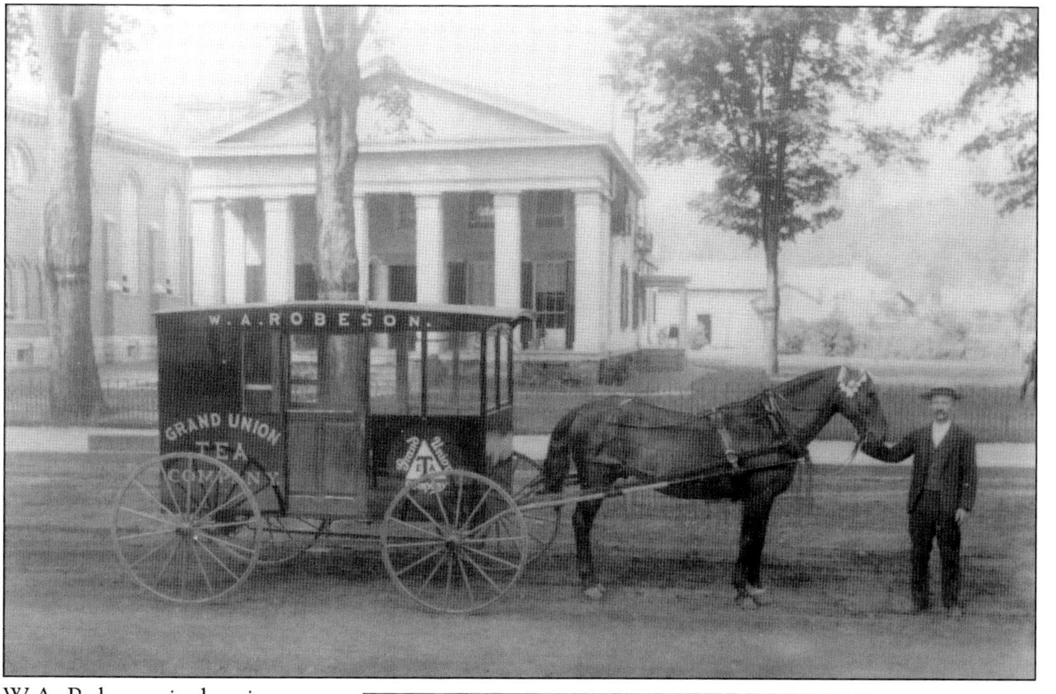

W.A. Robeson is showing off his Grand Union Tea Company horse and carriage on Milton Avenue in this c. 1910 photograph. His office was located at 31 Waterbury Street in Saratoga Springs. In the background is the rectory of St. Mary's Church. (Chris Morley collection.)

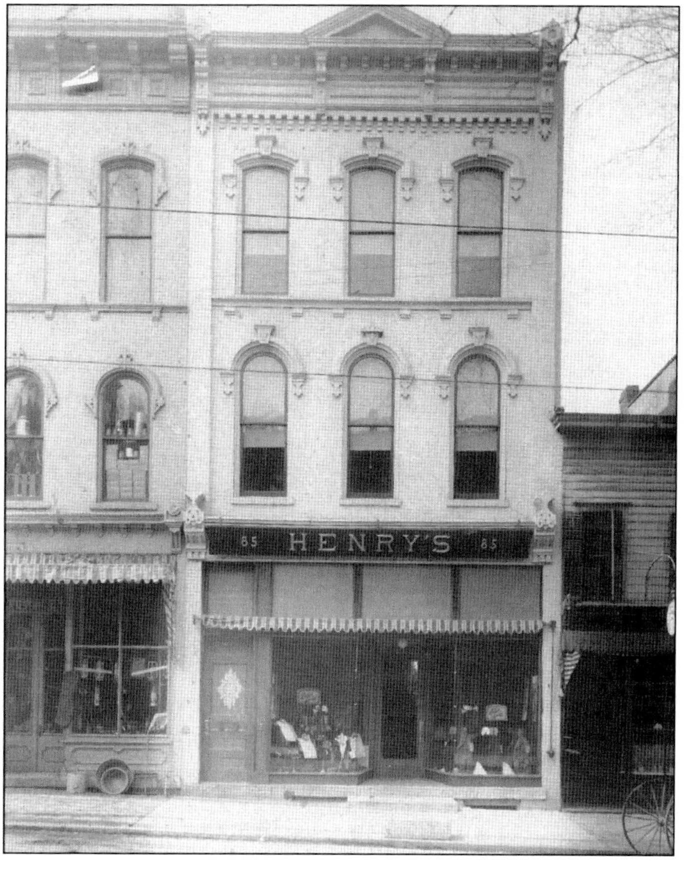

Louis Henry's clothing store was located at 85 Milton Avenue. On the left is Theodore Townley's hardware store, while E. H. Hayward's jewelry shop is on the right. (Saratoga County Historical Society at Brookside Museum.)

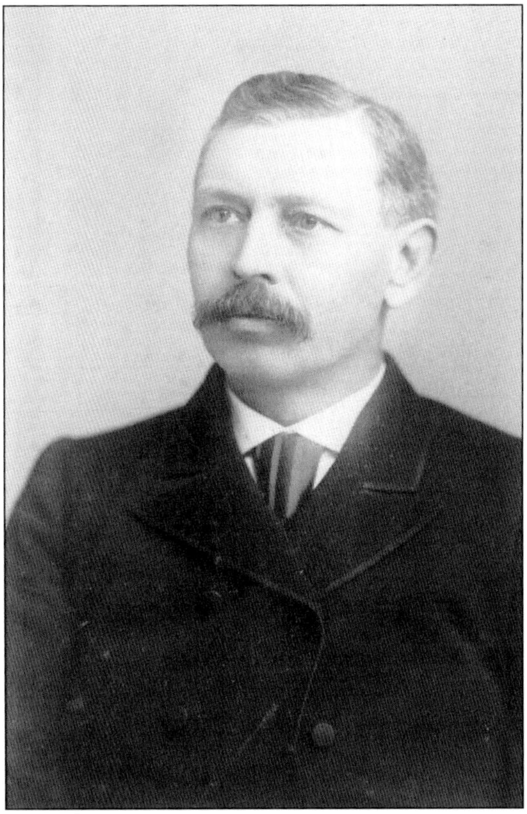

Ballston Spa resident Jesse L'Amoreaux (1837–1918) was one of Saratoga County's most prominent citizens. He was a highly successful attorney and county judge, as well as one of the founders and early officers of the First National Bank. (Saratoga County Historical Society at Brookside Museum.)

T.C. Kelley operated a millinery shop at 94 Milton Avenue for 30 years before selling it to Michael Sheehy in 1904. Sheehy advertised various lines of cloaks, furs, and clothing. The wagon is full of bunting, a lightweight material that is now used to manufacture flags and other decorations. (Saratoga County Historical Society at Brookside Museum.)

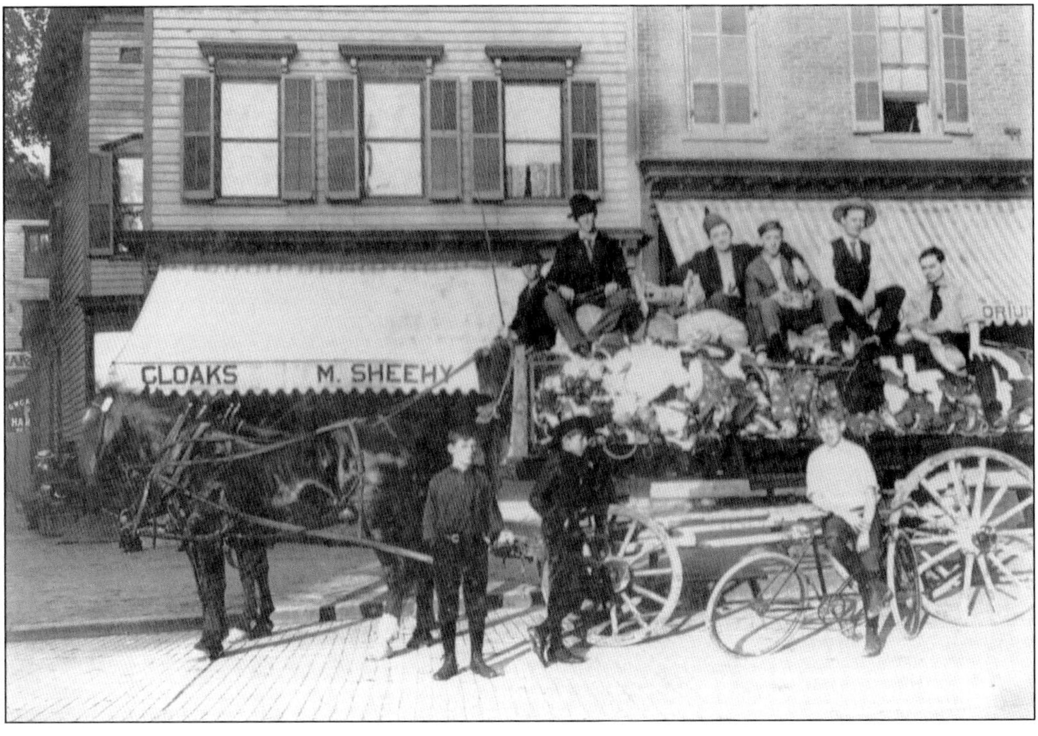

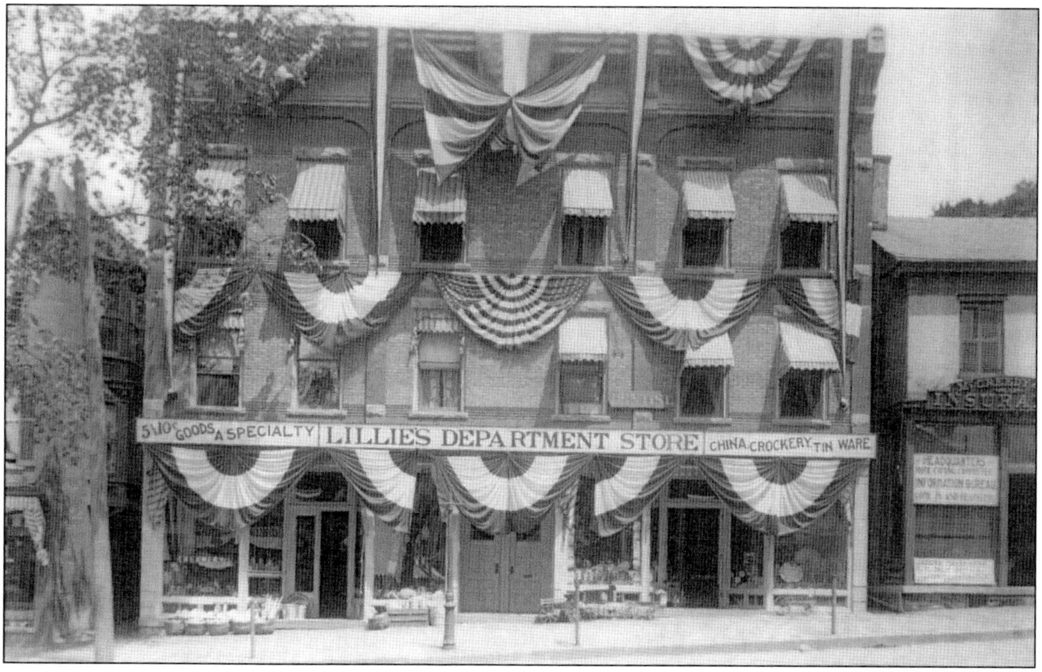

Lillie's Department Store, operated by Lula B. Lillie at 56 Milton Avenue, is all decked out for Ballston Spa's centennial celebration in 1907. For many years, a dentist named Dr. Tibbits occupied the second floor. Lillie's was part of the so-called Manogue Block, built and owned by contractor Dennis Manogue. The first tenant was the Sanford Briggs Grocery Store. (Chris Morley collection.)

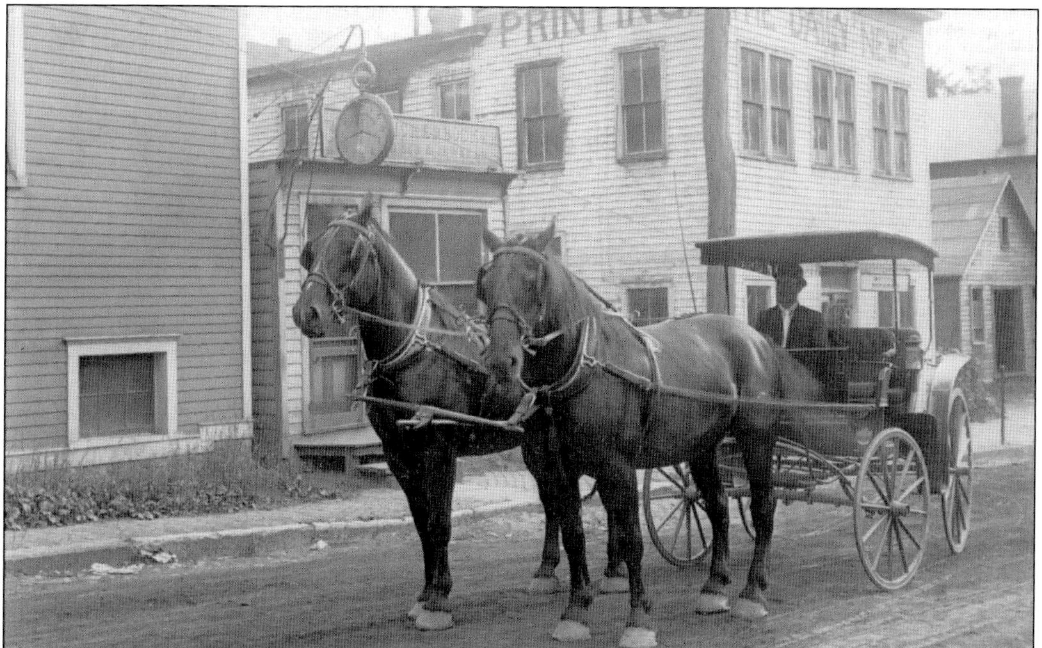

An 1800s version of the taxicab is pictured here on Milton Avenue in front of the Knickerbocker printing offices. (Chris Morley collection.)

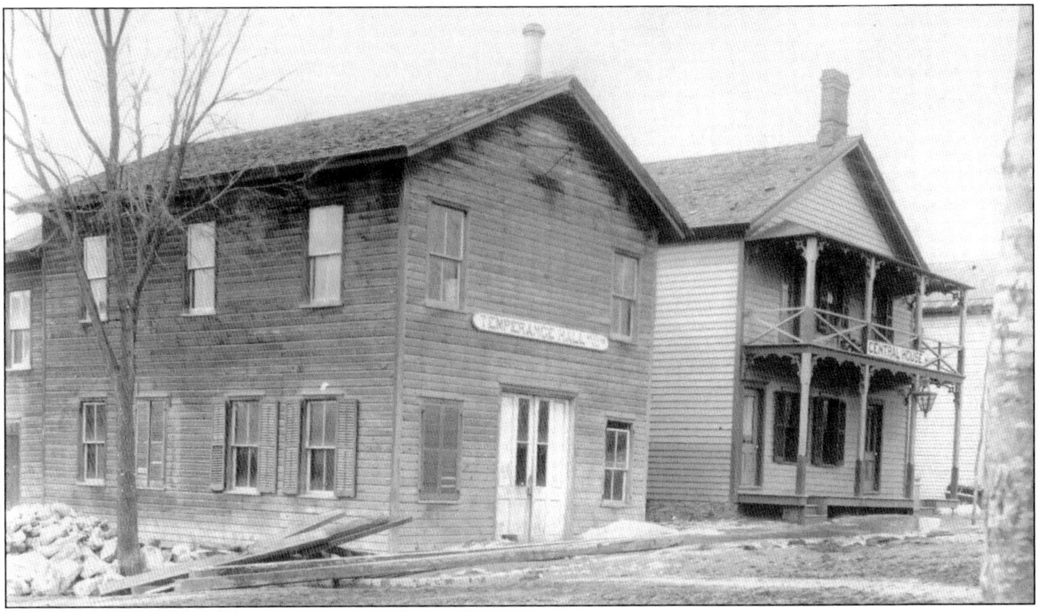

The temperance movement believed the only way to avoid the evils of drunkenness was to abstain from alcohol. One of the largest temperance societies in Milton was the Ballston Division of Sons of Temperance, with 316 members. The Temperance Hall was located on South Street next to a hotel called the Central House. Other societies included the Good Templars Lodge and the Woman's Christian Temperance Union. (Saratoga County Historical Society at Brookside Museum.)

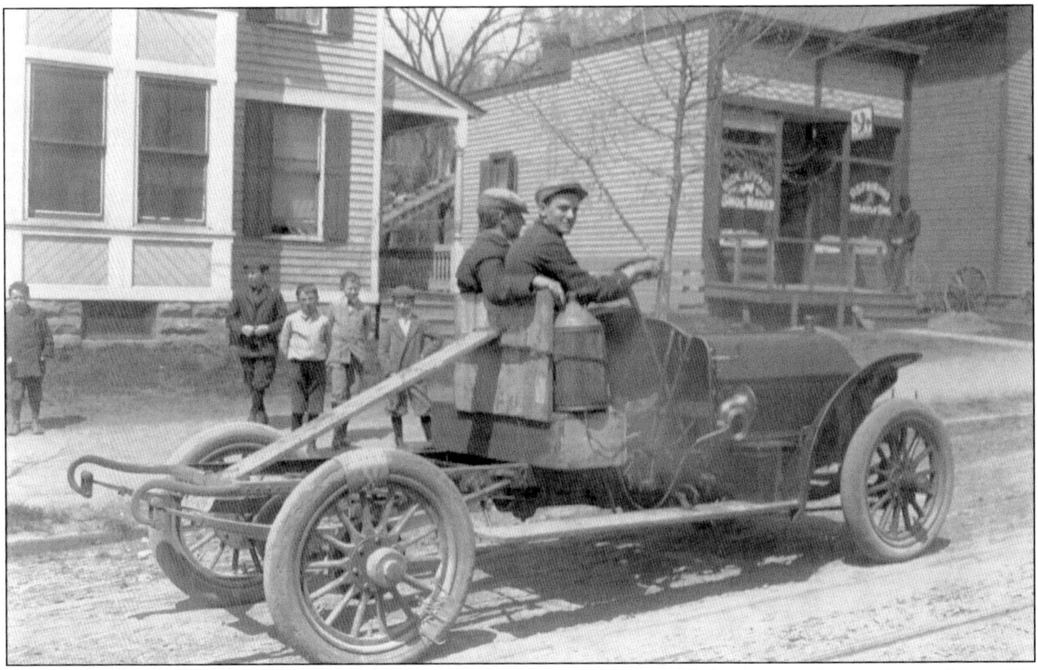

Fred Merrill converted this Buick automobile into a tow truck for use at his garage. Merrill's Garage is just visible to the right of Nick Auffiero's Shoe Repair Shop, seen in the center. Jesse Wooley took this 1914 photograph on Washington Street. (Saratoga County Historical Society at Brookside Museum.)

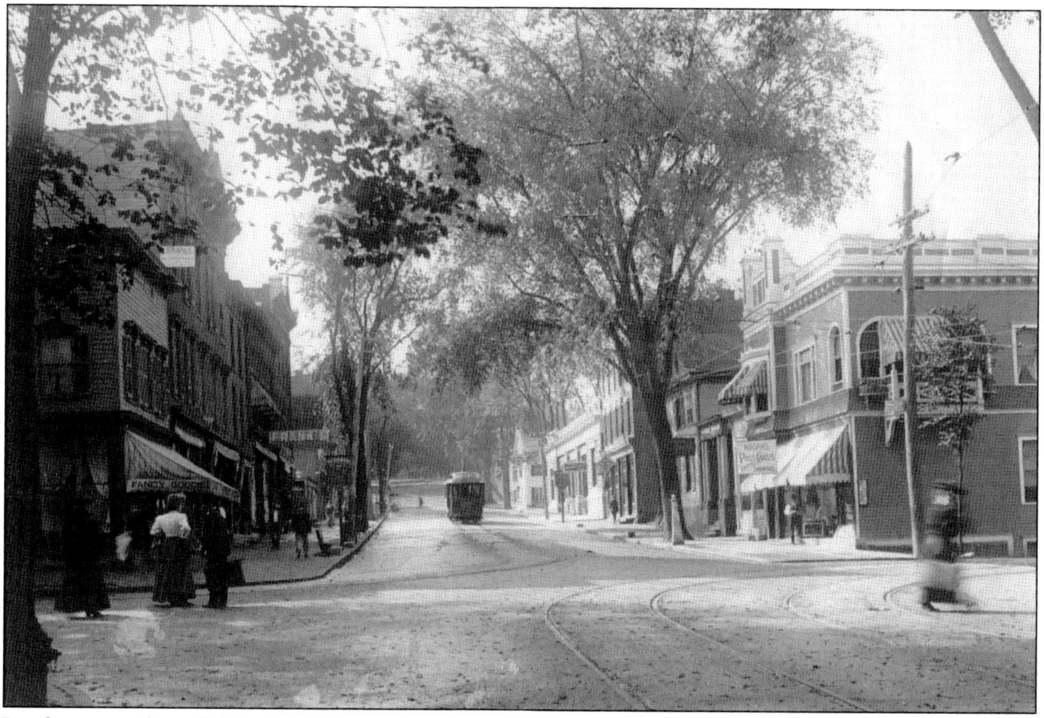

Looking south on Milton Avenue from Lincoln Corners are Jesse Wooley's photography studio (right foreground), the Carter Funeral Home, and the Eagle Hotel (right background). The W.A. Ten Eyck Café can be seen on the left. A Hudson Valley Railway car is making its way toward Malta Avenue. The foreground tracks are those of the Schenectady Railway. (Saratoga County Historical Society at Brookside Museum.)

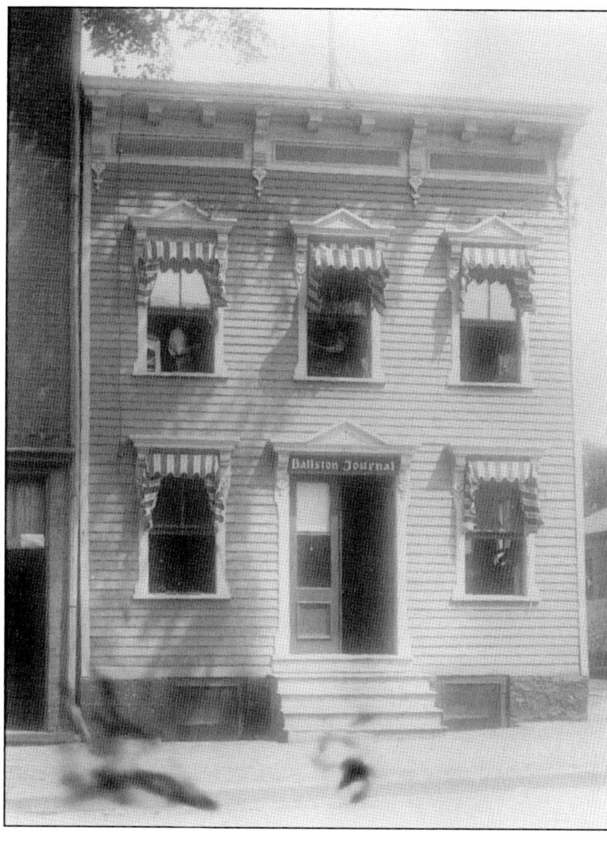

Various newspapers have been printed in Ballston Spa: *Saratoga Journal*, *Saratoga Courier*, *People's Watchtower*, *Ballston Spa Republican*, and *Ballston Daily News*, to name a few; however, only the *Ballston Journal* could boast a continuous print publication from 1798 to 2012. The publication office was on the corner of Bath and Walnut Streets. (Saratoga County Historical Society at Brookside Museum.)

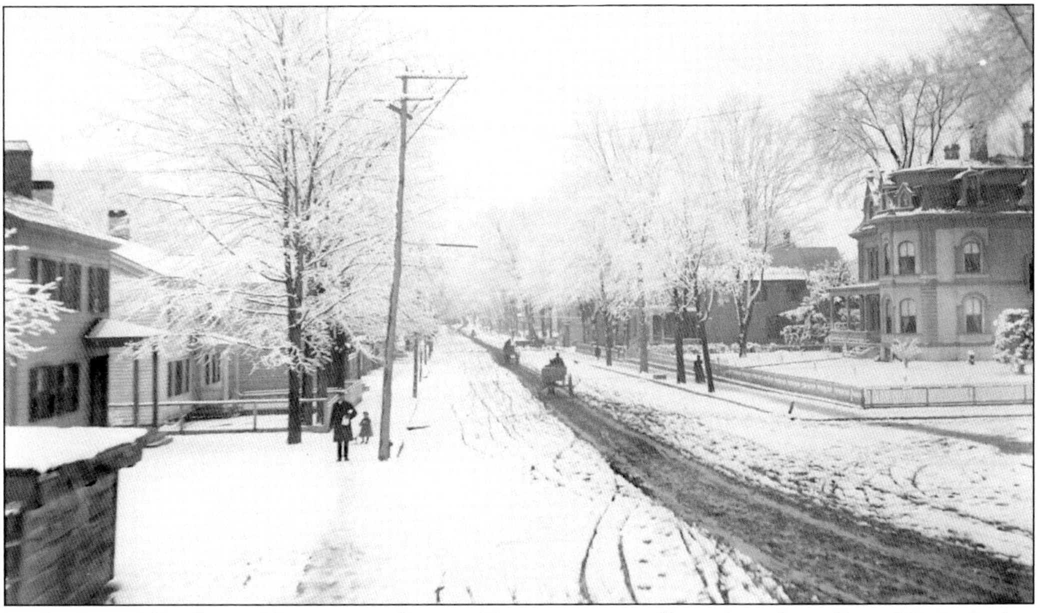

In the late 1860s, Jonas Hovey owned several large cotton mills within the village. He built this beautiful mansion (right) at the corner of Prospect Street and Milton Avenue for $70,000 (over $1.2 million today). After his untimely death in 1873, it was occupied by George West and, upon his death, Frederick Bischoff. The mansion was torn down in 1955 to make way for a gas station. (Chris Morley collection.)

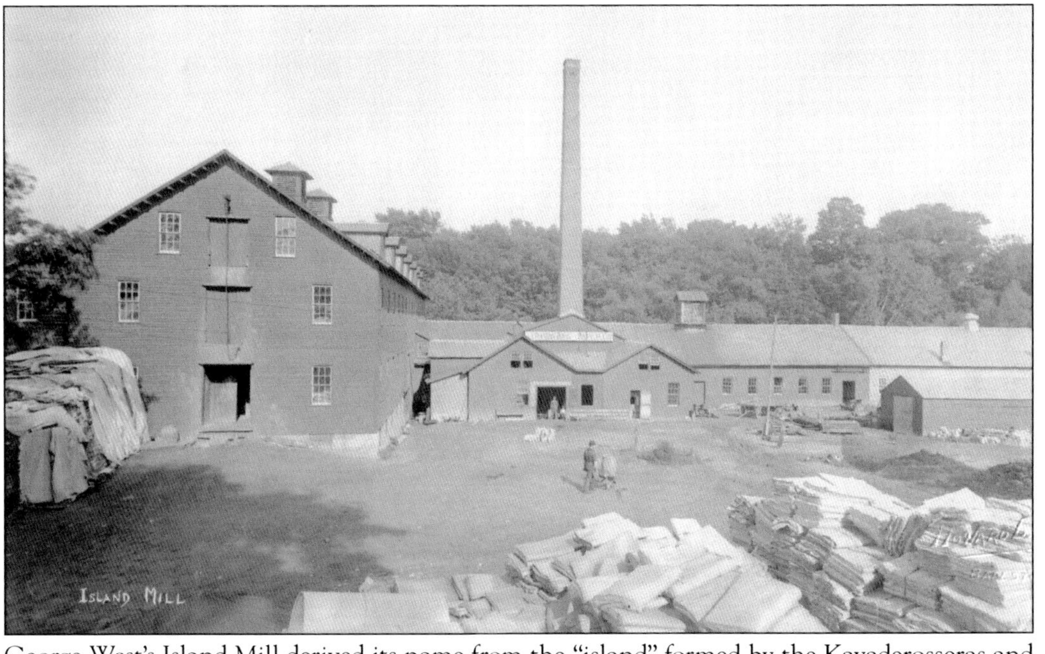

George West's Island Mill derived its name from the "island" formed by the Kayaderosseras and Gordon Creeks during the 1800s. It was first constructed in 1850 as a cotton mill, but later in the century West used it to produce manila paper. In 1899, it was purchased by the Union Bag & Paper Company, which continued operating it until 1915. (Saratoga County Historical Society at Brookside Museum.)

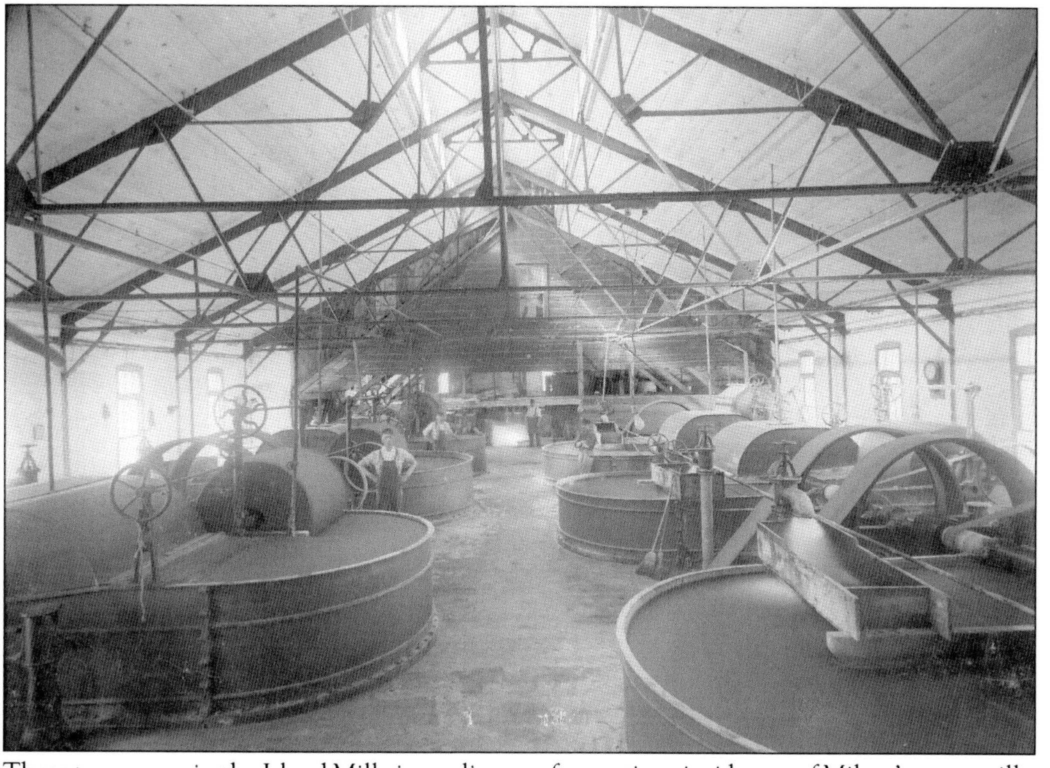

These two scenes in the Island Mill give a glimpse of operations inside one of Milton's paper mills. Processing tanks turned wood pulp into material suitable for paper (above), while machines turned the liquefied material into finished manila paper for shipment to the nearby bag factory (below). George West installed the latest machinery so that many tons of paper could be processed each day to keep up with the worldwide demand for his folding paper bags. (Both, Saratoga County Historical Society at Brookside Museum.)

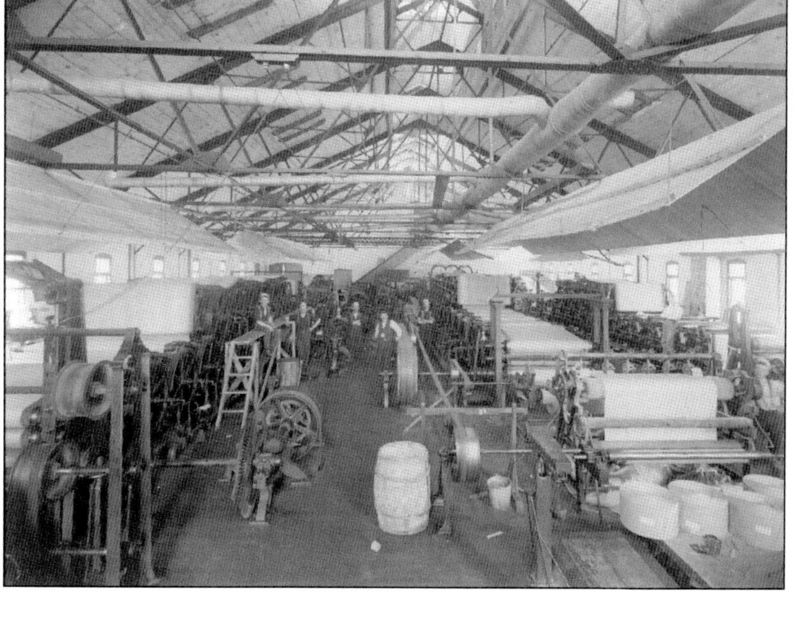

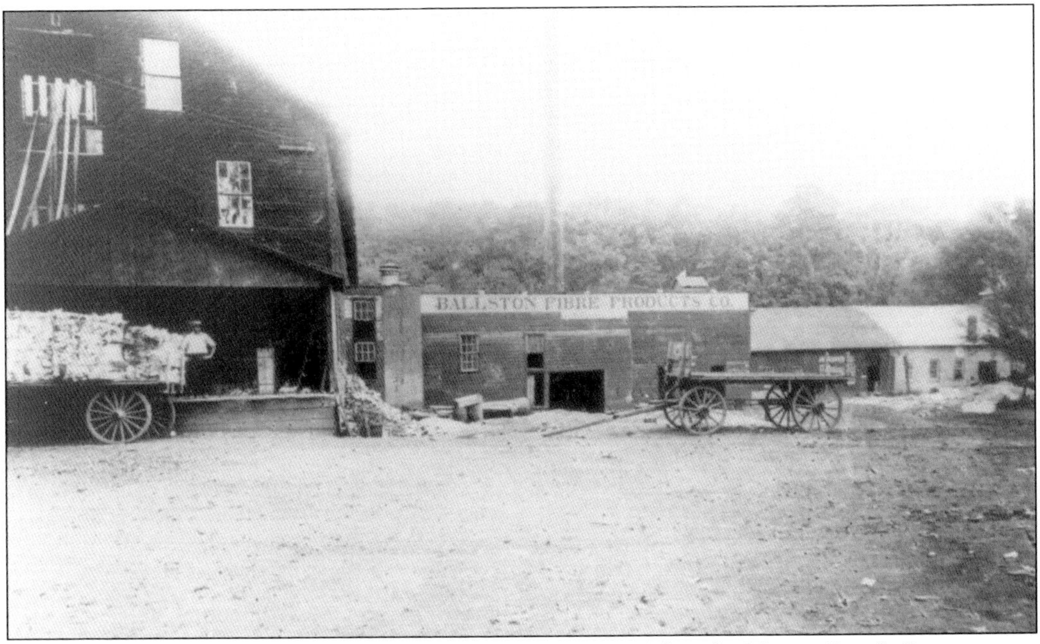

After the Union Bag & Paper Company relocated its paper-making operations to Hudson Falls in 1915, several concerns used the former Island Mill building before it closed down for good in the late 1920s. The short-lived Ballston Fibre Products Company is pictured here. (Chris Morley collection.)

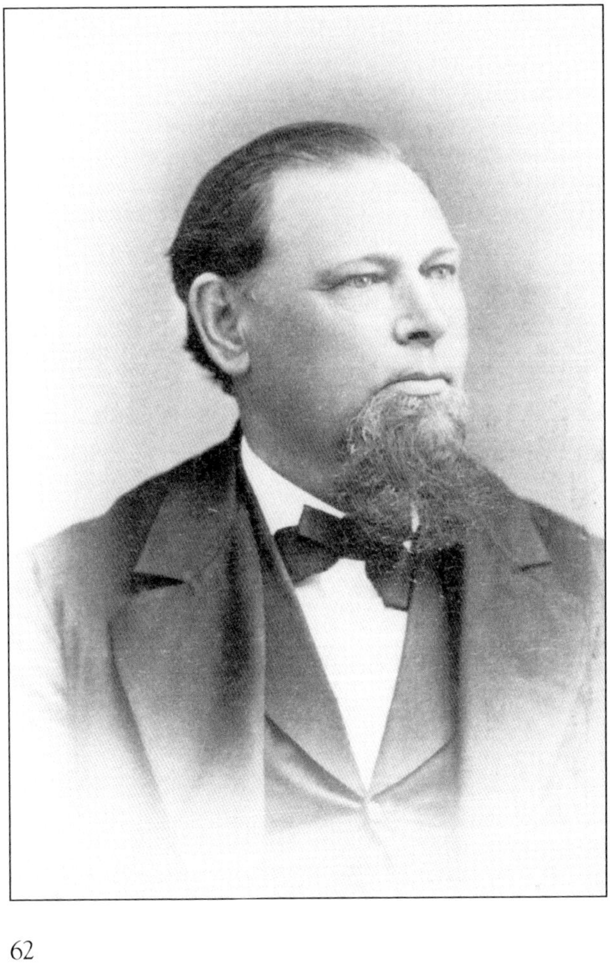

Born in the town of Ballston in 1829, Henry Mann Sr. was involved in many business enterprises over his lifetime. He owned the Blue Mill, partnered with Wells Laflin in a successful paper mill, conducted a general store with Charles Noxon, and invested in other businesses. He also held positions as county treasurer, vice president of the First National Bank, village trustee, and village president. (Saratoga County Historical Society at Brookside Museum.)

The Medbery family was well known in Ballston Spa during the late 1800s. This studio portrait shows, from left to right, Mary Clark, Stephen Jr., Annie, Neil, Stephen Sr., and Alicia. Stephen Sr. was the teller at the First National Bank, while his brother Horace was proprietor of the Glen Paper Collar Company. His father, Stephen B., operated the Medbery Hotel. (Saratoga County Historical Society at Brookside Museum.)

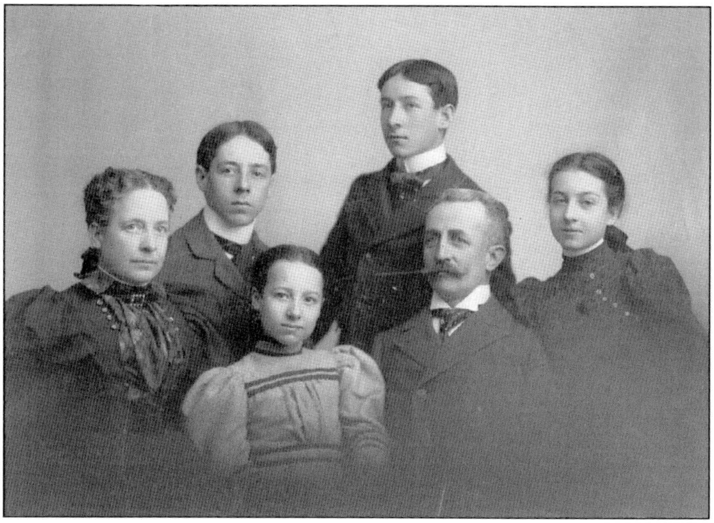

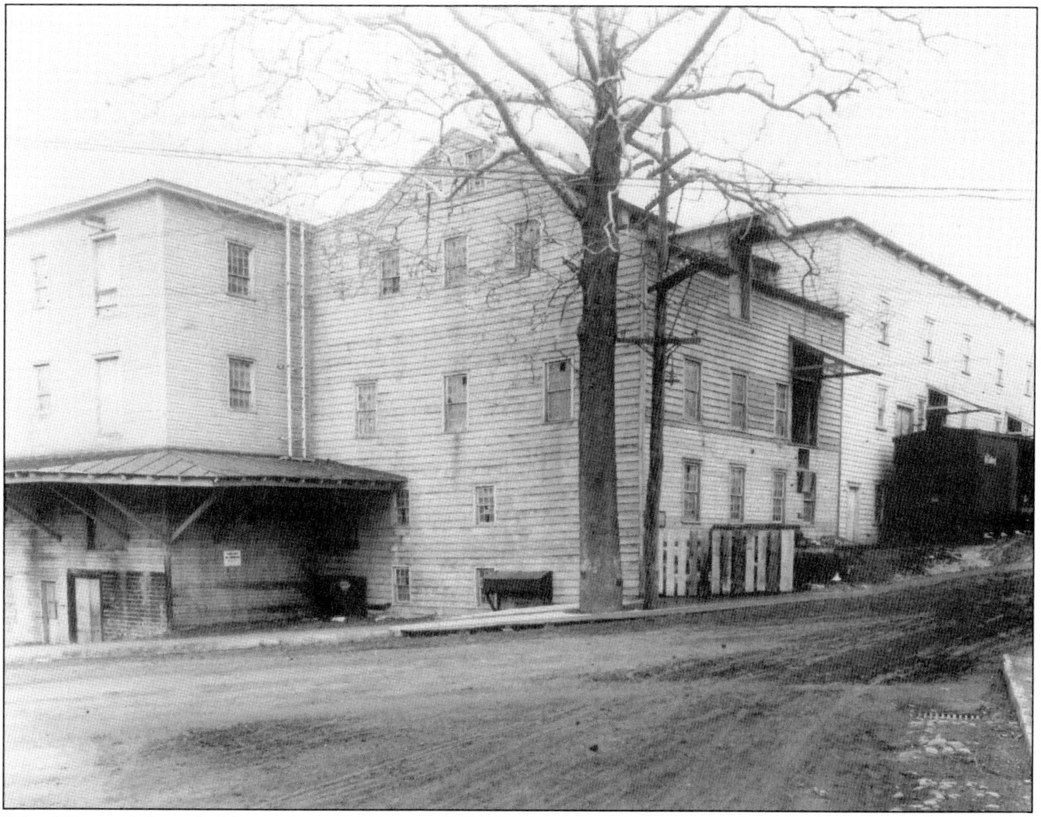

The Blue Mill on Milton Avenue opposite Saratoga Avenue is one of the village's most famous extinct buildings. It was constructed by Hezekiah Middlebrook as a gristmill in 1830 but achieved much greater fame as the site of the Glen Paper Collar Company in the 1880s. Frederick Bischoff of Bischoff Chocolates razed the building in the 1920s to create a park. (Chris Morley collection.)

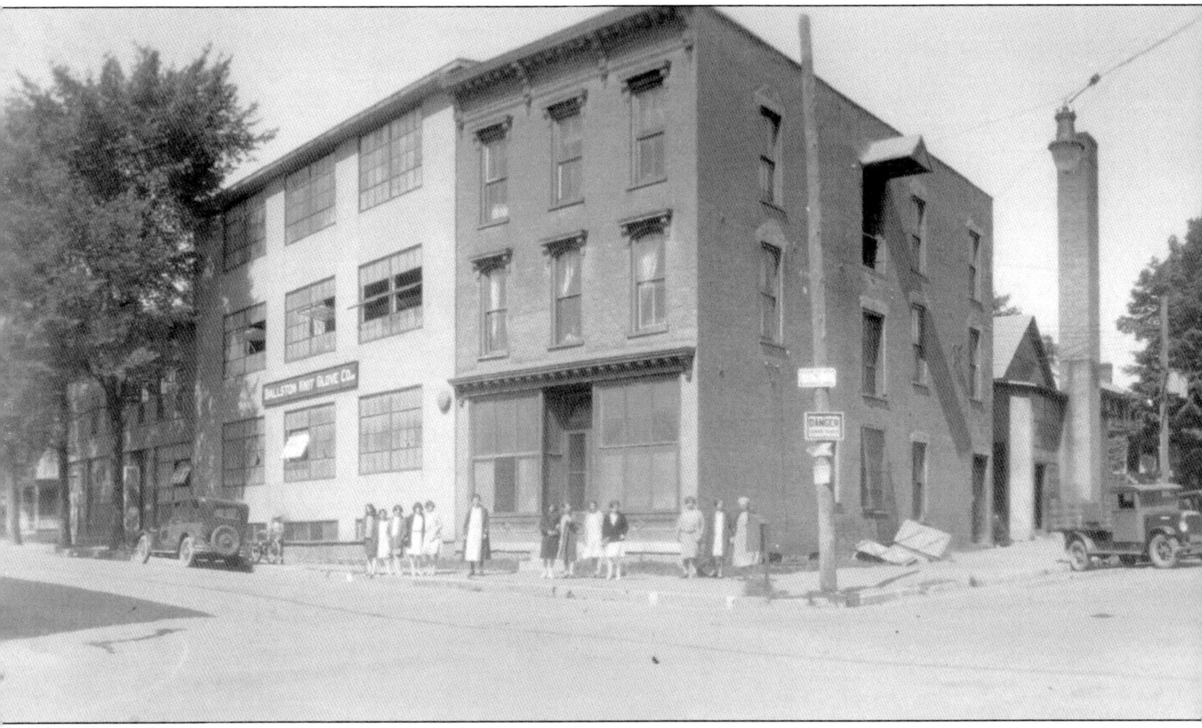

This c. 1920 view of the north end of the village shows both sides of Milton Avenue at the South Street intersection. On the left is the fledgling Ballston Knit Glove Company of Albert Ackerman. A staff of 40 women worked in the South Street factory, while 75 more worked from their homes to perform the "fingering" work. This business would later grow into the Ackshand

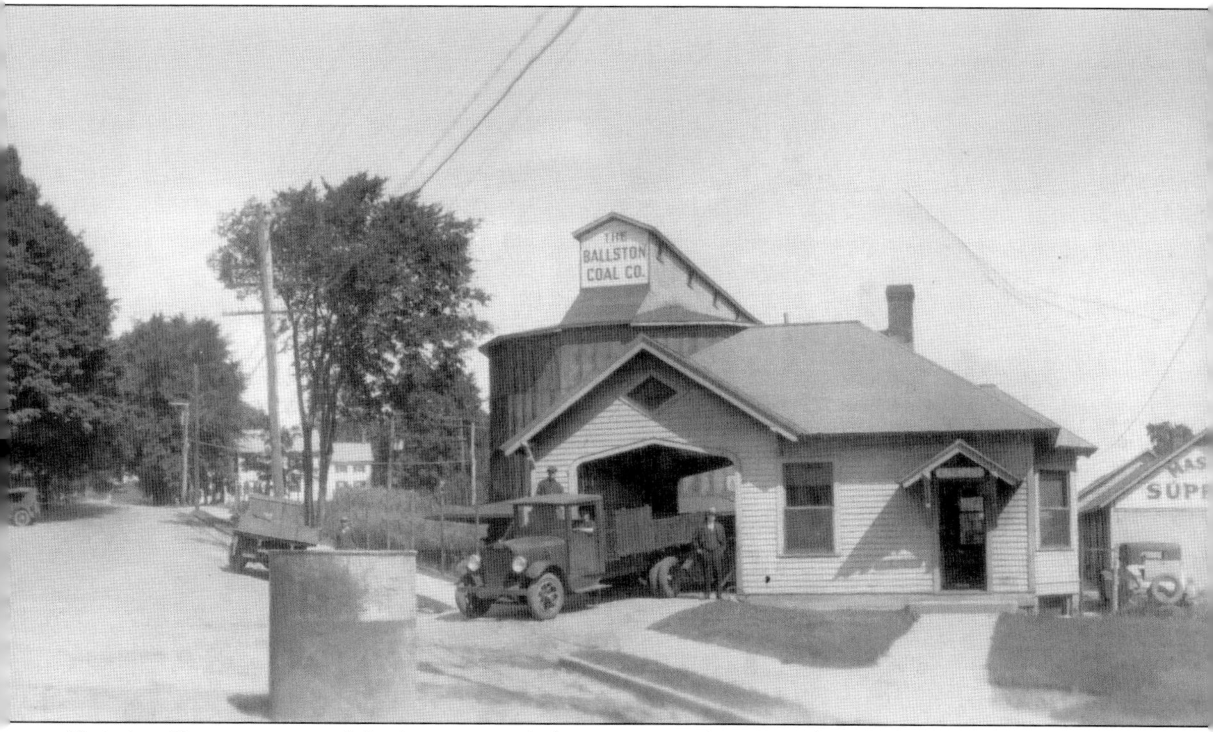

Knitting Company, one of the largest textile businesses in the town's history. On the right is the Ballston Coal Company, which was established in 1906 and operated for half a century. (Saratoga County Historical Society at Brookside Museum.)

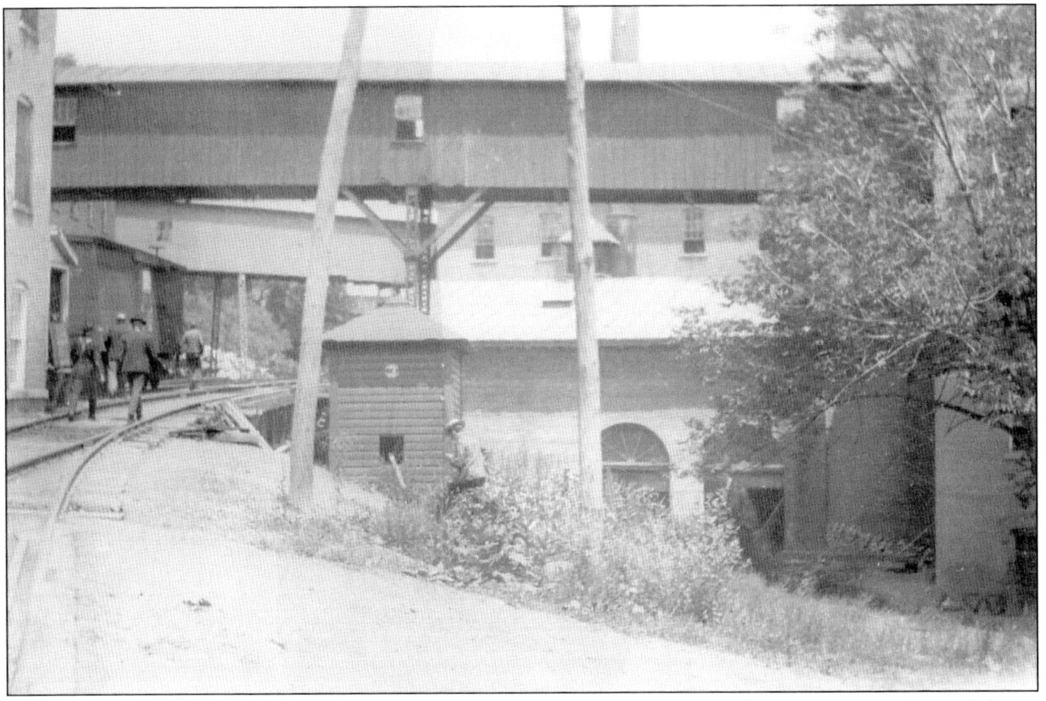

The photographer of this image stood on Prospect Street to take a close-up view of the Union Mill complex walkways. The building on the left is the bag factory, where millions of George West's square-bottomed paper bags were manufactured each week. The tracks are from the Ballston Terminal Railroad. (Chris Morley collection.)

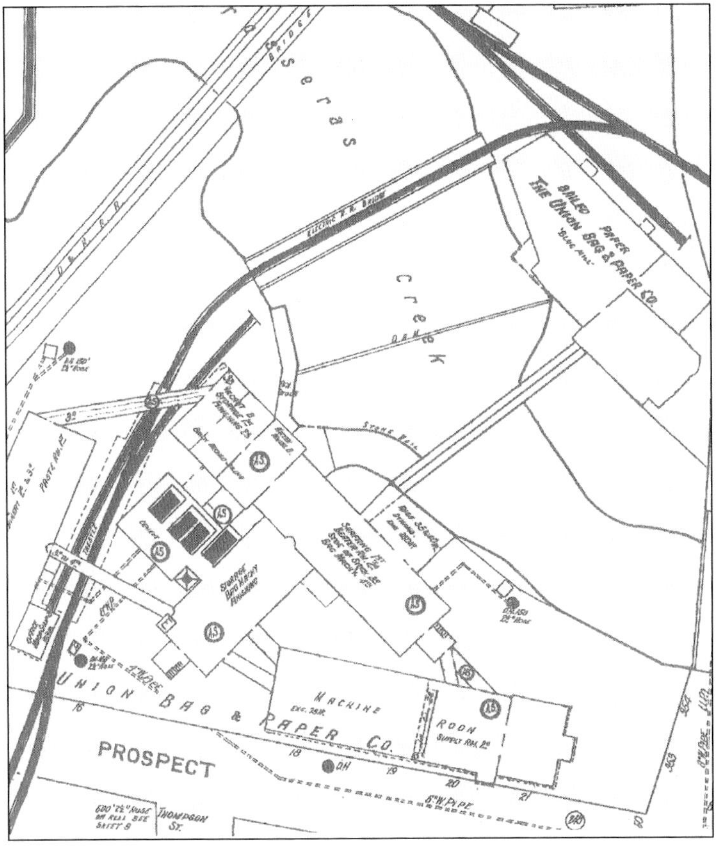

In 1911, a series of maps were drawn for each of the mills along Kayaderosseras Creek to analyze their fire-control systems. These maps give a clear understanding of the layout of each mill. Pictured in this sample are the Union Mill and bag factory (left) and the former Blue Mill (right). (Chris Morley collection.)

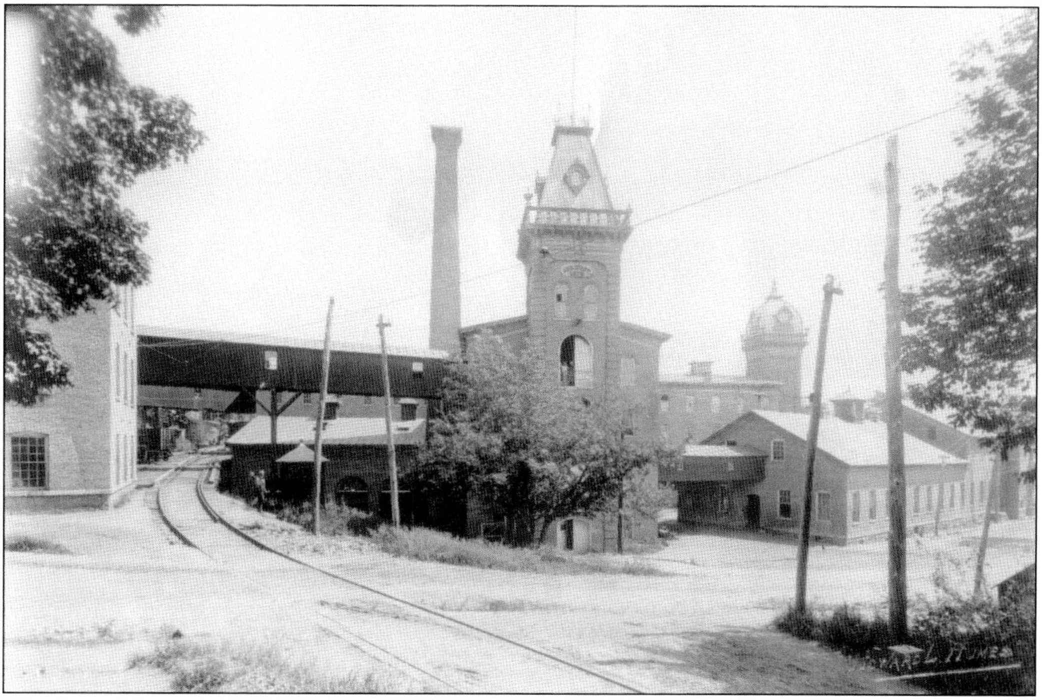

The large Union Mill complex owned by George West consisted of over a dozen buildings, including a paper mill and a bag factory. The walking bridge (left) connected the paper mill with the Blue Mill, which was used as storage. The truss bridge on the right belongs to the Ballston Terminal Railroad. Rolls of paper and raw materials for the mill are visible near the bridge. (Chris Morley collection.)

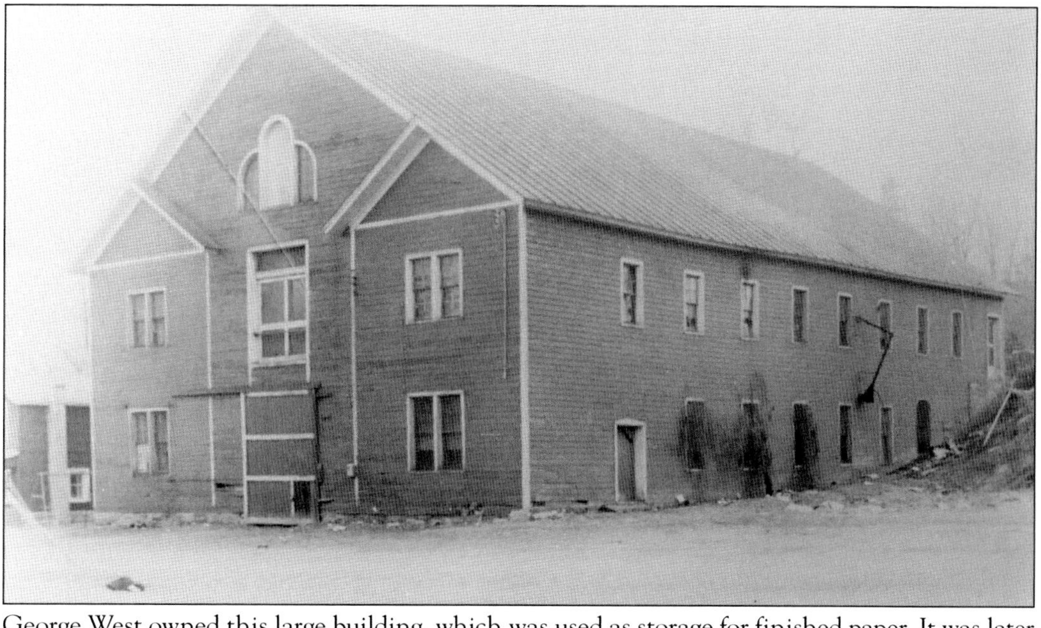

George West owned this large building, which was used as storage for finished paper. It was later used as the village garage until it burned down. Today, this site across Prospect Street from the Union Mill is a public parking lot. (Chris Morley collection.)

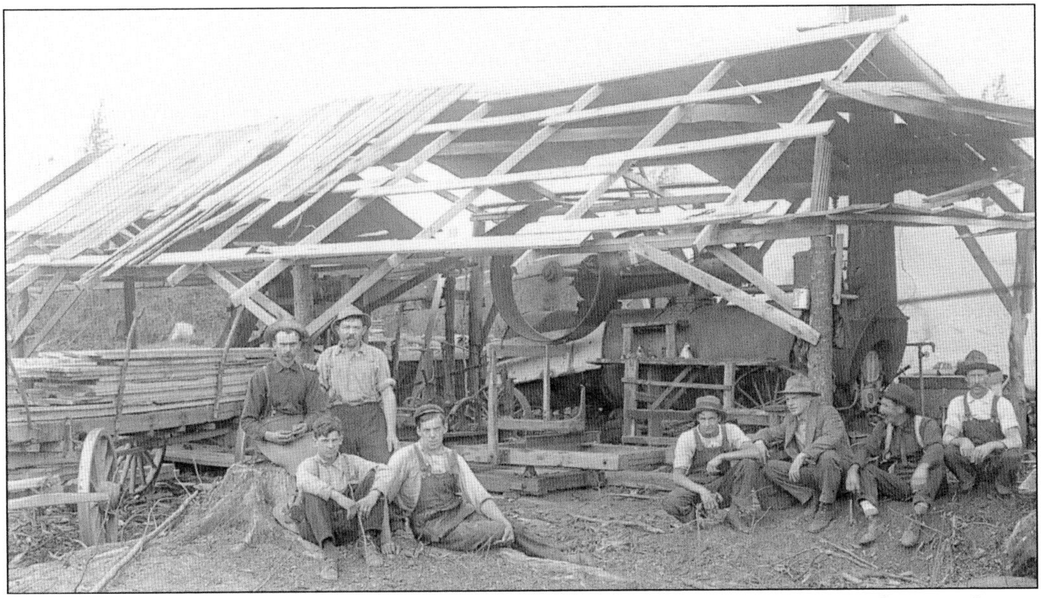

Established by Lester Streever in 1880, the Streever Lumber Company on Pleasant Street was one of the most successful and longest-lived sawmills in the history of Ballston Spa. The Streever family owned woodland around Saratoga County and set up portable sawmills at each location so that rough-cut lumber could be delivered to the main plant in Ballston Spa. (Chris Morley collection.)

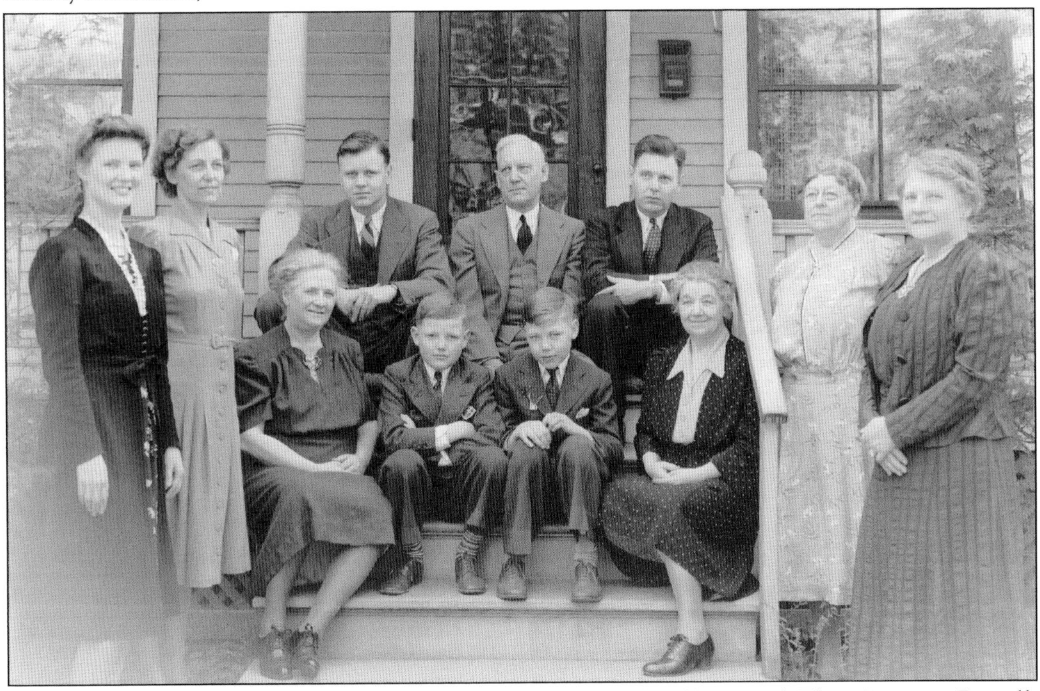

In this portrait of the Streever family are, from left to right, (first row) Elsie Streever Batzell, Doris Temple Streever, Imogene Granger, Donald Streever, unidentified, Carroll Streever, Mrs. Temple, and Caroline Streever; (second row) Ted Batzell, Lester Streever, and Donald Streever. (Streever collection, Saratoga County Historical Society at Brookside Museum.)

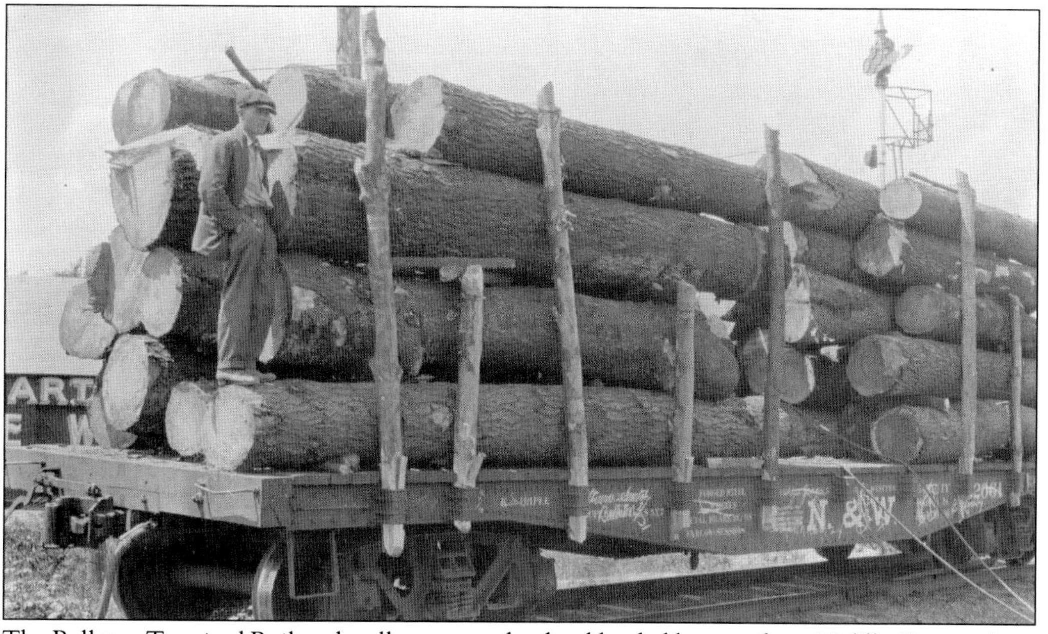

The Ballston Terminal Railroad trolley was used to haul loaded log cars from Middle Grove, where the Streevers owned vast woodlands, to the main sawmill in Ballston Spa. (Streever collection, Saratoga County Historical Society at Brookside Museum.)

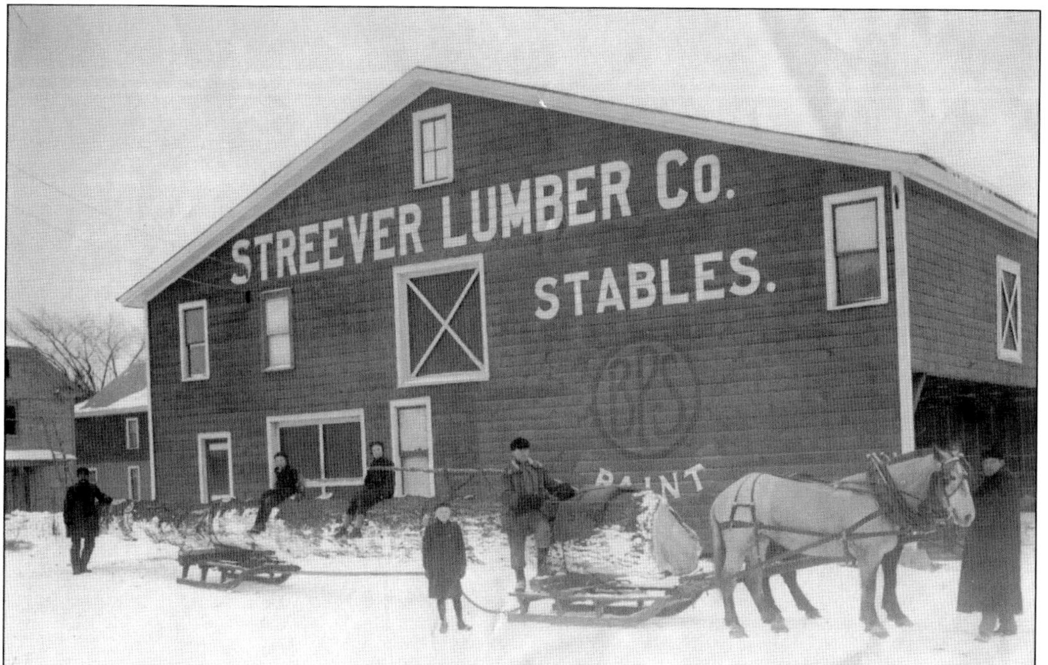

By the 1920s, the Streever sawmill had become so successful that it split into three companies: Streever Lumber Company, F.S. Streever Construction Company, and Streever Realty Company. Several generations of Streevers maintained the business into the 1940s. (Streever collection, Saratoga County Historical Society at Brookside Museum.)

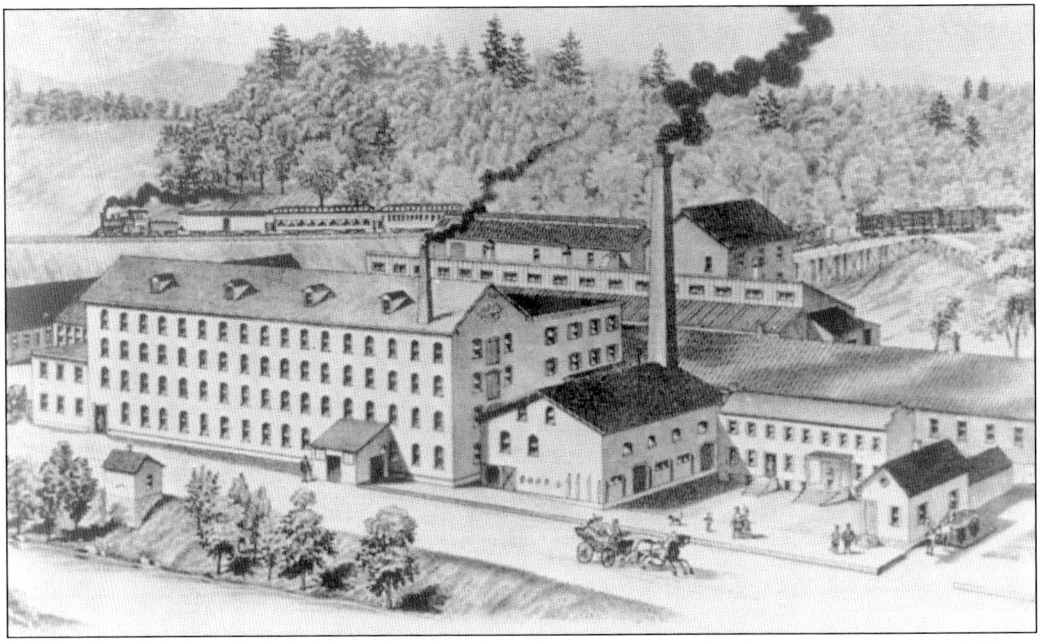

Samuel Haight and his brother-in-law Matthew Vassar operated a thriving tannery at Milton Center before it was destroyed by fire in 1878. Rather than rebuild, they decided to relocate to Bath Street in Ballston Spa, near the Delaware and Hudson main line. Within a short time, the Bull's Head Tannery was a thriving business that employed hundreds of men and boys. (Chris Morley collection.)

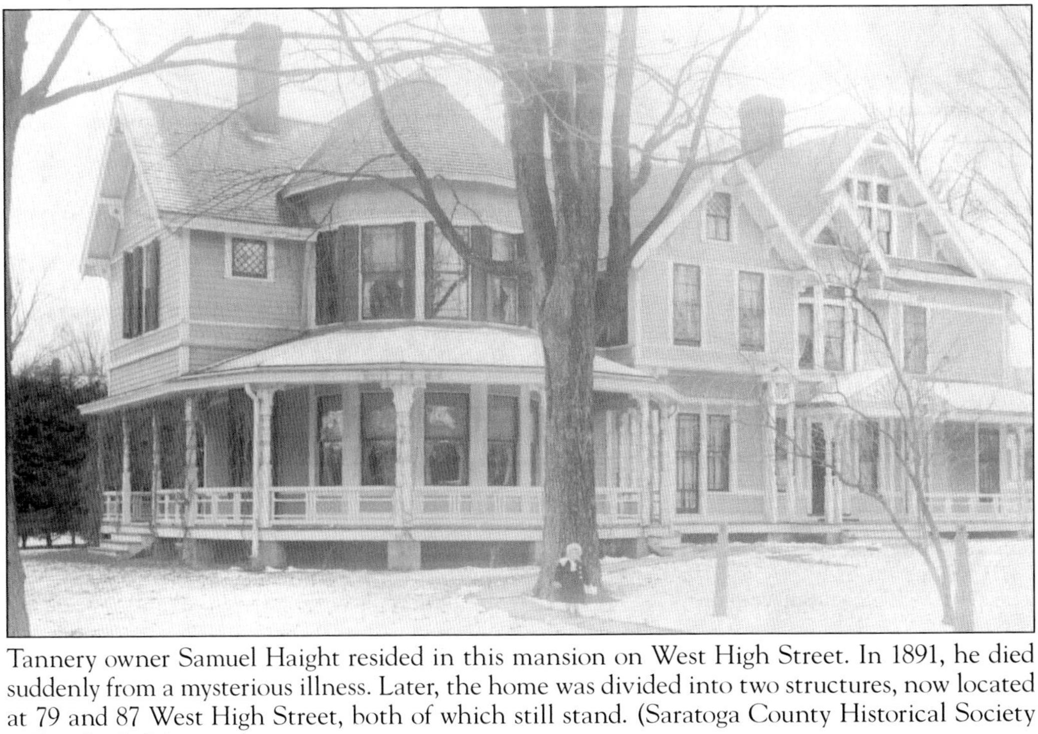

Tannery owner Samuel Haight resided in this mansion on West High Street. In 1891, he died suddenly from a mysterious illness. Later, the home was divided into two structures, now located at 79 and 87 West High Street, both of which still stand. (Saratoga County Historical Society at Brookside Museum.)

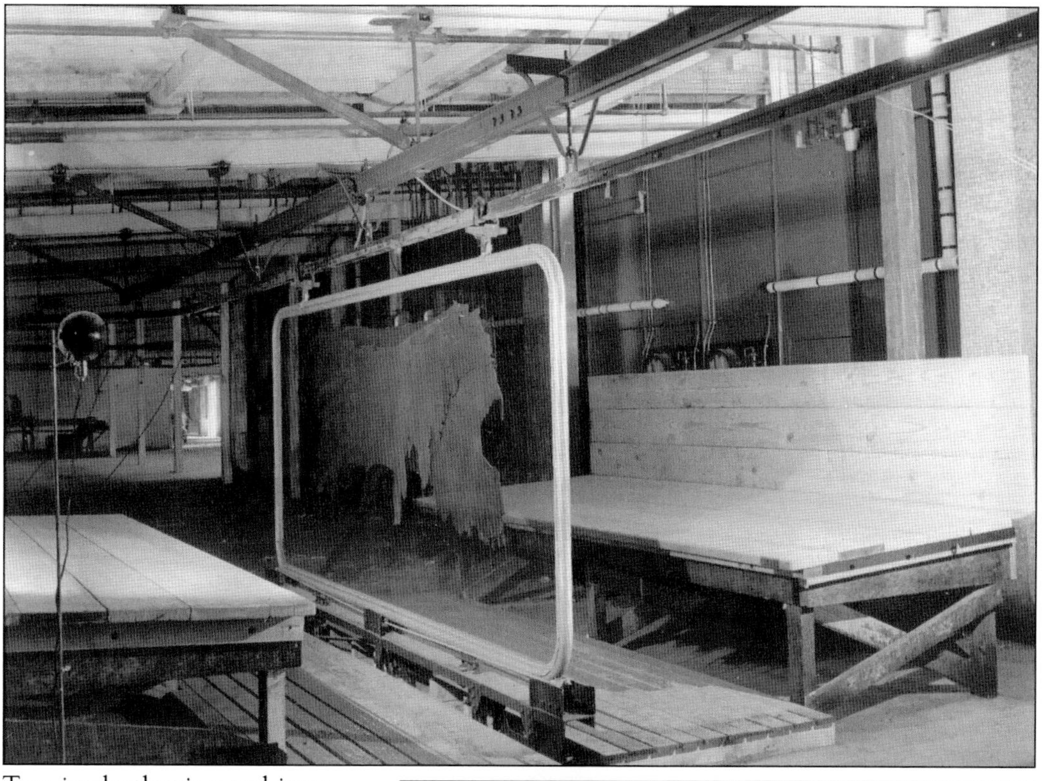

Tanning leather is a multistep process that involves "unhairing" the hides, adding chemicals, wringing them dry, coloring, and finishing. In the pasting room, hides were "pasted" to glass for stretching. Before this innovation, hides were tacked up and stretched manually. (Saratoga County Historical Society at Brookside Museum.)

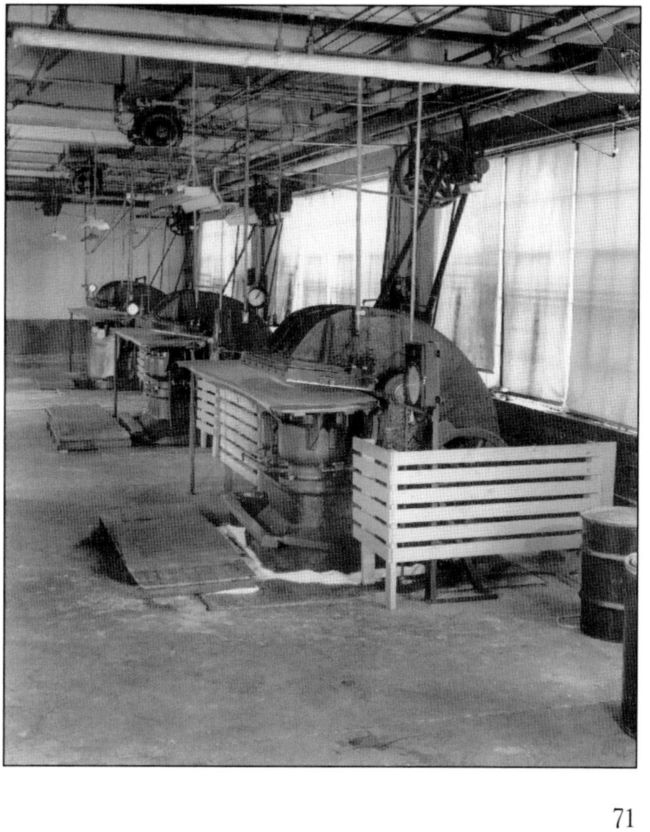

Hand ironing and polishing were no longer necessary once these machines were added to the tannery's automated processes. They were used to iron and polish the finished hides for a uniform finish, after which the hides merely needed to be dried, measured, and sorted. (Saratoga County Historical Society at Brookside Museum.)

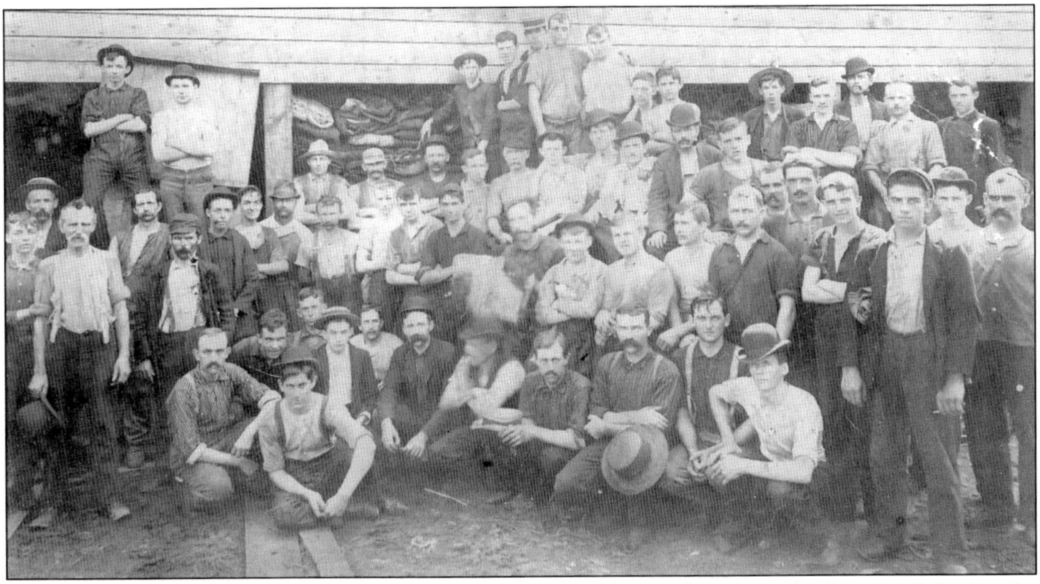

At the time this employee photograph was taken, the Bull's Head Tannery had reached the height of its success as an independent company before being absorbed by American Hide & Leather in 1899. (Chris Morley collection.)

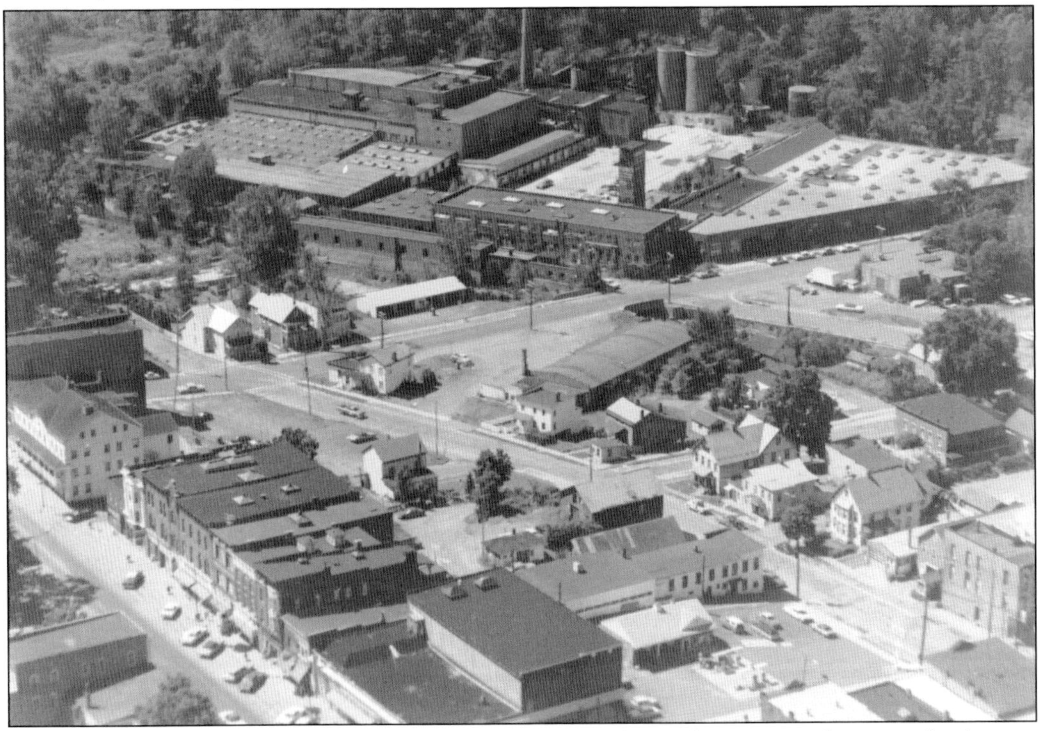

The American Hide & Leather tannery grew during the early 1900s to become the largest industrial complex in Milton, covering two acres of land from Bath Street to the Delaware and Hudson Railway main line. Most of the buildings survive, although their future is uncertain; the site had been used for industrial purposes for over 200 years. (Saratoga County Historical Society at Brookside Museum.)

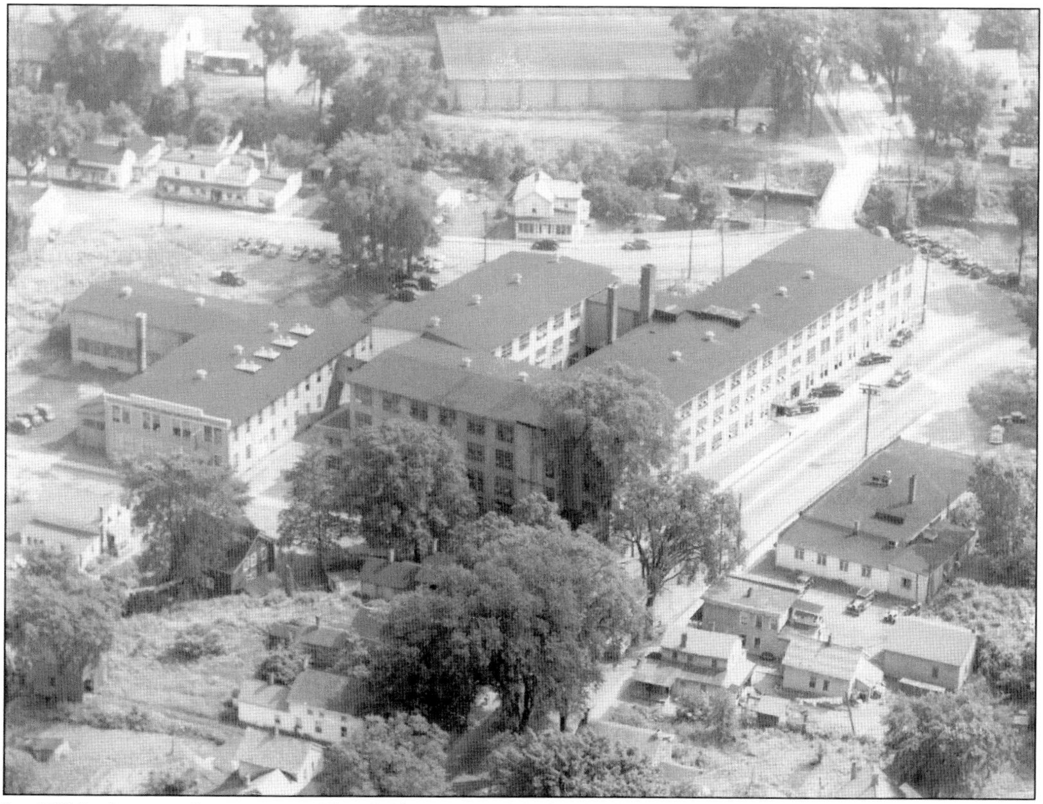

In 1920, Amsterdam native Floyd Shutts established what would later become known as the Ballston-Stillwater Knitting Company. The extensive building complex along Ralph Street is testimony to the company's success. By 1950, it employed 360 workers and produced 15 million knit socks per year. (Paul and Marilyn Pastore collection.)

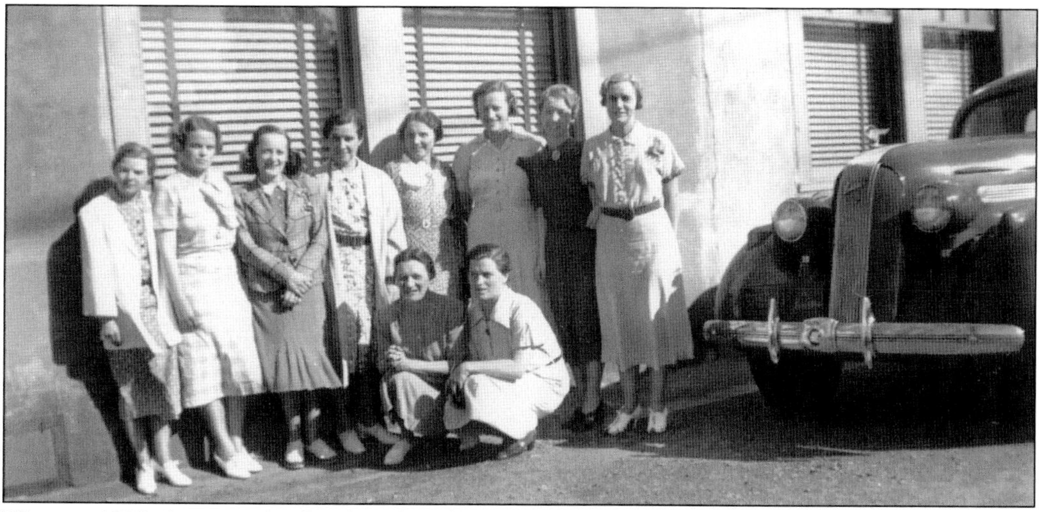

This is a 1937 photograph of 10 female Ballston-Stillwater Knitting Company workers. They are, from left to right, (standing) Ruth Heeney, Mildred Streifert, Mary Bilonis, Helen Flinton, Louise Wakefield, Laverna Frisbie, Mae Butler, and Emma Kvashnack; (kneeling) Mrs. Cox and Grace Knickerbocker. (Pat Streifert collection.)

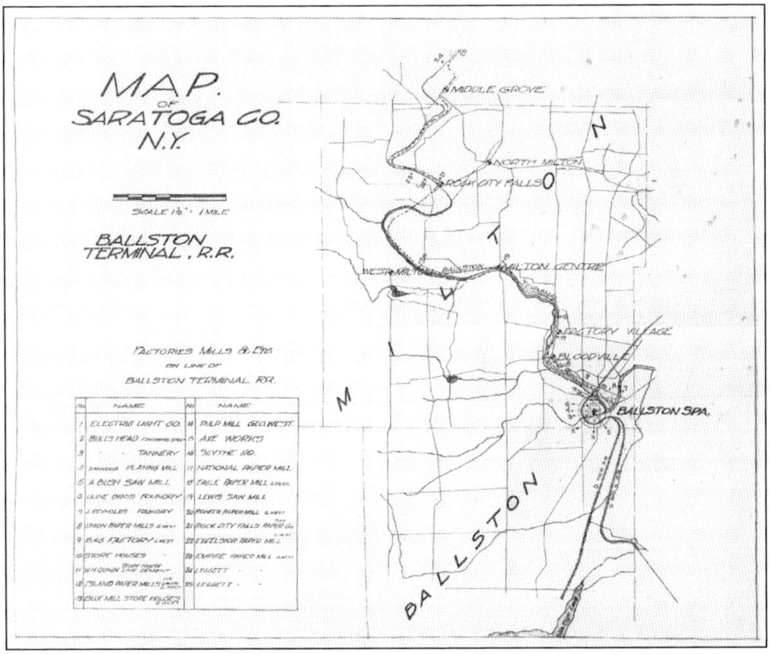

The Ballston Terminal Railroad was established in 1896 during the wave of electric trolley lines that were springing up all over the country. Despite the fact that most trolley railways carried passengers almost exclusively, this map clearly shows the main purpose of the Ballston line was to serve the two dozen factories along its route north to Middle Grove. (Ed Bond collection.)

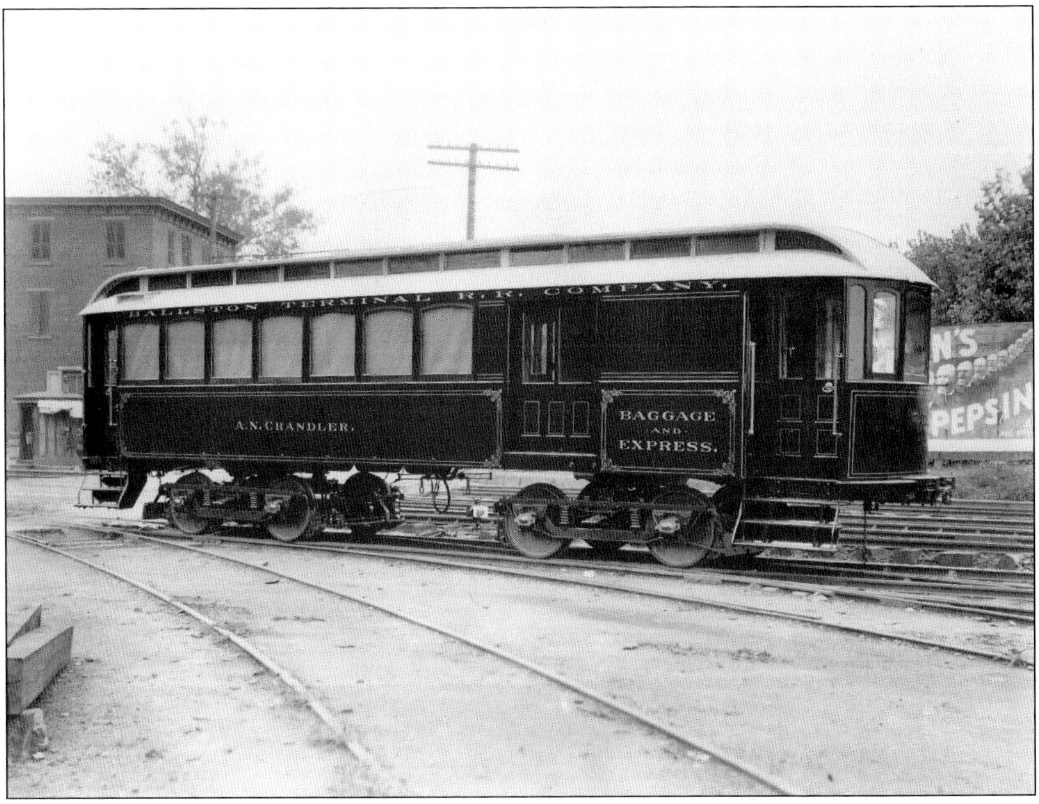

This builder's photograph shows the trolley car *A.N. Chandler* (named after one of the railroad's early investors) just off the assembly line. It would see active service between Ballston Spa and Middle Grove for the next three decades. (Ed Bond collection.)

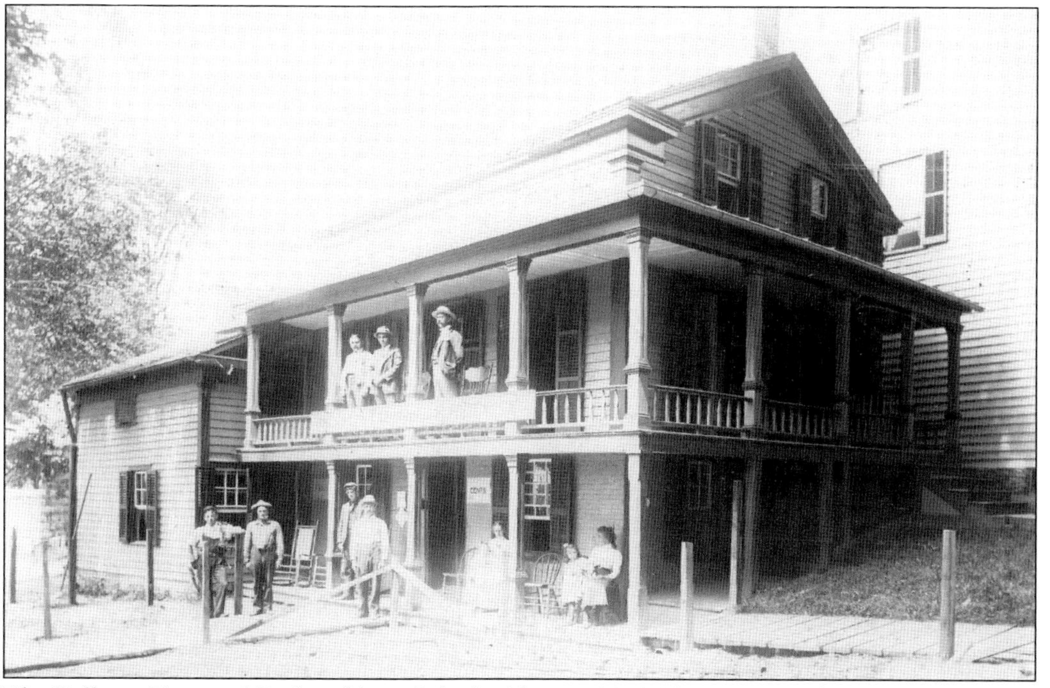

The Ballston Terminal Railroad leased the building at 309 Milton Avenue from George West as a passenger waiting station. Station agent Walter Estes is standing on the right on the second-story porch. The faded sign reads, "Ballston Terminal RR Office." The door on the left was for "Ladies," while the door on the right was for "Gents." (Town of Milton Historian.)

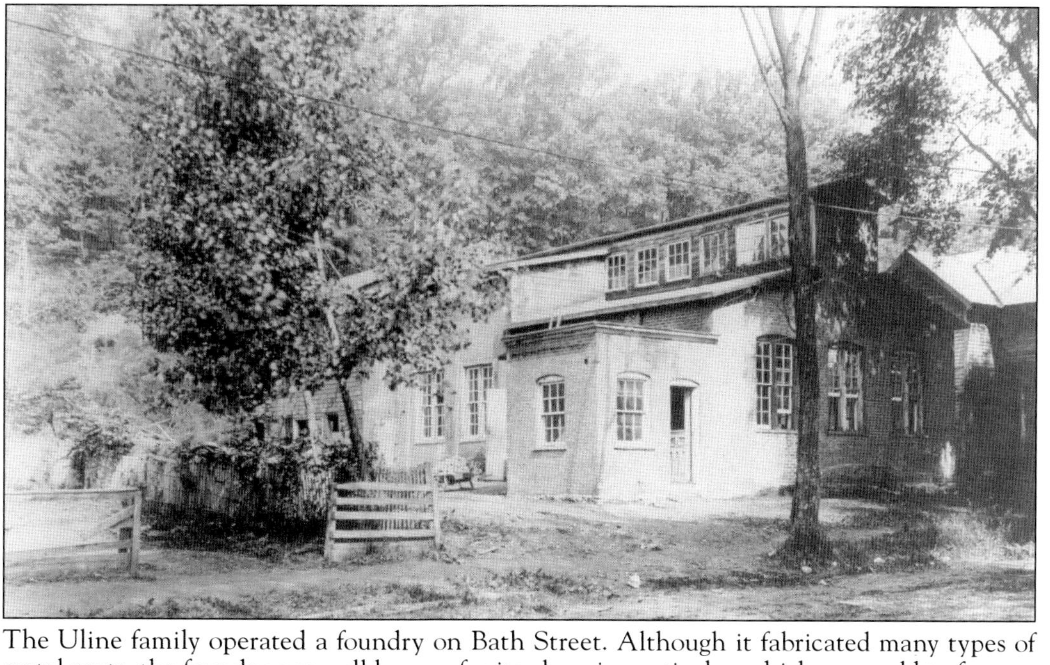

The Uline family operated a foundry on Bath Street. Although it fabricated many types of metal parts, the foundry was well known for its plows in particular, which were sold to farmers throughout the area. The building was sold to the Davison-Namack Foundry Company in 1905 before coming back into the family in 1913. (Chris Morley collection.)

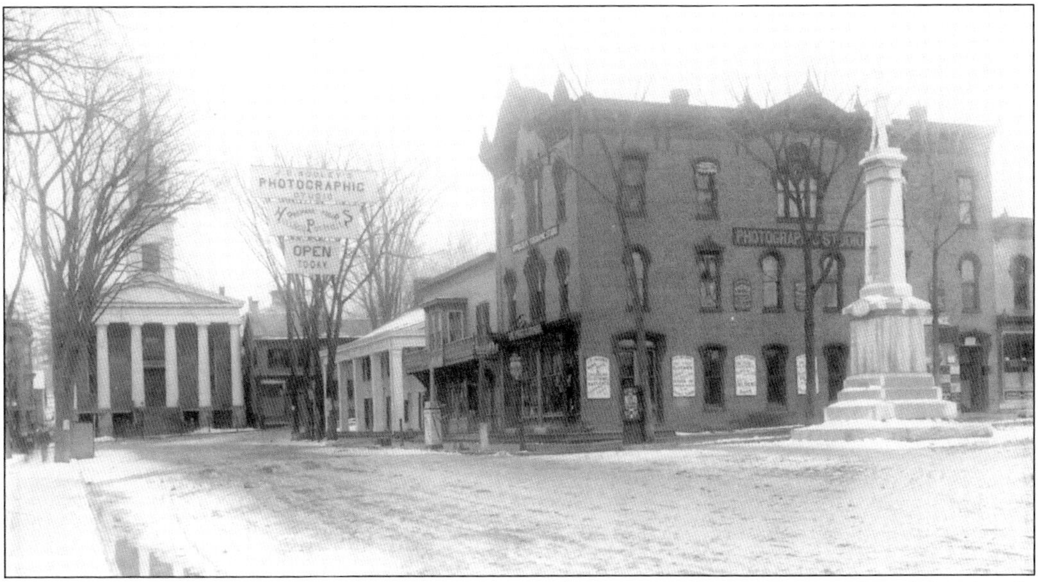

Photographer Jesse Sumner Wooley was born in Wilton in 1867 but later moved with his family to the geysers outside of Saratoga Springs. He first apprenticed with Baker and Record before going to work for Ballston Spa photographer T.J. Arnold. Wooley purchased Arnold's Monument Square studio on Front Street for $1,500 in 1887. He took many of the photographs appearing in this book. (Saratoga County Historical Society at Brookside Museum.)

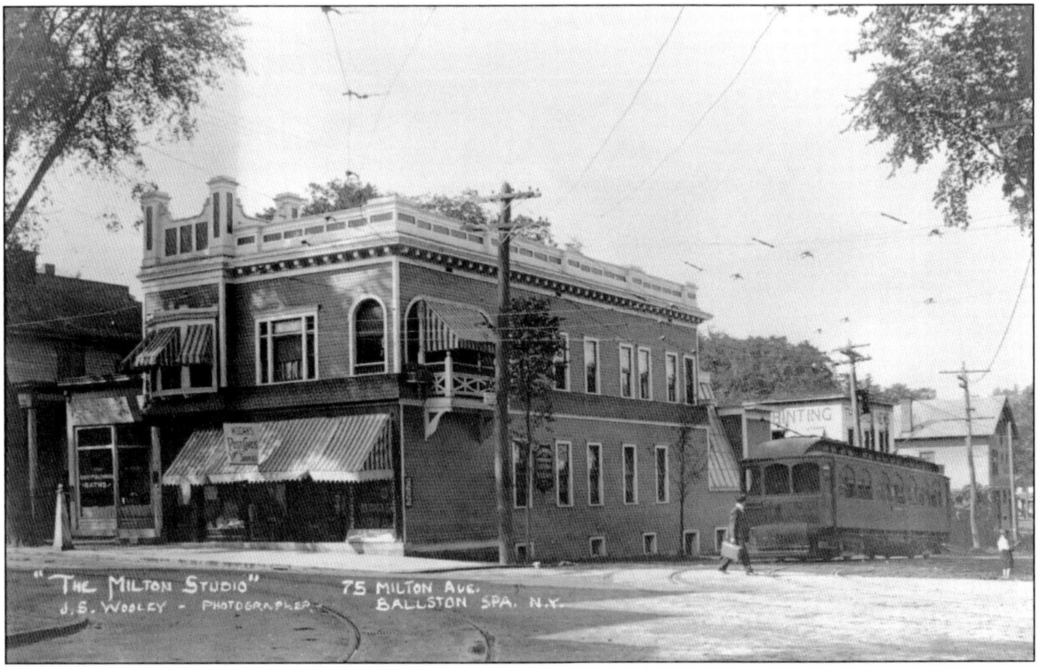

Once Jesse Wooley was established as the primary photographer in Ballston Spa, he became known for conducting photographic tours of Europe and parts of the United States. In 1903, he commissioned the construction of a new studio on the corner of Milton Avenue and Washington Street. When he retired, the building was sold to photographer Howard Humes. (Saratoga County Historical Society at Brookside Museum.)

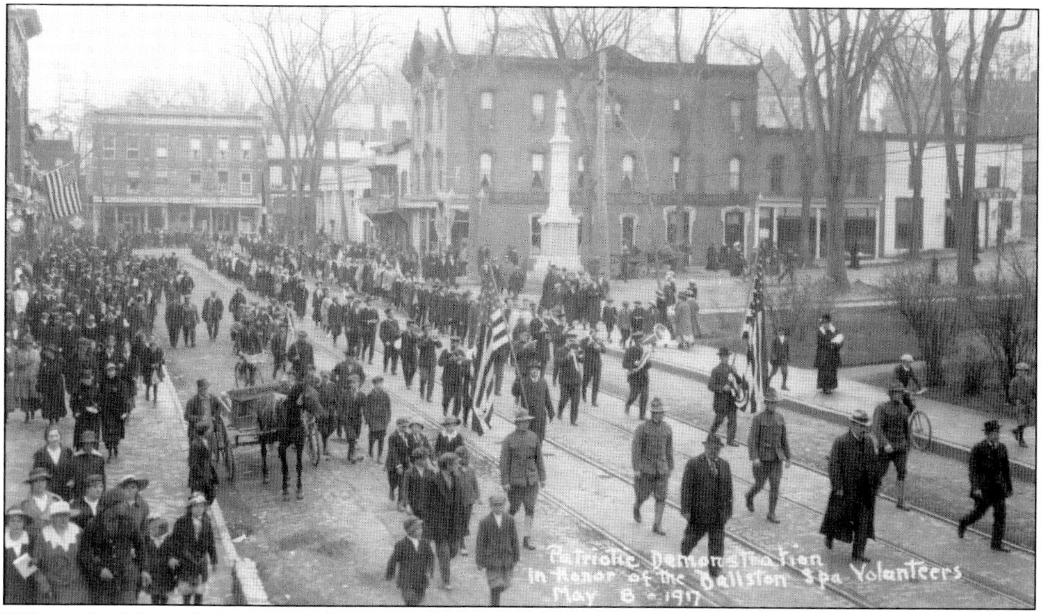

When the United States finally entered World War I in 1917, three years after it started, there were plentiful volunteers who signed up to join the effort. These volunteers are lined up in front of the Bath Street railroad station, just out of view on the right. Lillie's Department Store is in the distance. (Saratoga County Historical Society at Brookside Museum.)

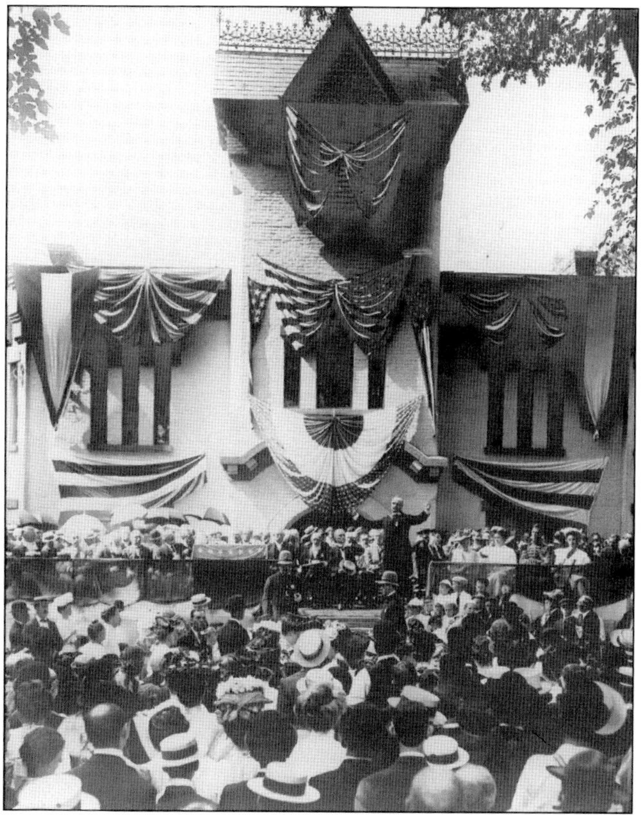

The armory on the corner of West High Street and Milton Avenue was the site of Ballston Spa village president Irving Wiswall's centennial address before an enthusiastic crowd on June 25, 1907. The building was first constructed in 1858 for the 29th Regiment of the New York State Militia. When the militia disbanded in 1873, it was purchased by the Christ Episcopal Church. (Saratoga County Historical Society at Brookside Museum.)

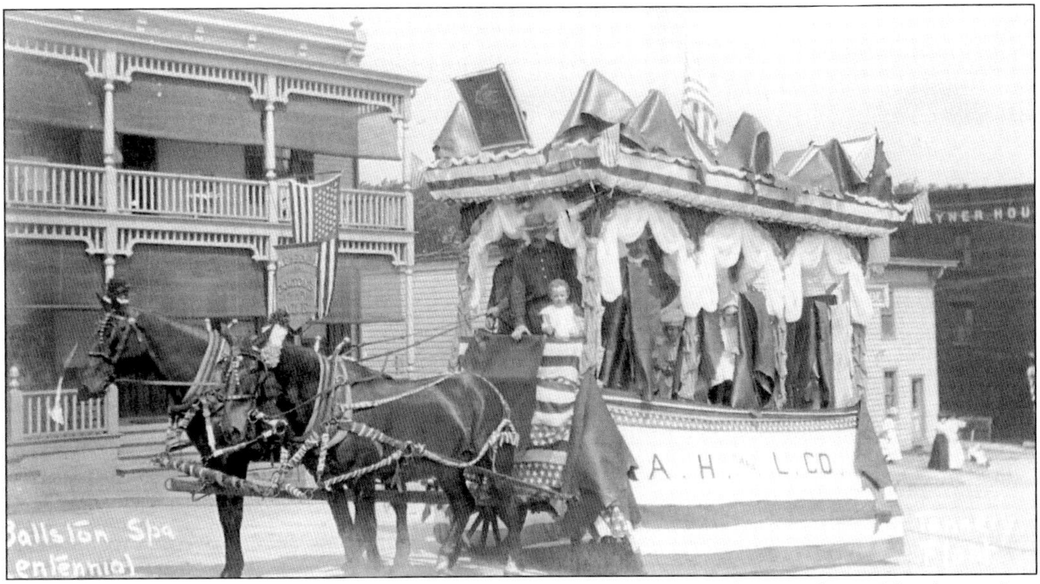

The 1907 centennial celebrations were marked by parades, speeches, and a public festival at Brookside. In that year, Edward Grose published the *Centennial History of the Village of Ballston Spa*, which, despite some errors, is still the definitive history of the village itself and the town of Milton as a whole. (Saratoga County Historical Society at Brookside Museum.)

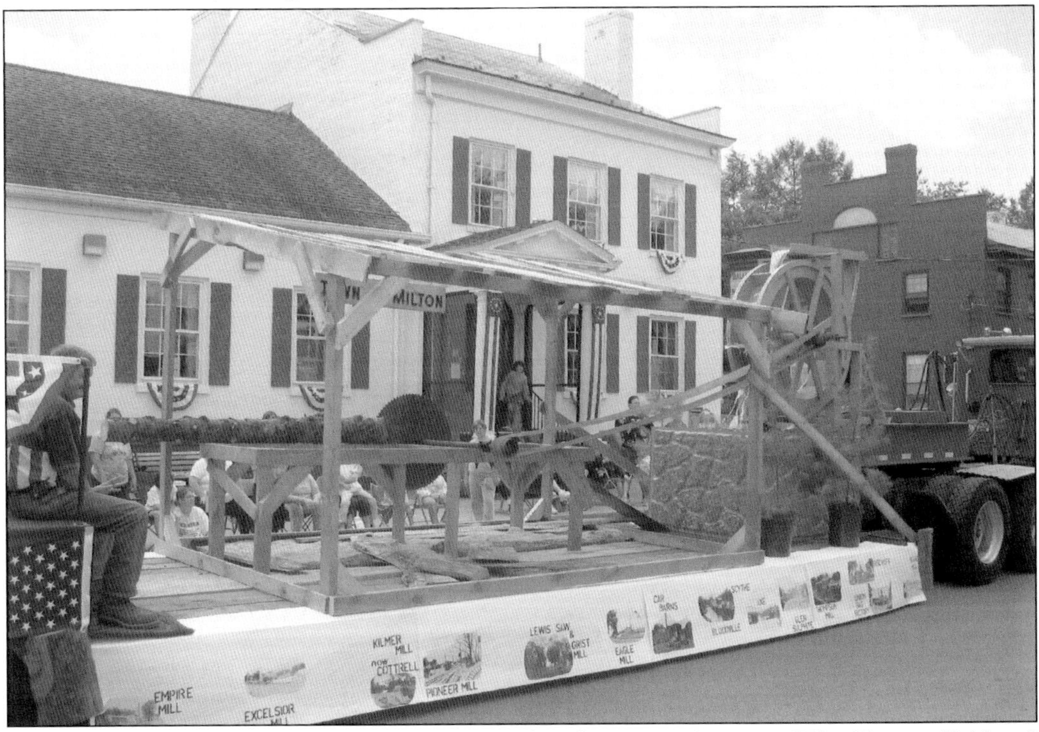

In 2007, Ballston Spa celebrated its bicentennial with a year of events. "The Town of Milton" float depicted a sawmill, along with photographs of the individual mills that played such an important role in the town's history as the float's skirting. The Ballston Spa National Bank is in the background. (Author's collection.)

Four

BLOODVILLE

Sylvester Blood was a scythe maker who had a small shop on the Mourning Kill two miles south of Ballston Spa. When his shop burned down, he decided to purchase a tract of land along the Kayaderosseras in what was then called "the Hollow." Young Isaiah learned the business under his father's apprenticeship, and in 1837 he was able to take over its operations when the elder Blood sold the business to him.

The area grew in prosperity once the scythe factory was enlarged to increase production. Blood proved to be a generous employer, selling lots to his employees or providing low-cost tenement housing. Wages were more than competitive, and while he was alive there is no record of worker unrest or strikes.

It is believed that one of his workers named the growing hamlet Bloodville in his honor in 1850. That same year, Blood expanded his business by acquiring land about a half mile south of his scythe factory and began the production of axes and other hard-edge tools. During the next decade, Bloodville grew rapidly as the capacity and production of the factories increased. Once all the lots were occupied along Maple Avenue, two more streets were laid out named Division and Middle Streets. The inconvenience of having to travel to Ballston Spa for supplies was alleviated as stores and other mercantile interests moved in to serve the growing population. A schoolhouse was built for the children as more workmen settled down and started raising families.

At the peak of operations, the Ballston Scythe and Axe Works gave employment to over 350 men. After Isaiah Blood died in 1870, his son-in-law Henry Knickerbocker inherited the business and continued its operation, although he spent most of his time in New York City and left the day-to-day management to others. A hard-edge tool trust called the American Axe & Tool Company assumed control in 1892, and many hoped that operations would continue. However, both the scythe and axe factories were destroyed in separate fires in 1900, never to be rebuilt.

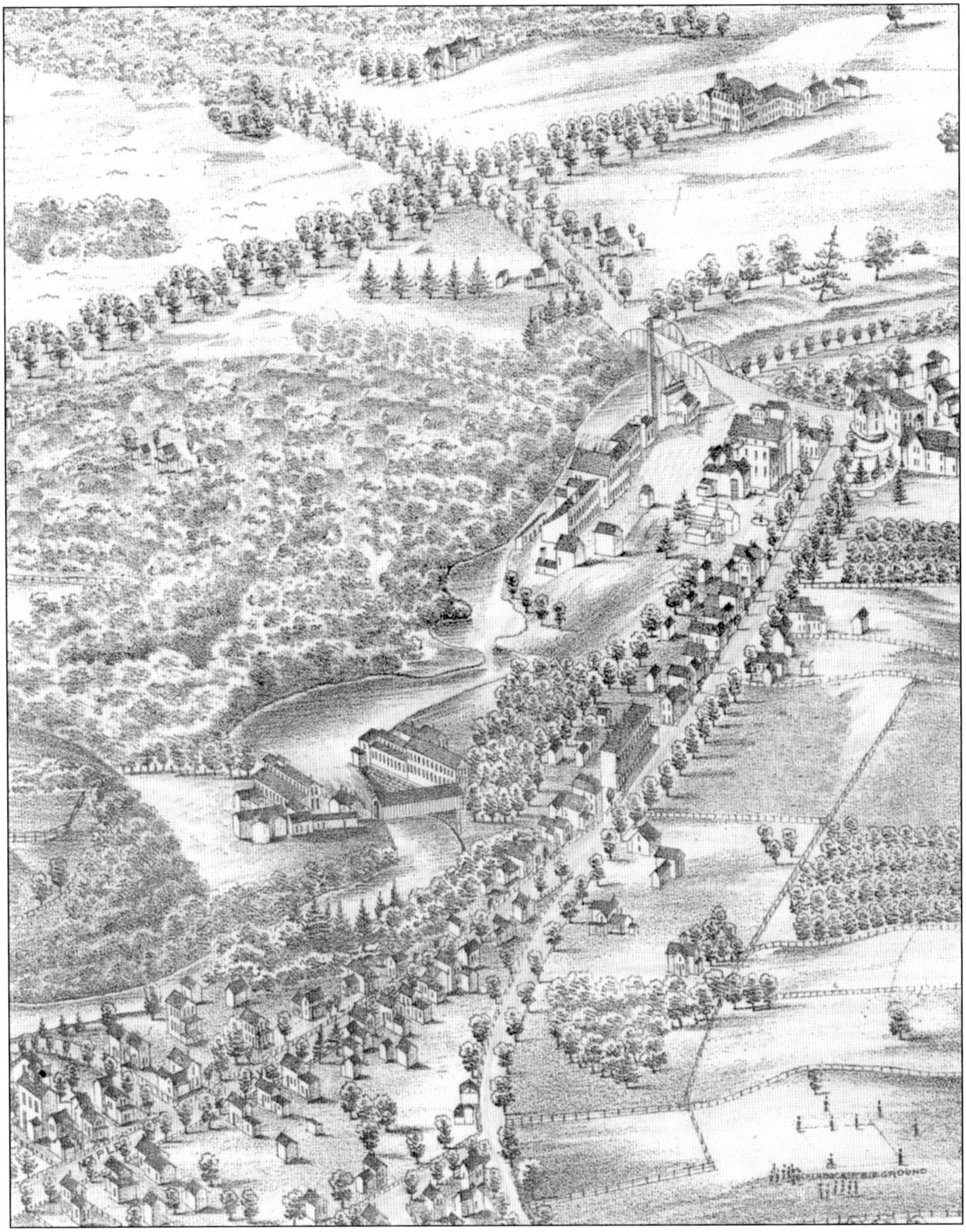

This c. 1870 drawing is an excellent representation of the layout of Bloodville. Maple Avenue is depicted on the east side of Kayaderosseras Creek, while County Farm Road led over a bridge (no longer in existence) to the Saratoga County Alms House (top). Isaiah Blood's mansion, offices, and scythe factory are situated at the north end of the hamlet, while the axe factory occupied both sides of the creek at the south end. (Chris Morley collection.)

This 1866 map depicts the compact yet thriving hamlet of Bloodville near its peak of industrial activity. It is obvious from the business directory listing that the economy was almost completely dependent upon the axe and scythe factories; however, Benjamin Barber also operated a sash and blind factory (bottom). Next door was a woolen mill that operated intermittently beginning in 1835. (Chris Morley collection.)

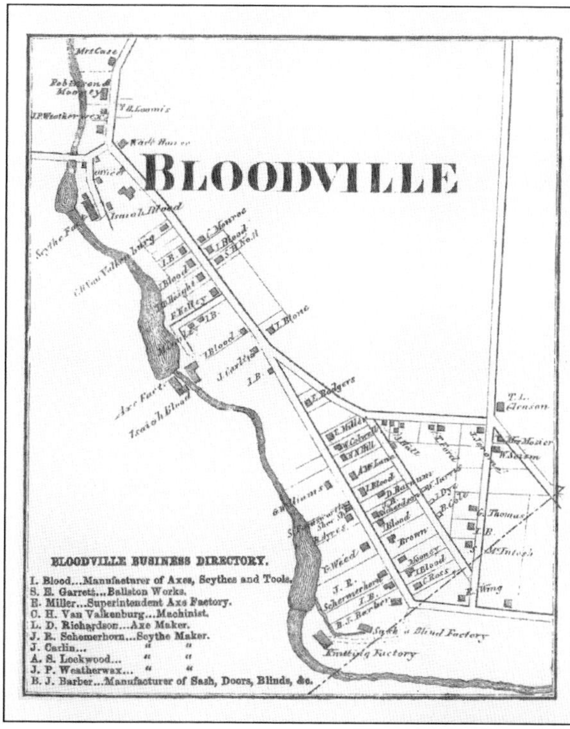

After Isaiah Blood died in 1870, his mansion, known as the Maples, remained in the family for another 20 years, first occupied by his widow and then sporadically by his daughter and son-in-law. In 1892, it was acquired by the hard-edge tool trust and used by factory managers. Later, it was renovated as apartments, but then destroyed by fire in 1995. Today, an apartment complex occupies the site. (Paul and Marilyn Pastore collection.)

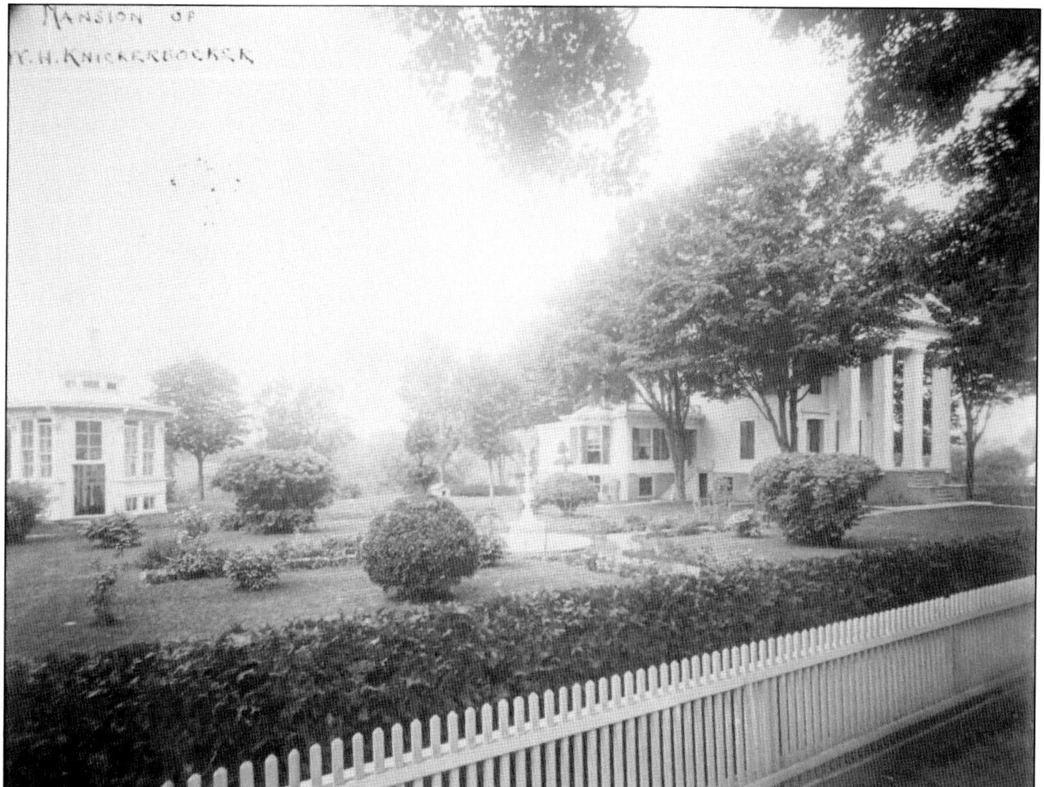

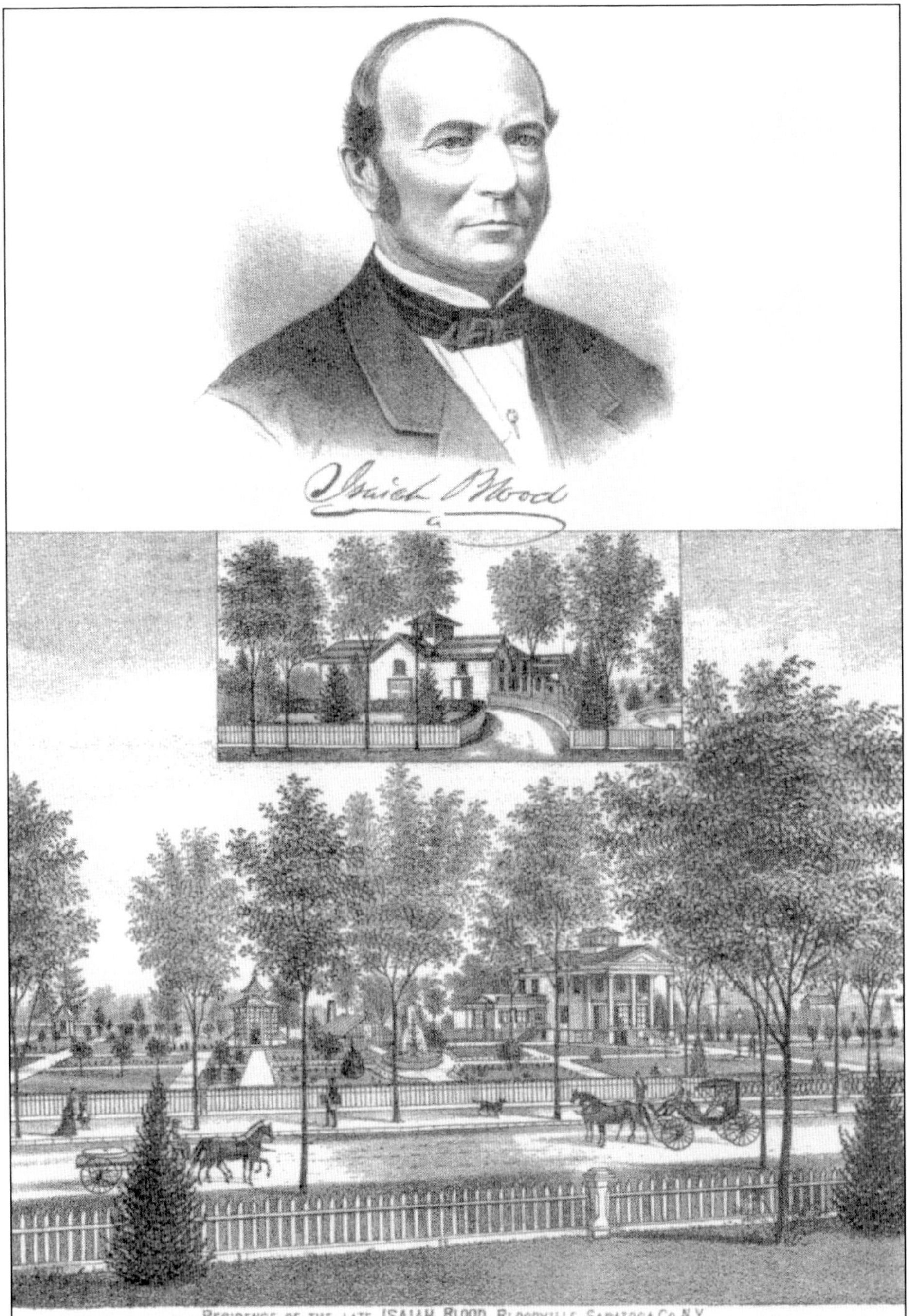

Born in the town of Ballston on February 13, 1810, Isaiah Blood is considered one of the most popular citizens in Milton's history. When his hard-edge tool business became successful, he began giving his employees zero-interest loans so that they could build their own houses. Blood was also active in politics, serving as Milton town supervisor, a member of the assembly, and state senator. His funeral in 1870 was perhaps the largest in town history. (*History of Saratoga County, New York*, 1878.)

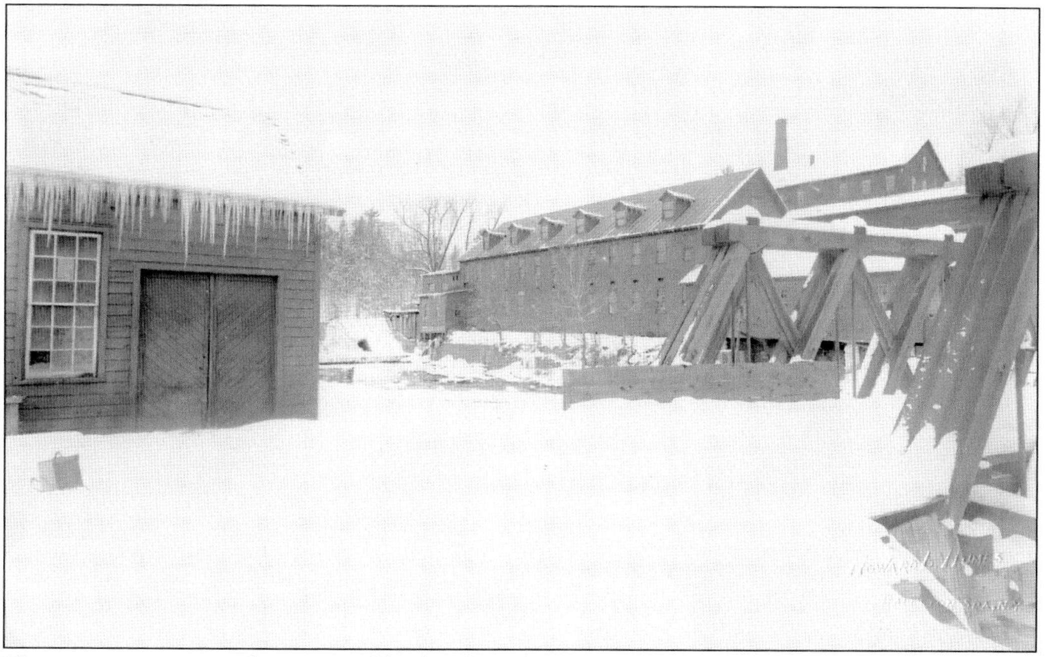

The extensive axe works occupied both sides of the Kayaderosseras. To the left is the machine shop, which was connected to the forge shop (out of view). Across the river were the grinding, handle-fitting, and packing rooms. Part of the dam and flume can be seen to the right of the machine shop. (Saratoga County Historical Society at Brookside Museum.)

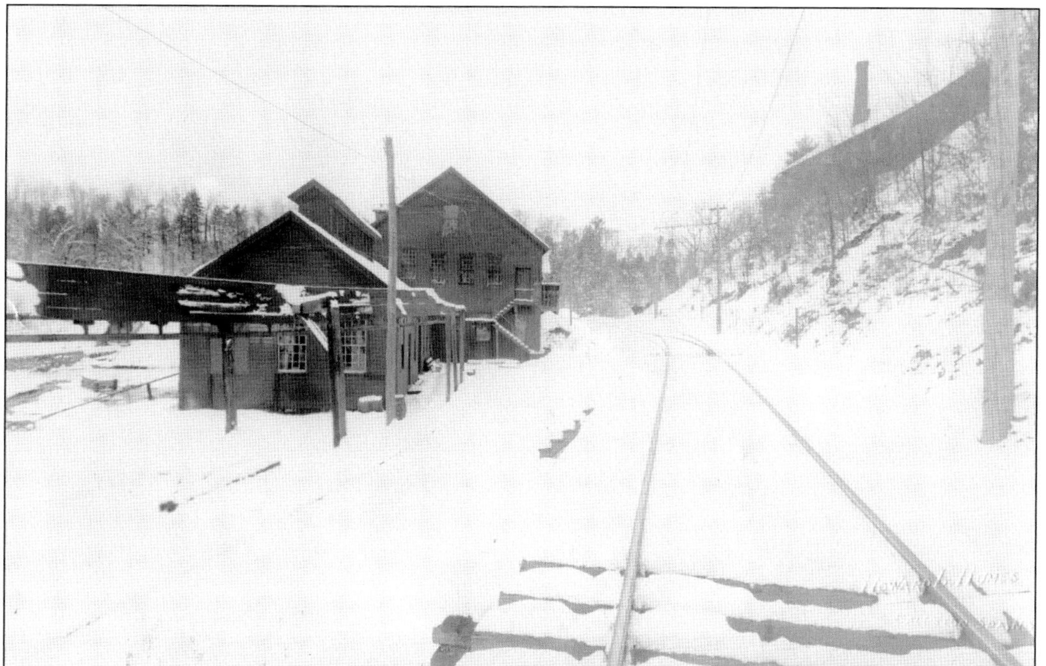

The Ballston Terminal Railroad main line ran between the polishing houses and packinghouses of the axe works and the steep embankment that led to street level. The partially frozen Kayaderosseras Creek can just be made out on the left. (Chris Morley collection.)

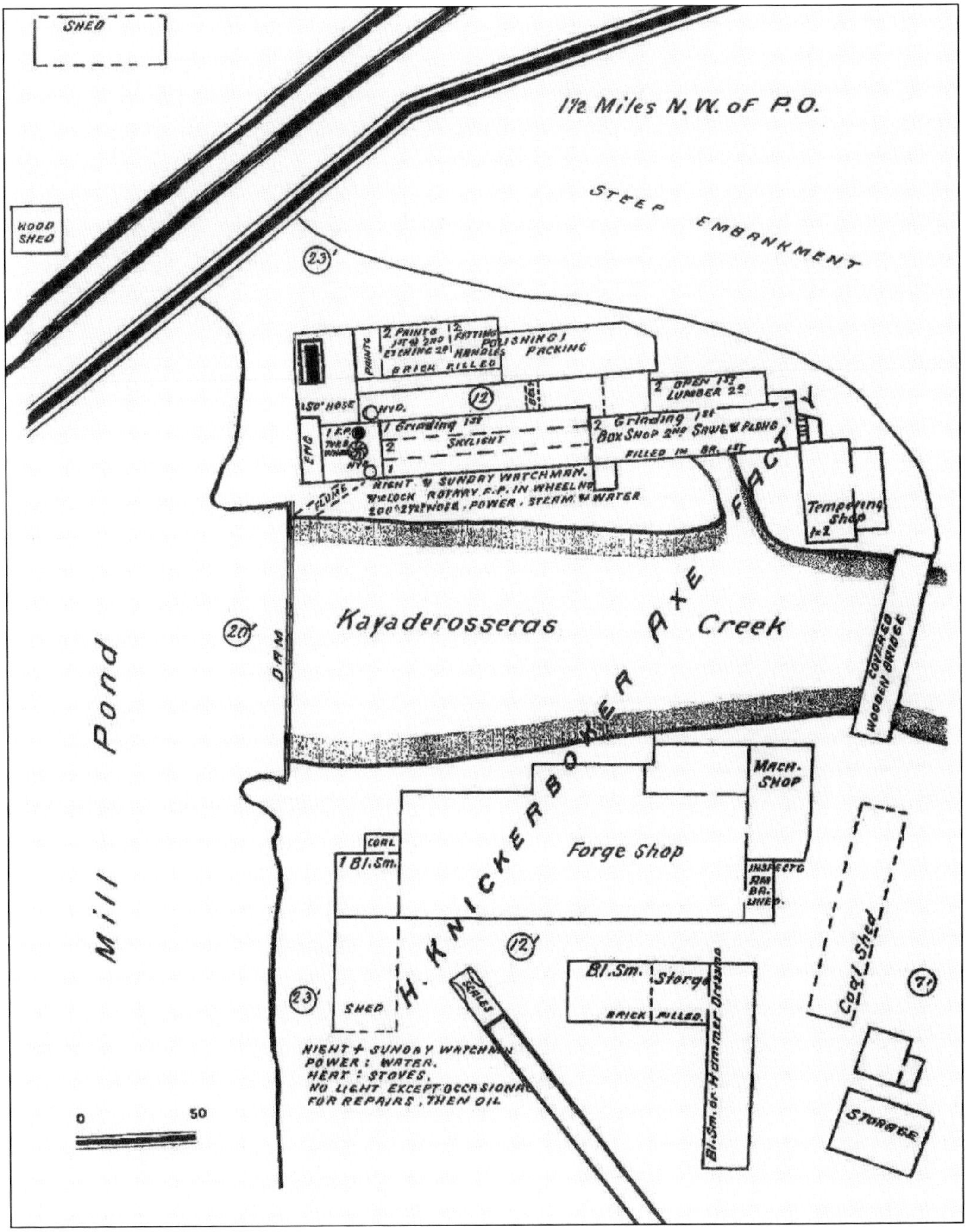

This c. 1900 fire equipment map shows the layout of the axe works along both banks of Kayaderosseras Creek. By this time, it had become known as the Knickerbocker Axe Factory, named after Isaiah Blood's son-in-law Henry Knickerbocker. The lines on the top of the drawing represent the Ballston Terminal Railroad main line and spurs. (Chris Morley collection.)

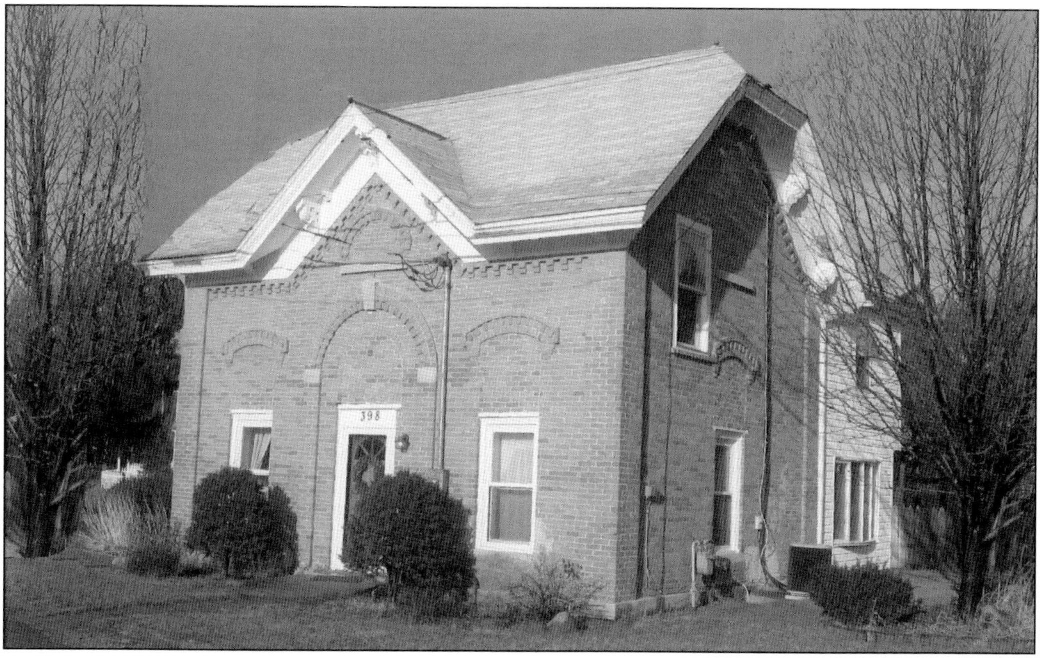

This charming brick building, located on Maple Avenue, served as Isaiah Blood's office, conveniently situated near his mansion and scythe factory. After the factories burned down, it was renovated as a residence. It is one of the few buildings of the former tool factory complex to survive. (Author's collection.)

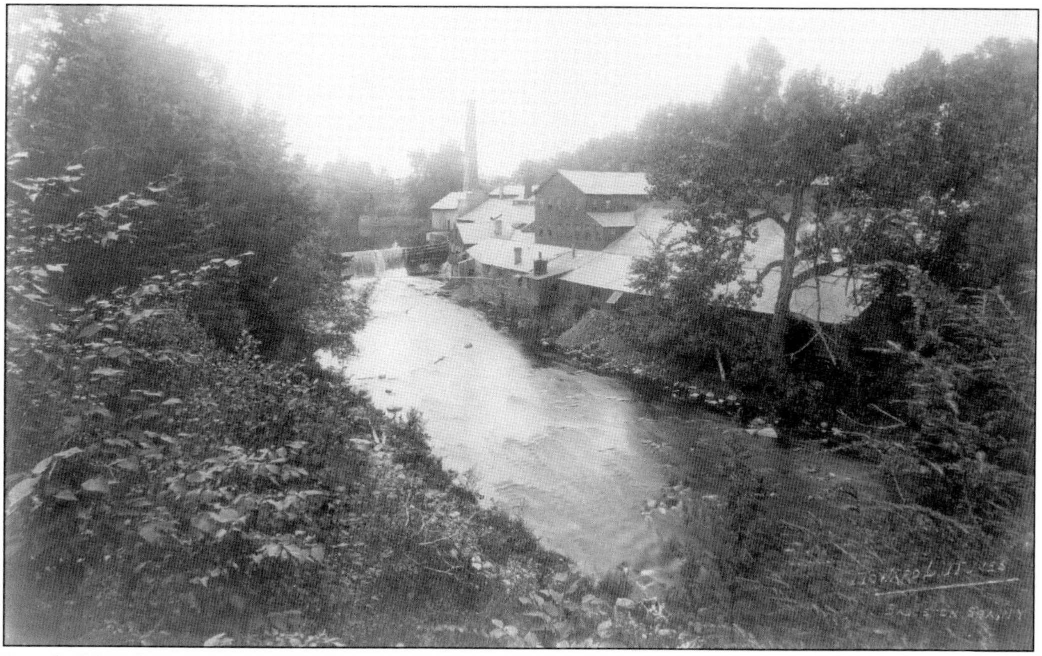

Isaiah Blood's massive scythe factory was built on the banks of Kayaderosseras Creek to take advantage of its waterpower. At its peak in the 1890s, the factory produced 1,200 scythes per day. The bridge in the extreme background led to the Saratoga County Alms House. (Chris Morley collection.)

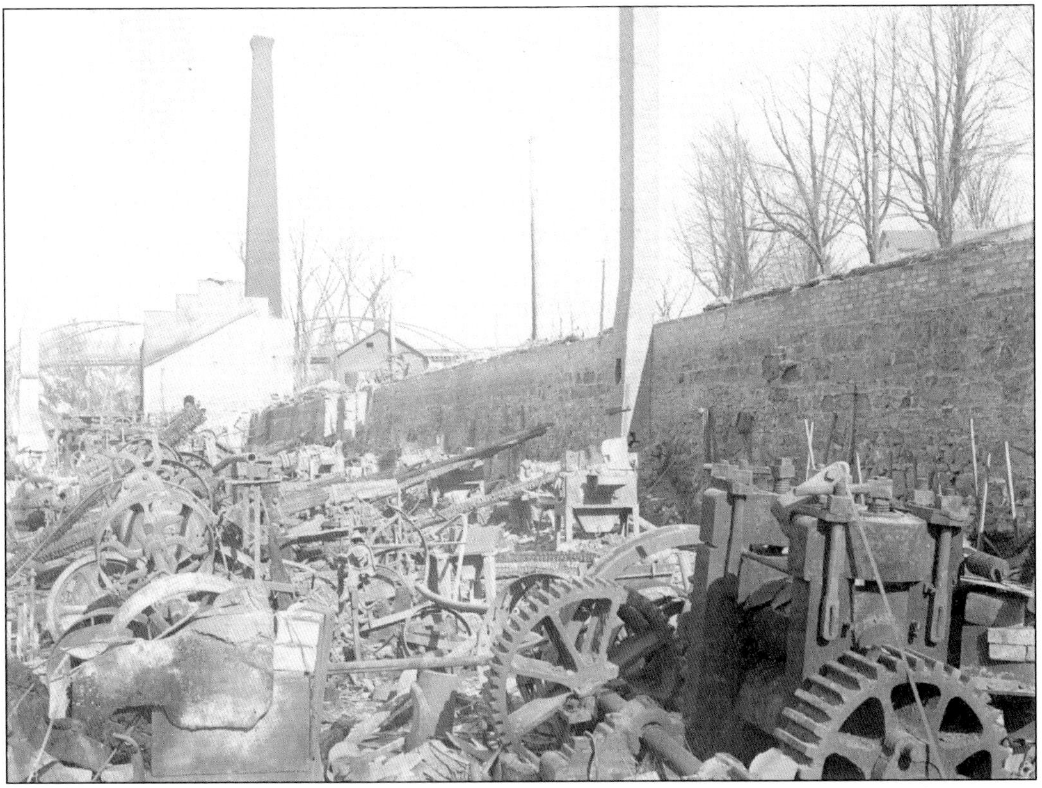

In May 1900, a massive fire almost completely destroyed the scythe factory, causing $70,000 in damages. It turned out to be a devastating blow to Bloodville. Regional trust American Axe & Tool Company had assumed control of the works in 1892. Since the business was not profitable enough to warrant a complete rebuild, operations were moved elsewhere, leaving hundreds of men out of work. (Both, Saratoga County Historical Society at Brookside Museum.)

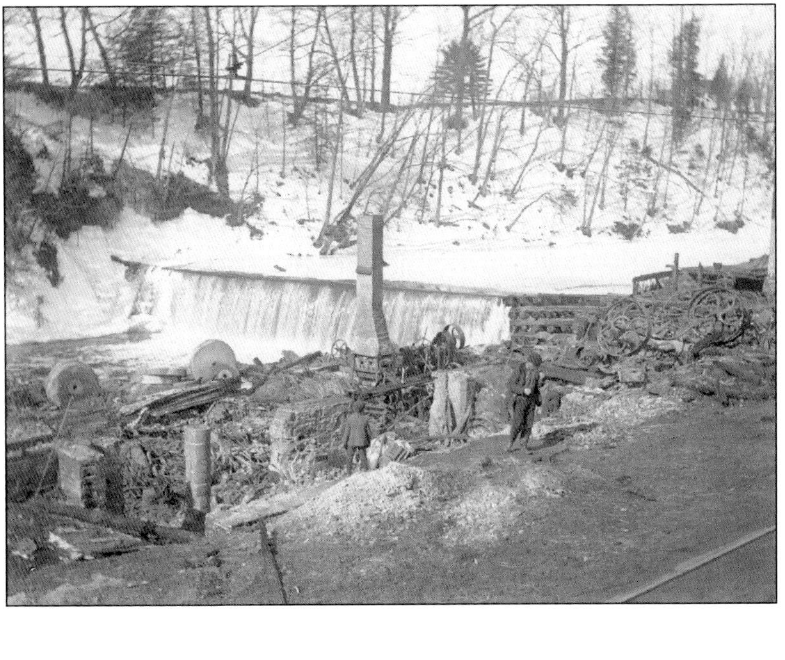

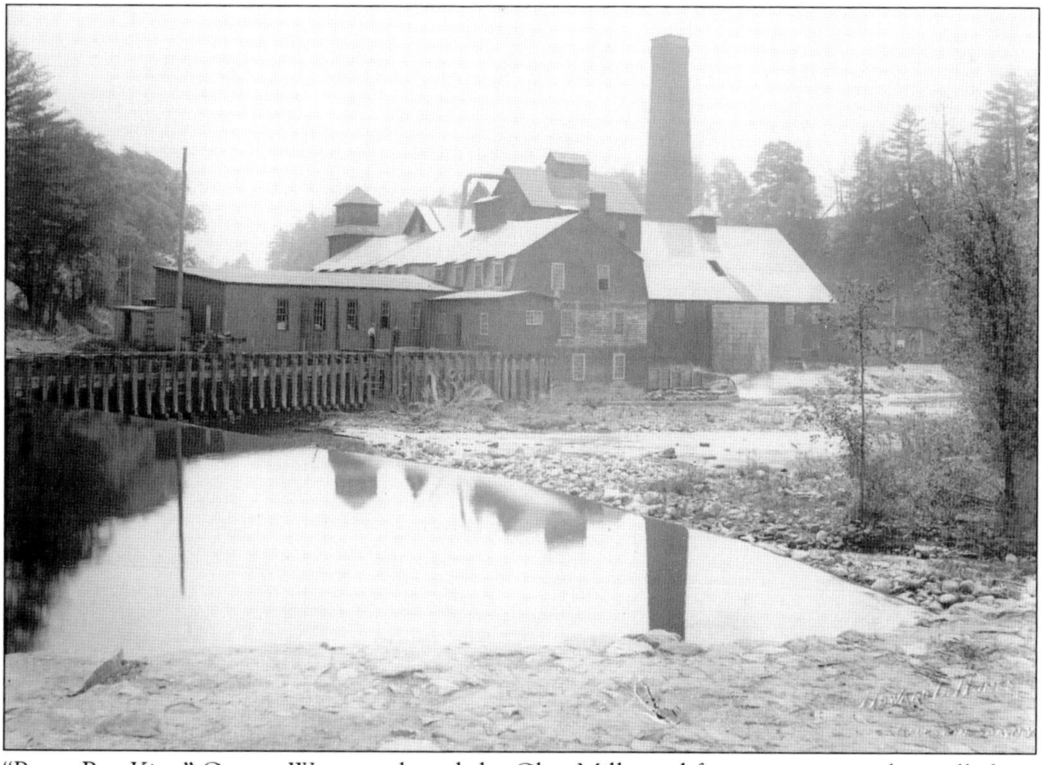

"Paper Bag King" George West purchased the Glen Mill, used for years as a woolen mill, from the Jonas Hovey estate in 1875. He refitted the building to process raw lumber into paper pulp, which would then be turned into paper at his other mills. It was located on the north side of Blue Mill Pond, just outside of the Ballston Spa village limits. (Saratoga County Historical Society at Brookside Museum.)

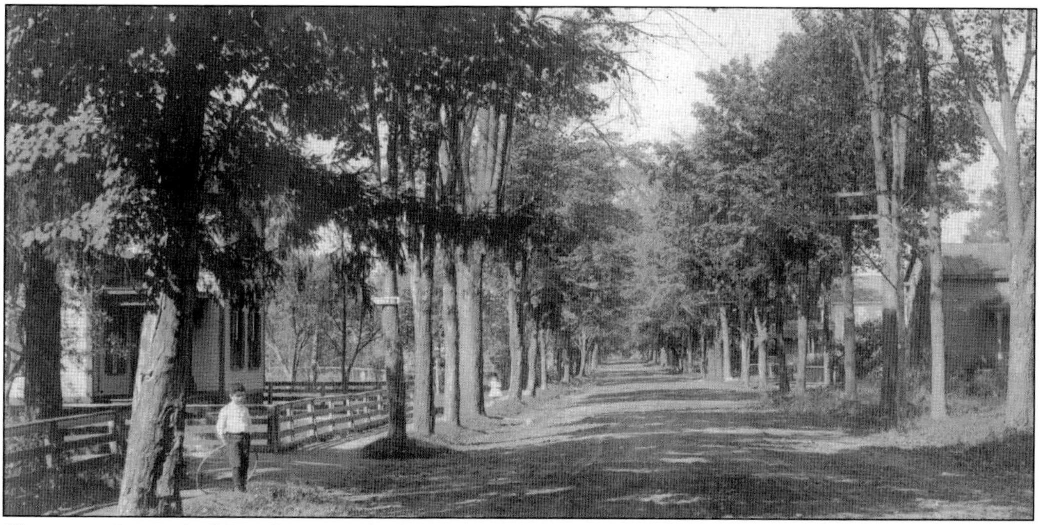

Shown is the end of South Street looking toward Bloodville and Maple Avenue. The sign on the tree reads Barber Street, which led to Benjamin Barber's Eagle Wood and Iron Works foundry and sawmill. Today, the steep embankment makes it hard to imagine a navigable street once existed here. (Saratoga County Historical Society at Brookside Museum.)

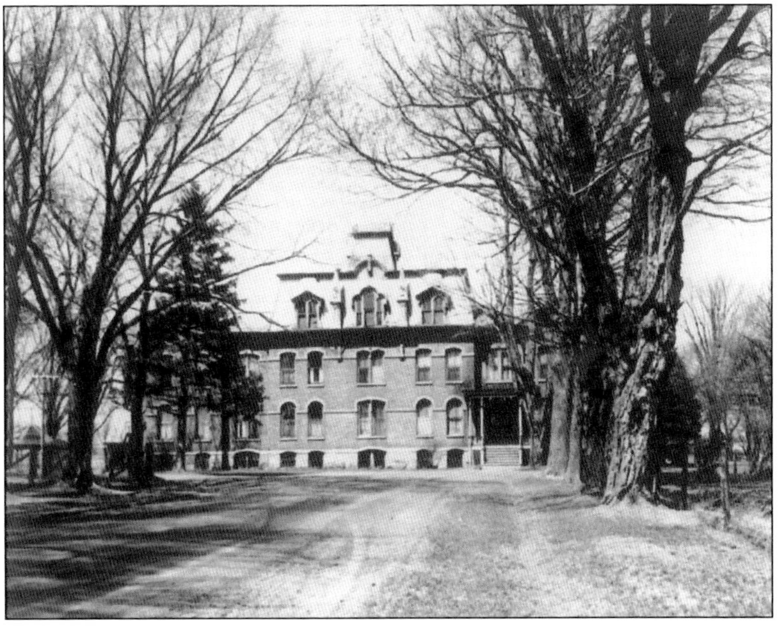

This version of the Saratoga County Alms House (also known as the poorhouse) was built in 1876 to replace one in disrepair. Women lived in the east wing, men lived in the west wing, and the administrative offices were in the center. Census records indicate that, on average, about 125 "inmates" resided there. A small farm was kept to offset some of the expenses. (Saratoga County Historian.)

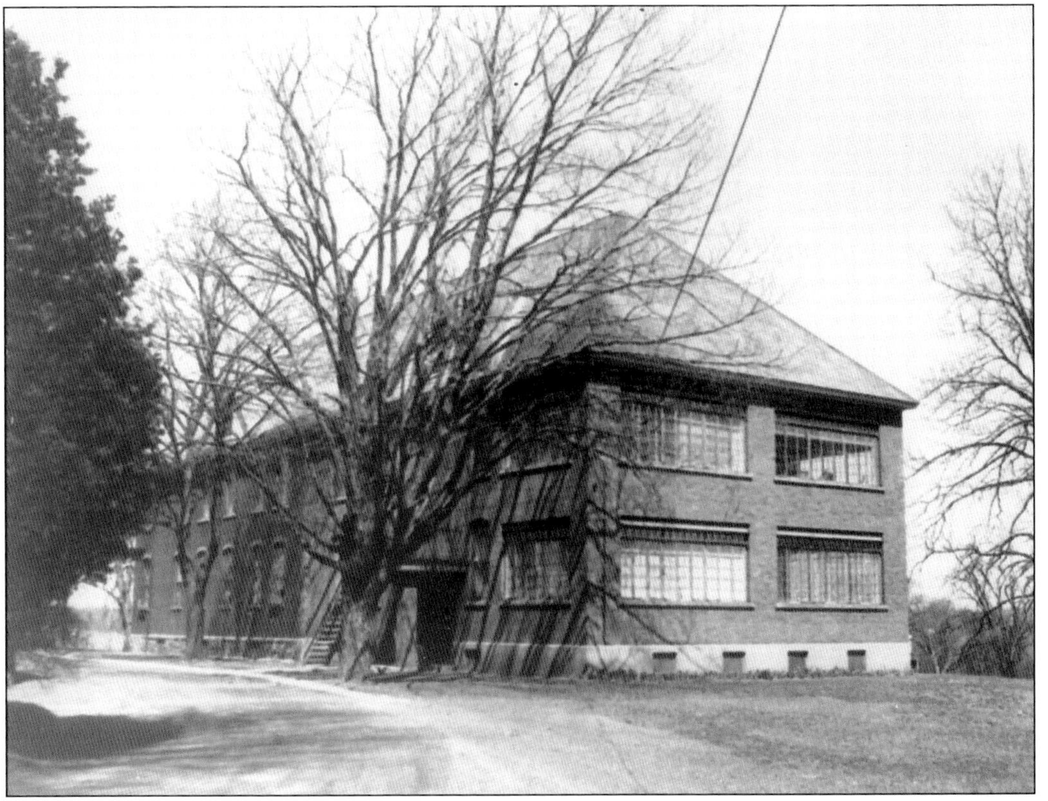

Until this hospital was built adjacent to the almshouse, paupers and the mentally ill were all kept in one building, with little provision for medical services. It was not uncommon for a quarter of the residents to be listed as "insane." The poorhouse and infirmary were torn down in 1960, and the land is now used by the county jail and highway department. (Saratoga County Historian.)

Five

Rock City Falls

Rock City Falls was first settled before 1800 at the western end of the hamlet, then known as Hatch Mills. An early sawmill and gristmill were situated on Kayaderosseras Creek. Valentine Rathbone and Elisha Swann are believed to have built the first crude paper mill in addition to a hotel and store. Their early effort at settlement had limited success, but in 1845 Chauncey Kilmer built a more substantial paper mill on this site. After several partnership changes, it was sold to George West and became known as the Empire Mill. This quickly became the hub of West's paper bag operations. West also built a substantial home across the street that still stands.

Kilmer erected another paper mill a short distance to the east on the corner of what is now Route 29 and Rock City Road. Known as the Stone Mill, it was one of the first US paper mills to manufacture paper from rye straw using a new process after a long period of painstaking experiments.

Before the construction of the Ballston Terminal Railroad, geographic distances to urban centers and poor roads forced Rock City Falls to become self-sufficient. A variety of merchants and craftsmen set up businesses to support the paper mill workers and local farmers. A Methodist church was established just after the first paper mill was built. St. Paul's Catholic Church was constructed in 1874 on a lot donated by Chauncey Kilmer. Children were educated at one of three school districts, designated as No. 4, No. 5, and No. 12. A quarry was excavated near Kilmer's mill to provide lime to manufacture his paper in addition to the lime brought in from nearby Rowland's Hollow. Two hotels, a general store, post office, and approximately 100 dwellings rounded out the hamlet.

Until the turn of the century, the three paper mills provided economic stability and dependable employment to dozens of men. However, George West and Chauncey Kilmer both passed away just as new technologies were making single-owner, water-powered mills obsolete. The Empire and Excelsior Mills shut down, leaving only the Cottrell Paper Company in operation. Even so, many families have remained and carried on small-town life to the present day.

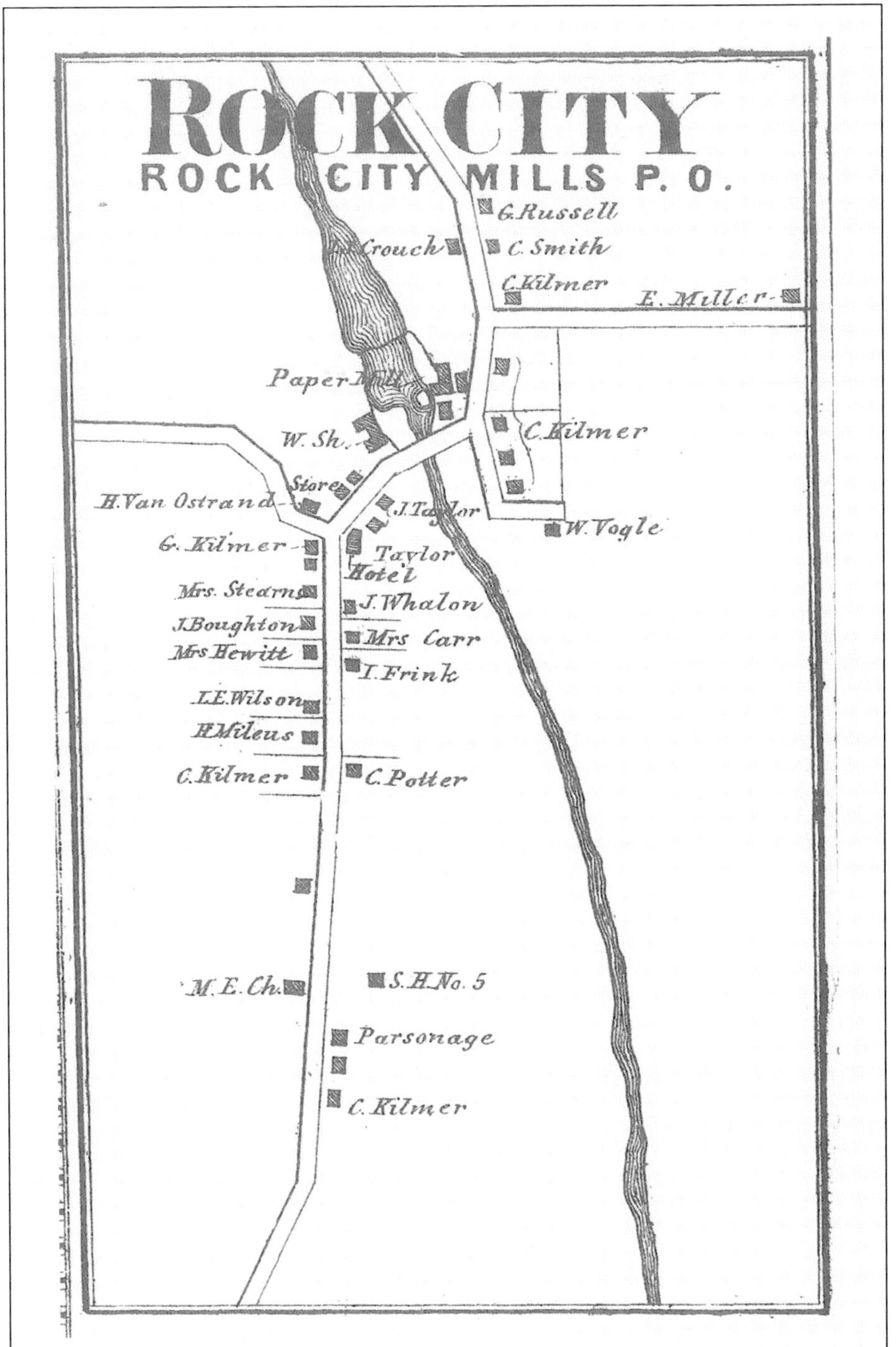

The paper mill indicated on the map was owned by Chauncey Kilmer, who had become a millionaire by manufacturing straw printing paper for the *New York Sun*. George West also became wealthy manufacturing manila paper at his mills (not shown). This map represents the "lower" portion of Rock City Falls; "upper" Rock City Falls was to the north and contained West's two paper mills, a bag factory, and a mansion. (Author's collection.)

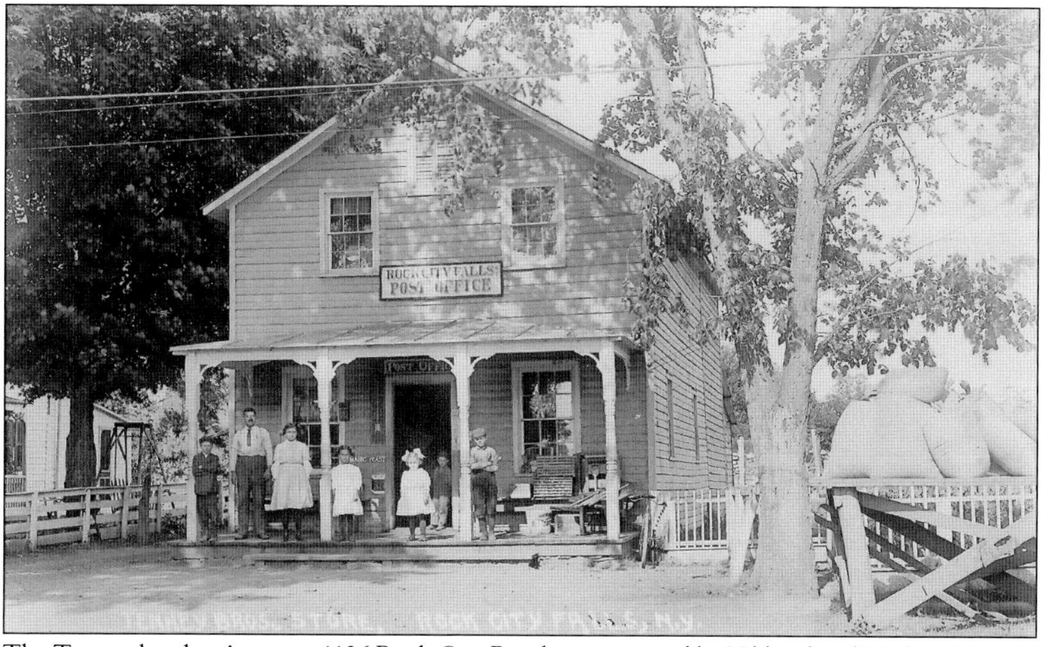

The Tenney brothers' store at 1106 Rock City Road was operated by Vibbard and Herbert Tenney, who lived next door. The store also served as the post office. Prominent resident Harlow Van Ostrand was the first postmaster, a job he held from 1849 until his death in 1879. The store was later converted to a residence. (Paul and Marilyn Pastore collection.)

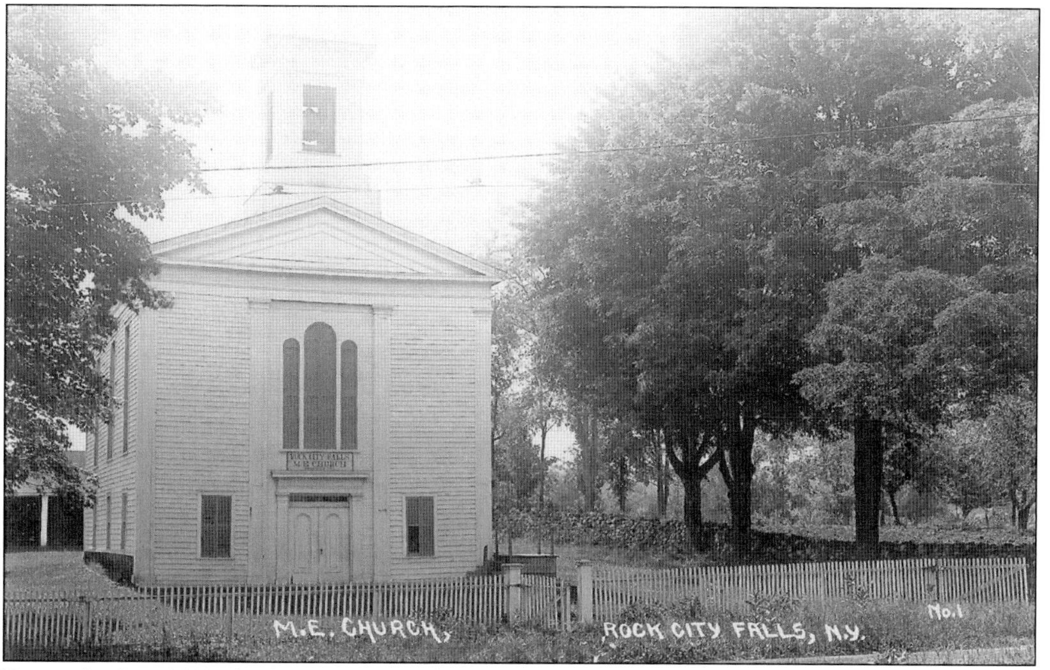

Dating back to 1810, the Simpson United Methodist Church was the first church founded in Rock City Falls. A wooden structure was built in 1844 that stood for more than 75 years until it was destroyed by fire and replaced by the present-day edifice. (Paul and Marilyn Pastore collection.)

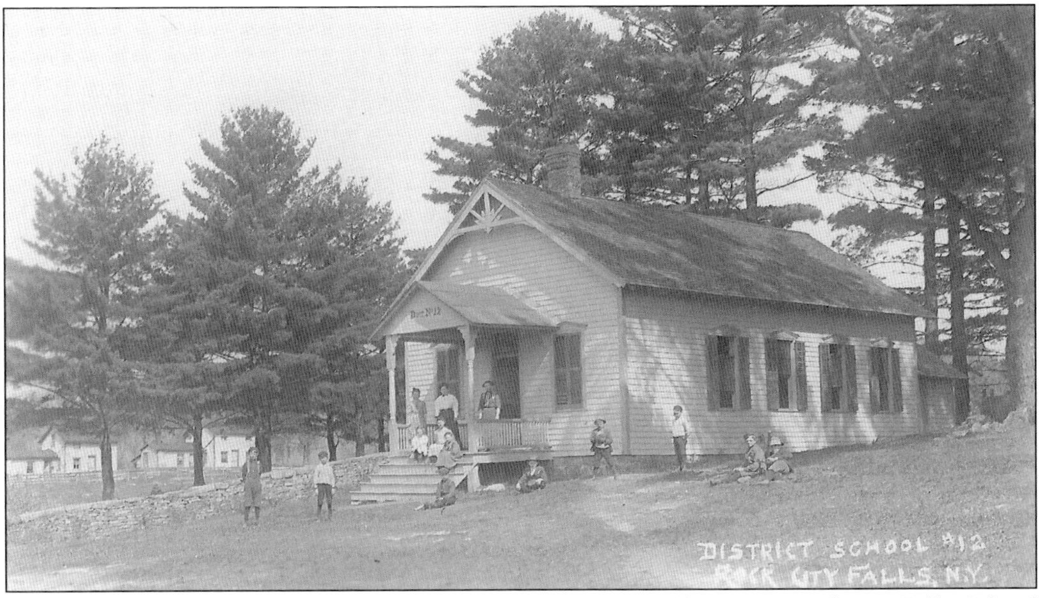

Throughout the 19th century, there were three one-room schoolhouses in Rock City Falls. School No. 12, shown here, was located on Route 29, across the street from the Excelsior Paper Mill. The houses in the background are on Emigh Road. Like Schools No. 5 and No. 13, the building has survived and was renovated as a small residence. (Paul and Marilyn Pastore collection.)

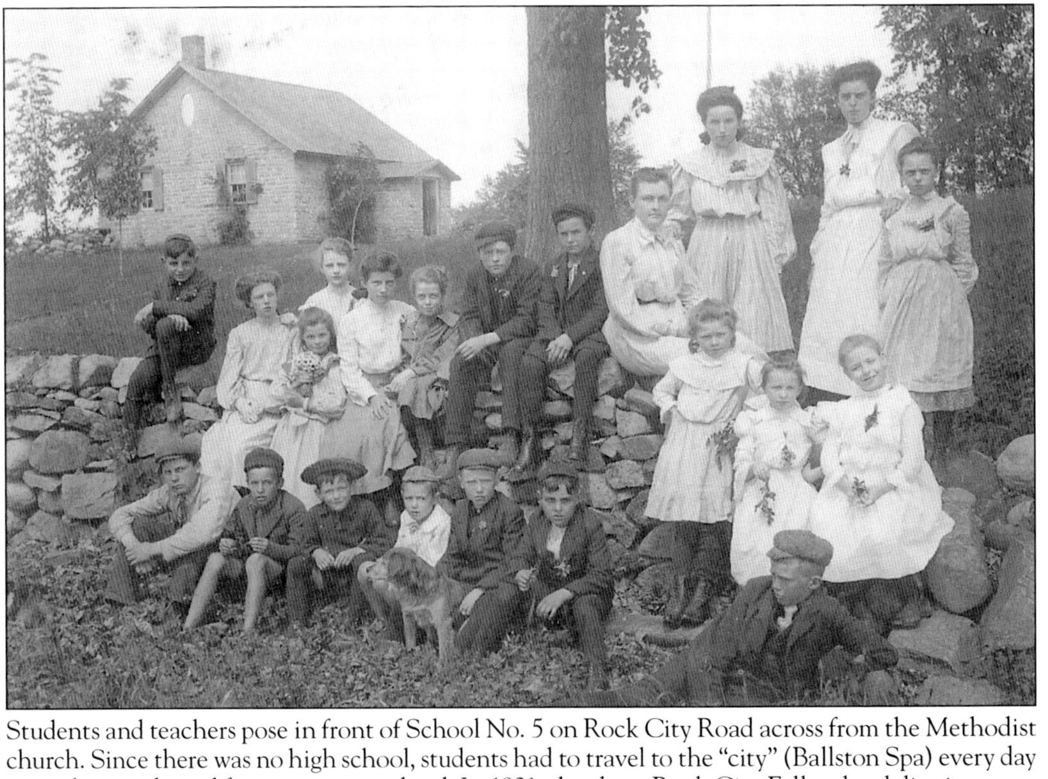

Students and teachers pose in front of School No. 5 on Rock City Road across from the Methodist church. Since there was no high school, students had to travel to the "city" (Ballston Spa) every day once they graduated from grammar school. In 1921, the three Rock City Falls school districts were consolidated into a new building. (Saratoga County Historical Society at Brookside Museum.)

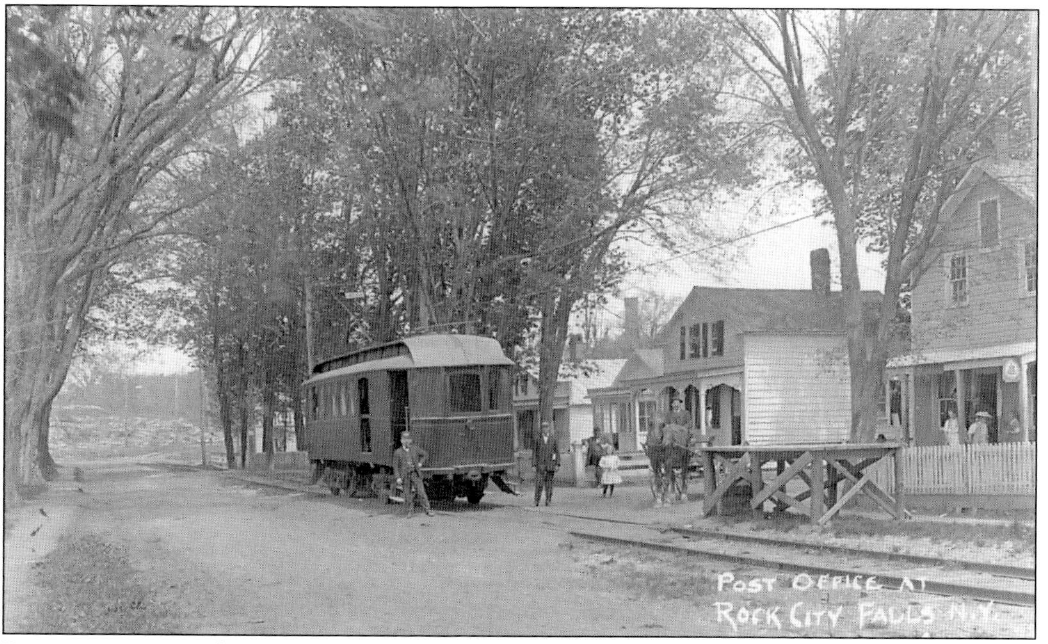

Beginning in 1898, the Tenney store and post office were served by the Ballston Terminal Railroad, which emerged from the woods of West Milton just a short distance out of view. The next stop would be the Rock City Falls Hotel. (Saratoga County Historical Society at Brookside Museum.)

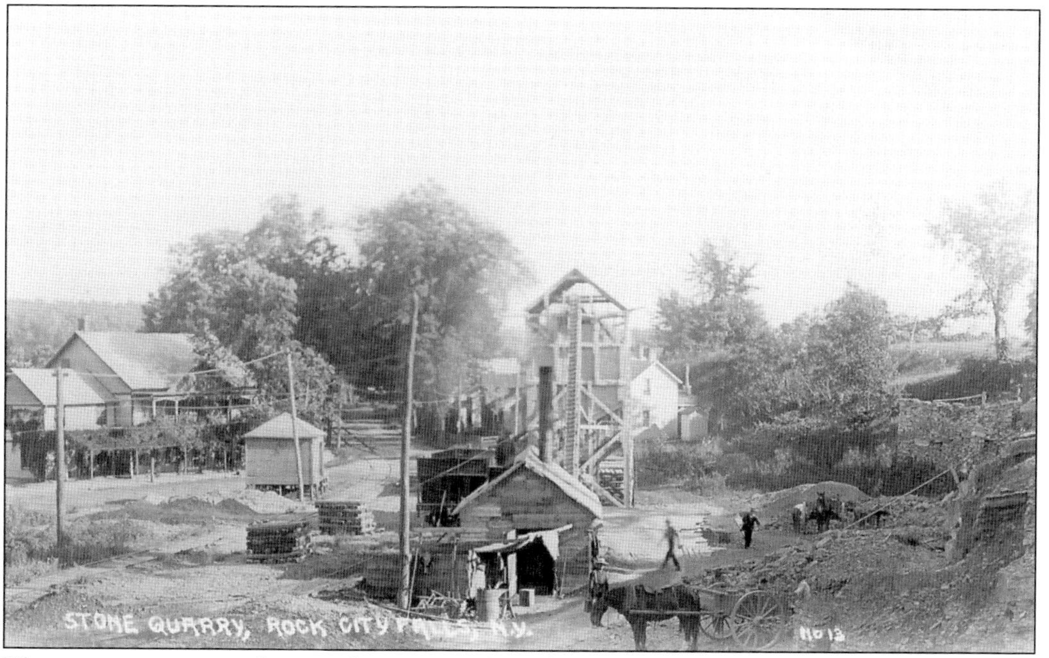

The stone quarry was first used to extract lime for manufacturing straw paper at the nearby Kilmer Mill. In 1905, a new venture called the Big Falls Stone Company commenced operations to provide limestone to local builders. Directly across the street was the Rock City Falls Hotel. At center is the Ballston Terminal Railroad that served the quarry. Today, the Rock City Falls Fire Department occupies this site. (Chris Morley collection.)

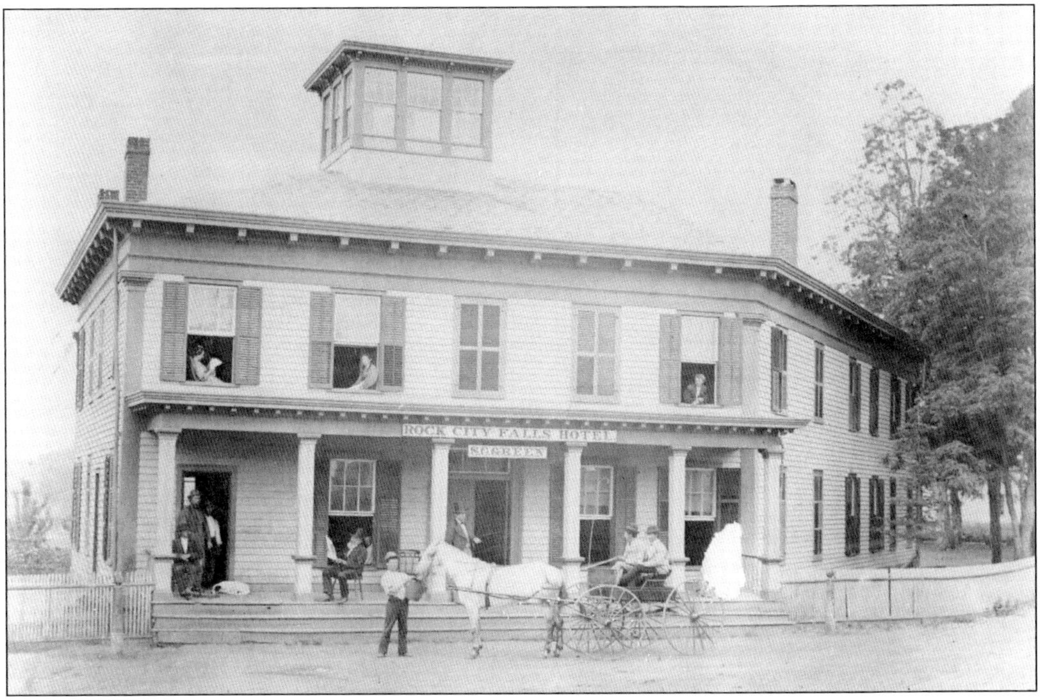

This first version of the Rock City Falls Hotel, once located opposite the present-day firehouse near the end of Rock City Road, was erected by Seymour Green in 1865. After Green sold it in 1877, it passed through various owners before being destroyed by fire in 1884. (Paul and Marilyn Pastore collection.)

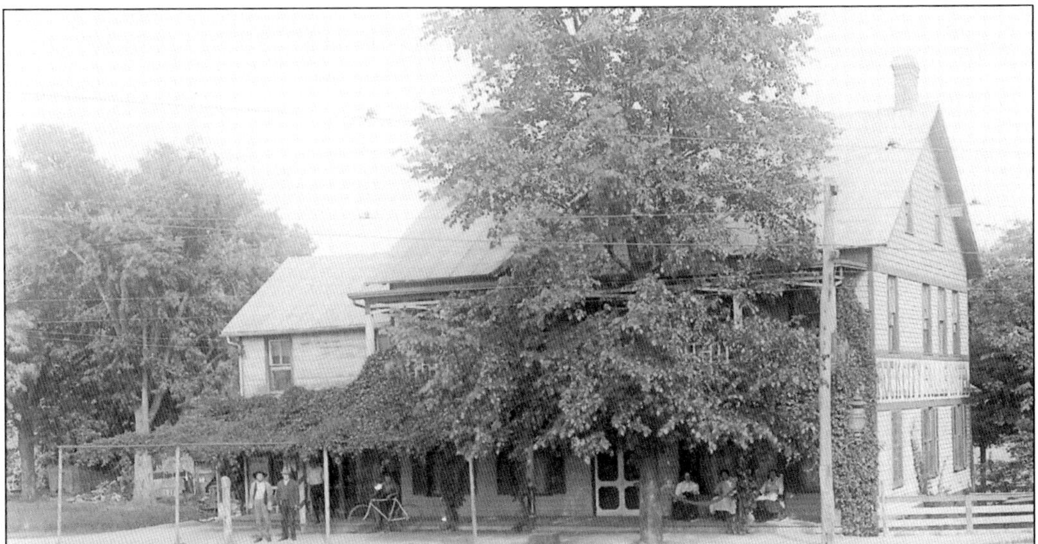

The rebuilt Rock City Falls Hotel was owned and operated by Elijah Horton for almost 30 years. It served as a waiting station for passengers of the Ballston Terminal Railroad, which passed near its front porch. The hotel burned down for the last time two days before Christmas in 1918 and was replaced a few years later by the Rock City Falls consolidated school, a building that still stands. (Paul and Marilyn Pastore collection.)

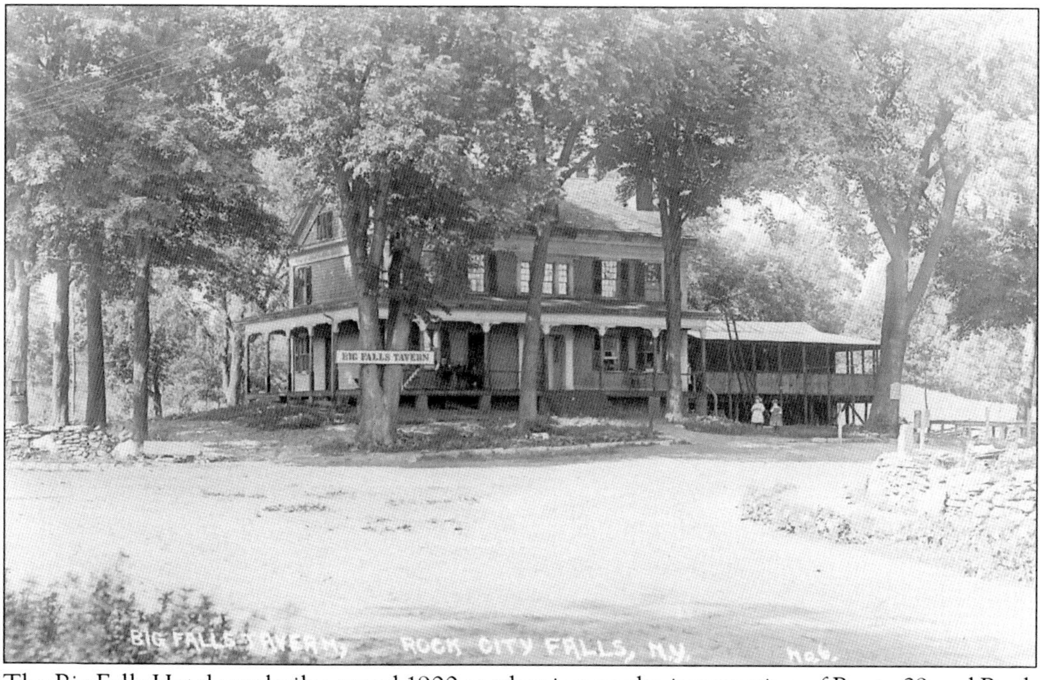

The Big Falls Hotel was built around 1900 at what is now the intersection of Route 29 and Rock City Road. James Moran, superintendent of the Kilmer Mill, was proprietor until 1907, when it passed on to various owners. When this photograph was taken, it was known as Big Falls Tavern and used as a boardinghouse. It burned down in the spring of 1927 and was not rebuilt. (Paul and Marilyn Pastore collection.)

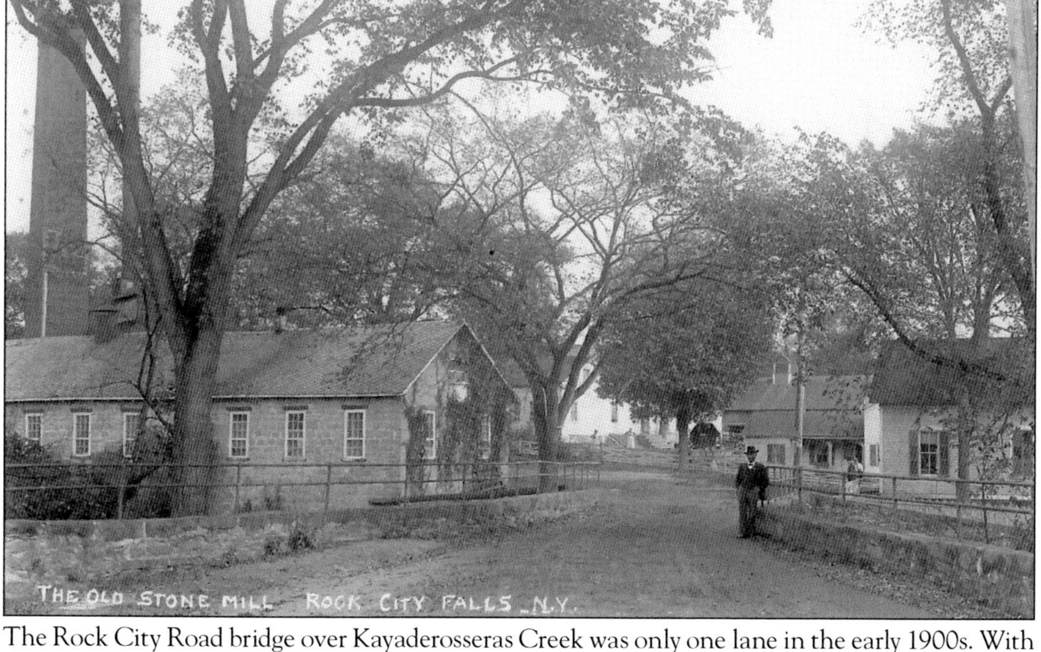

The Rock City Road bridge over Kayaderosseras Creek was only one lane in the early 1900s. With the Kilmer Stone Mill (left), stores, hotels, the post office, and residences, this area was the hub of activity in the 1800s and early 1900s. (Paul and Marilyn Pastore collection.)

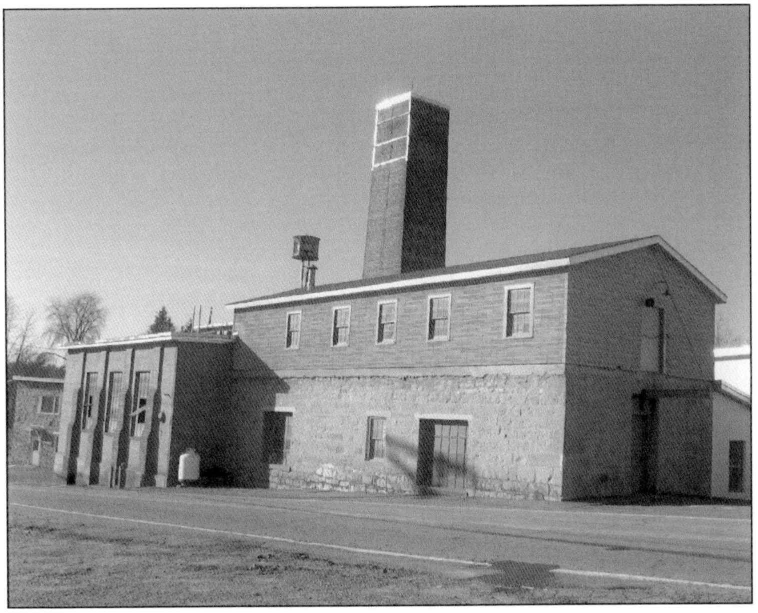

In 1919, the former Kilmer Stone Mill was acquired by the Cottrell family, who continue to operate it today as a manufacturer of specialty paper. Numerous additions to the original stone buildings over the years are apparent. (Author's collection.)

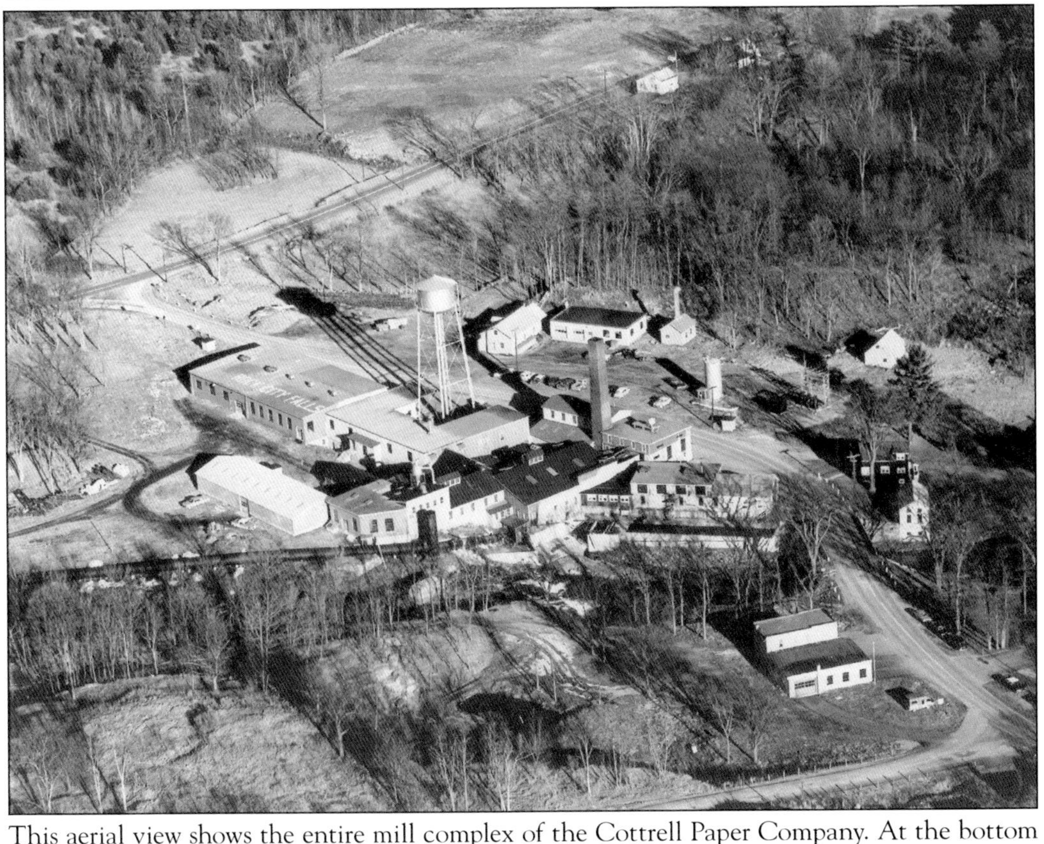

This aerial view shows the entire mill complex of the Cottrell Paper Company. At the bottom right was the former lime quarry used by the mill (now a firehouse). Rock City Road snakes around the mill and ends at Route 29 (top). The original c. 1850 stone mill is located at the bottom right side of the complex, next to the bridge. (Chris Morley collection.)

George West was among the most famous citizens in Milton's history. He was born in England in 1823 and immigrated to the United States at the age of 26. After working in various paper mills, he purchased the Empire Mill in Rock City Falls and went on to acquire a dozen other mills. At one time, he was the largest manufacturer of manila paper in the world. (Saratoga County Historical Society at Brookside Museum.)

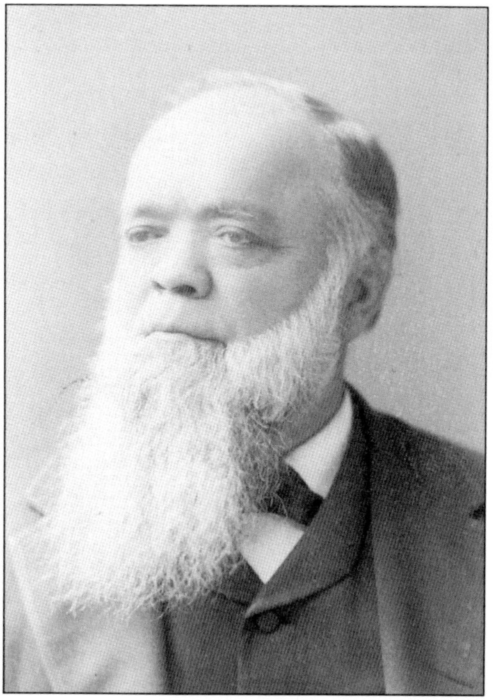

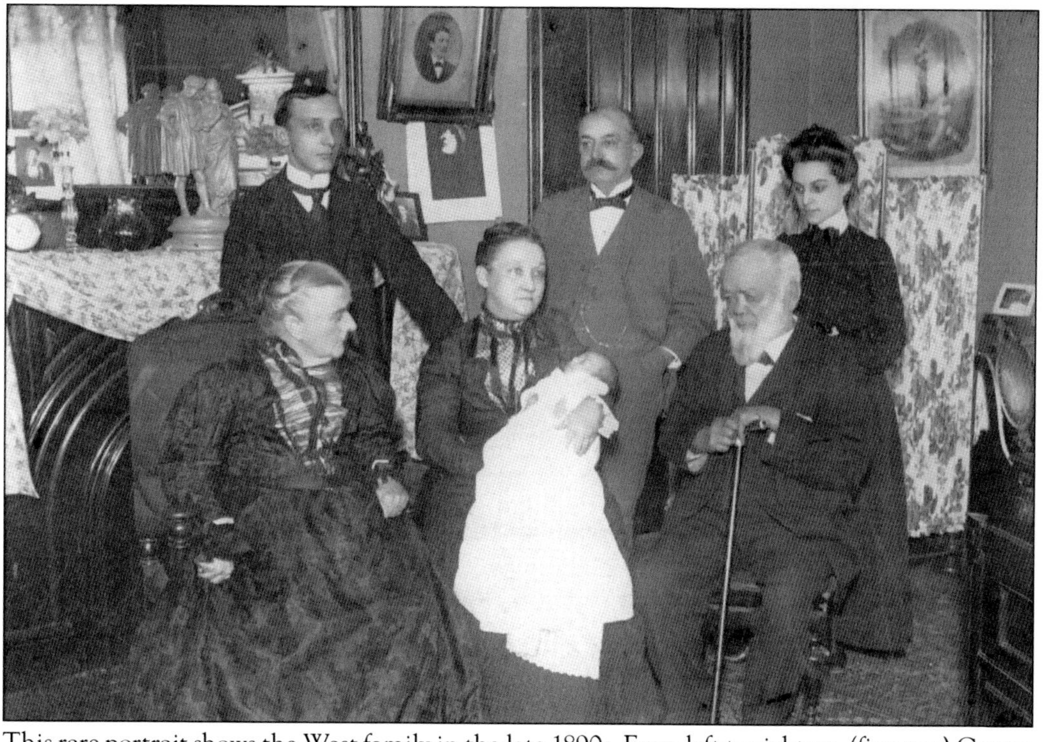

This rare portrait shows the West family in the late 1890s. From left to right are (first row) George Sr.'s wife Louisa, his daughter Florence holding George Jr.'s baby, and George Sr.; (second row) George Sr.'s son Walter (who passed away soon after this photograph was taken), George Jr., and George Jr.'s wife Emily Hathorn. (Saratoga County Historical Society at Brookside Museum.)

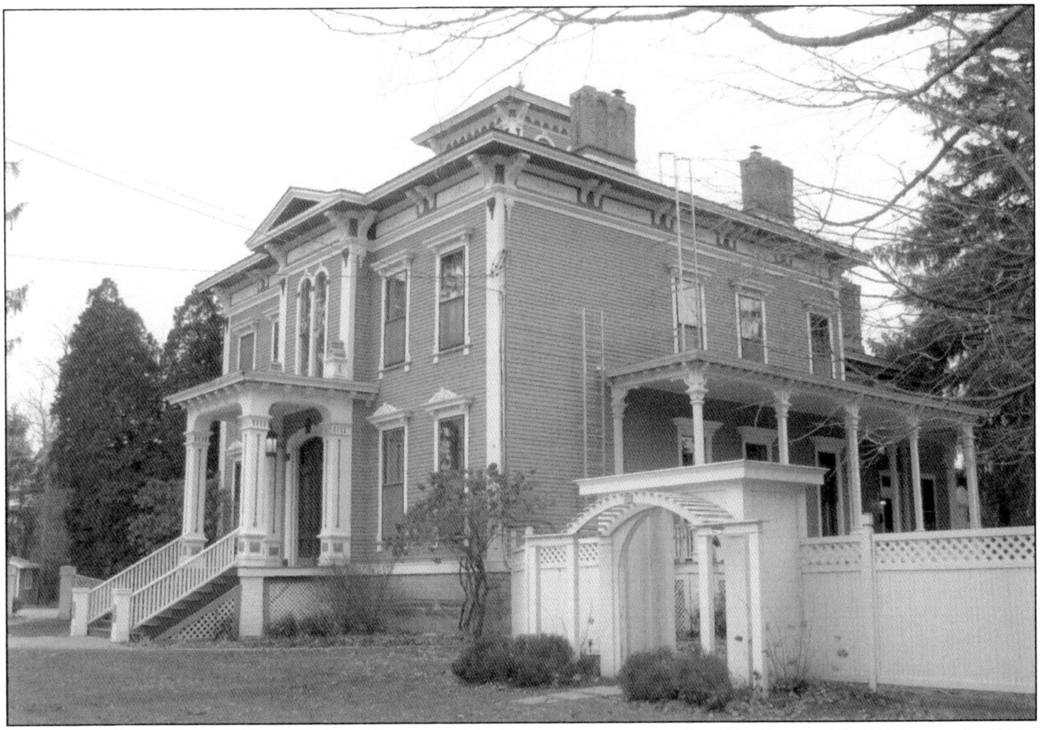

The success of George West's line of paper bags beginning in the 1860s enabled him to build a 23-room, Venetian-style mansion in Rock City Falls across the street from his two paper mills. The building currently serves as a bed-and-breakfast and has been maintained in excellent condition. It was added to the New York State Register of Historic Places in 2005. (Author collection.)

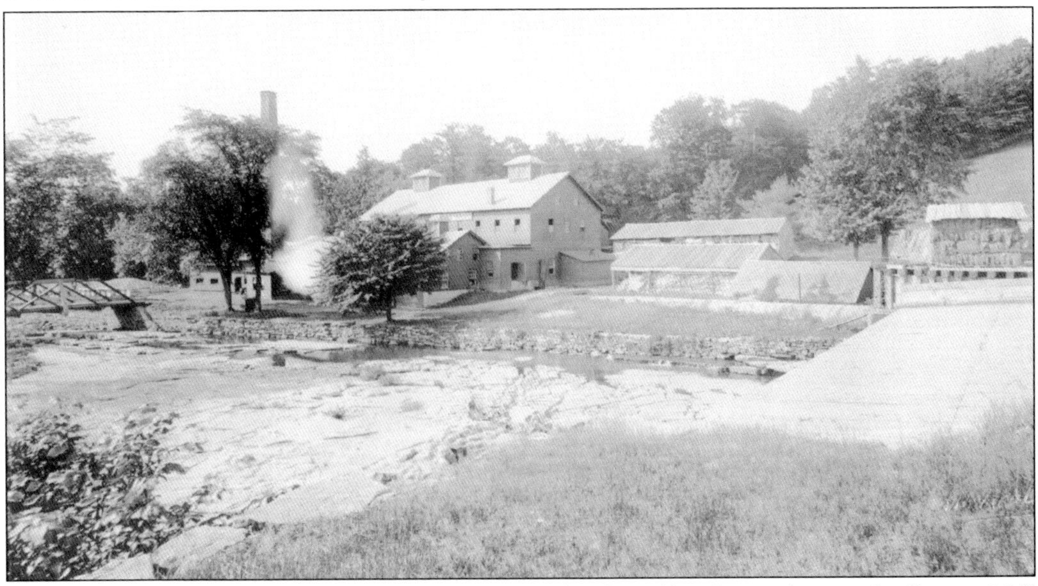

In 1866, George West built the Excelsior Mill on undeveloped land next door to the Empire Mill to keep up with the nationwide demand for his line of manila paper and paper bags. There was a footbridge (left) for workers and a plank bridge (right) for transporting finished paper to the main road. (Saratoga County Historical Society at Brookside Museum.)

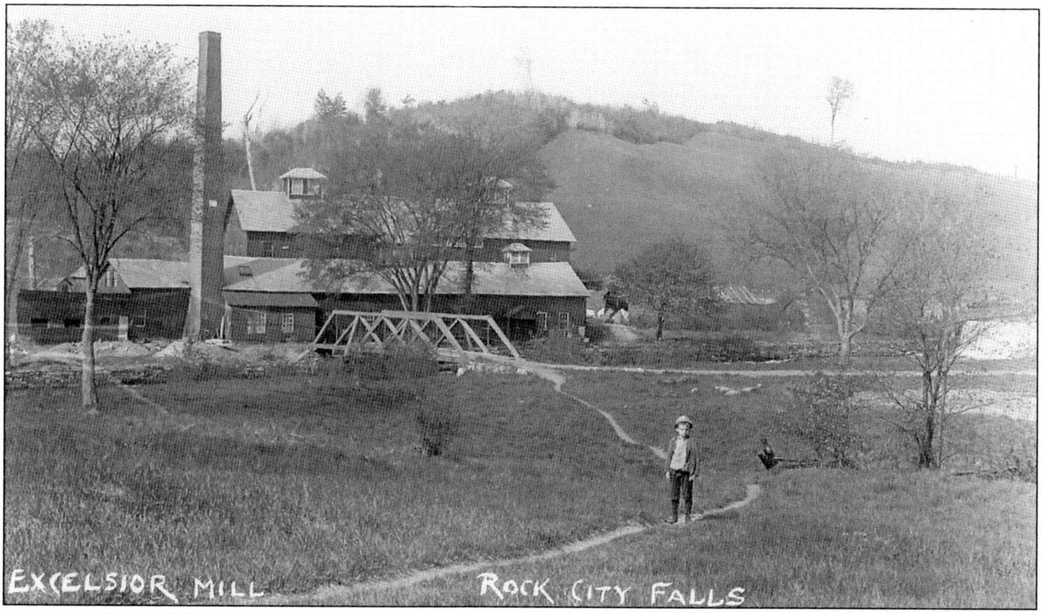

The Excelsior Mill was most successful under its original builder George West. After West retired in 1899, there were a number of owners who had limited success. Although it operated until 1925, the mill was subject to periods of disuse. The Cottrell family used it for storage but finally tore it down in 1976. Only the stone foundations remain today. (Paul and Marilyn Pastore collection.)

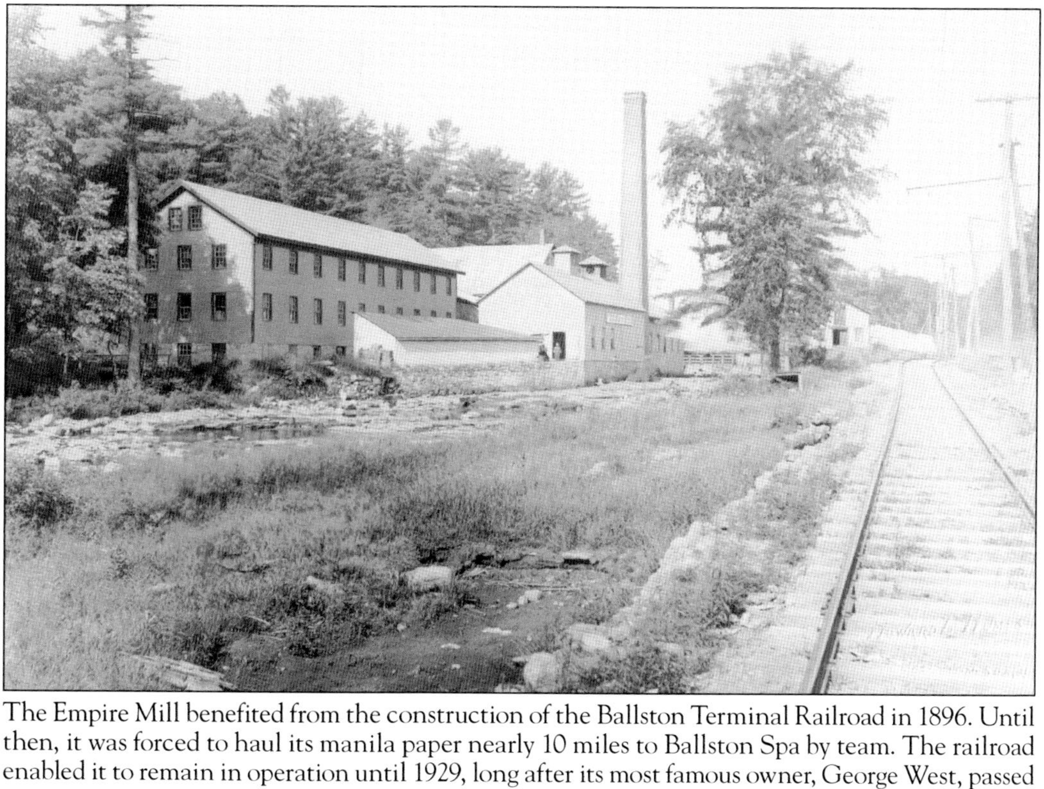

The Empire Mill benefited from the construction of the Ballston Terminal Railroad in 1896. Until then, it was forced to haul its manila paper nearly 10 miles to Ballston Spa by team. The railroad enabled it to remain in operation until 1929, long after its most famous owner, George West, passed away. It was one of the last paper mills in Milton to shut down. (Chris Morley collection.)

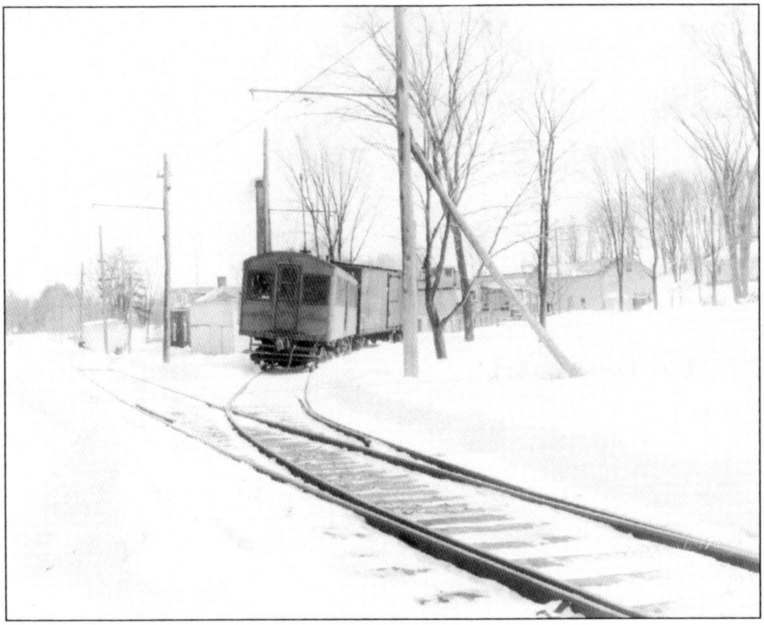

Winters are tough in the Northeast, but snow rarely stopped railroad operations for long. A spur at the Empire Mill allowed the George West trolley car to deliver coal and load finished goods directly at the factory. This spur crossed Kayaderosseras Creek just below the paper mill's dam. (Chris Morley collection.)

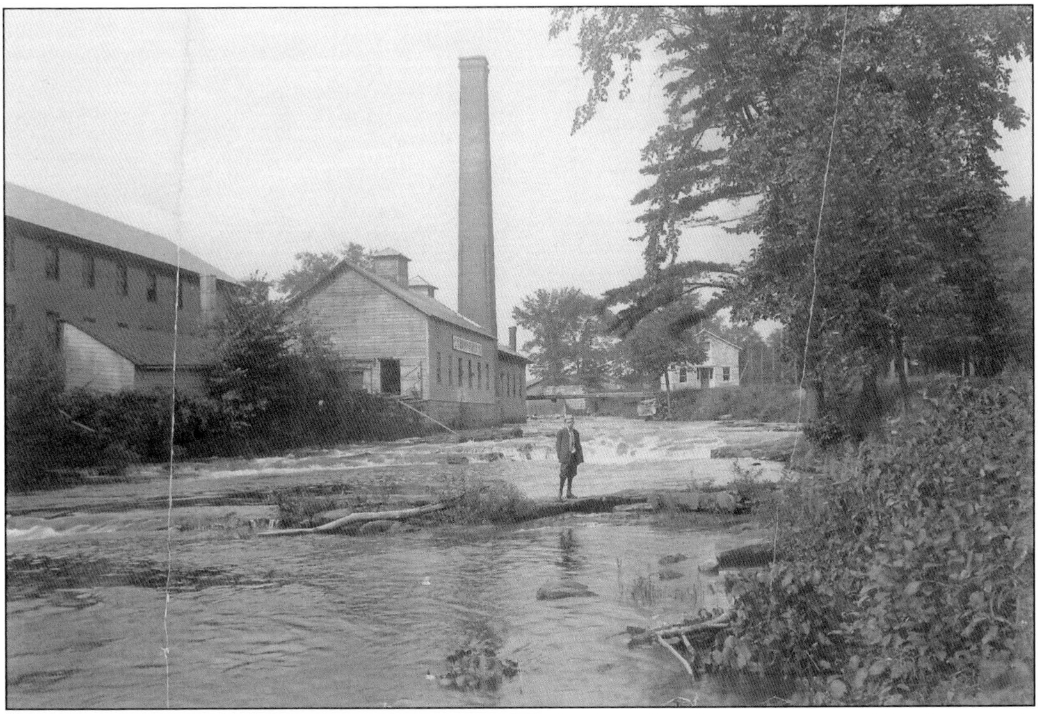

Here is another view of the Empire Mill, taken from the bank of Kayaderosseras Creek. The photograph probably dates from the early 1900s, when it was owned by Edward Brown. The stone residence in the background, now abandoned, still stands. (Paul and Marilyn Pastore collection.)

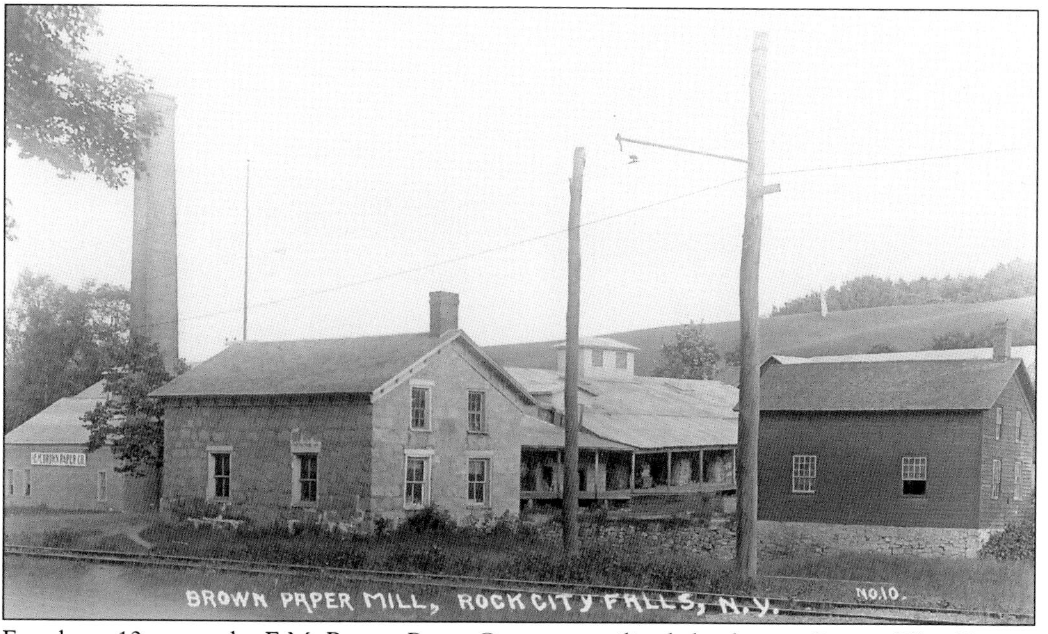

For about 10 years, the E.M. Brown Paper Company utilized the former George West Empire Mill to manufacture card middles. In 1918, Edward Brown stepped in to save the electric trolley from going bankrupt since he used it to transport paper goods to Ballston Spa. (Paul and Marilyn Pastore collection.)

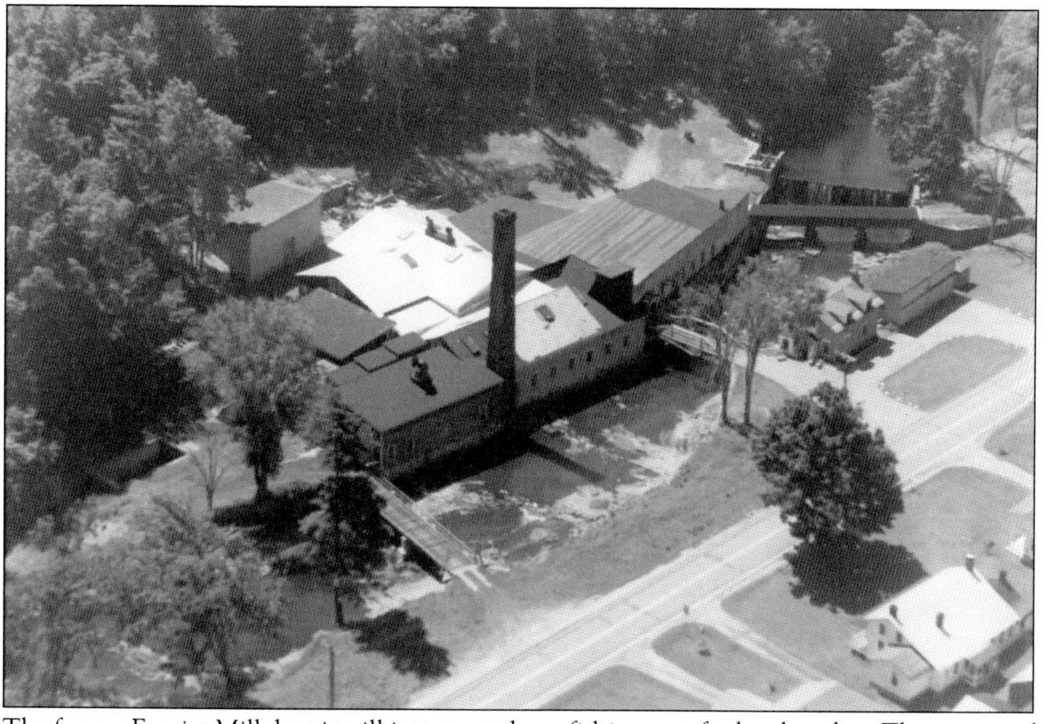

The former Empire Mill dam is still intact, used as a fishing spot for local anglers. The success of the paper mill over a period of decades resulted in the reconstruction of many buildings throughout the complex, but few of the original structures survive. (Chris Morley collection.)

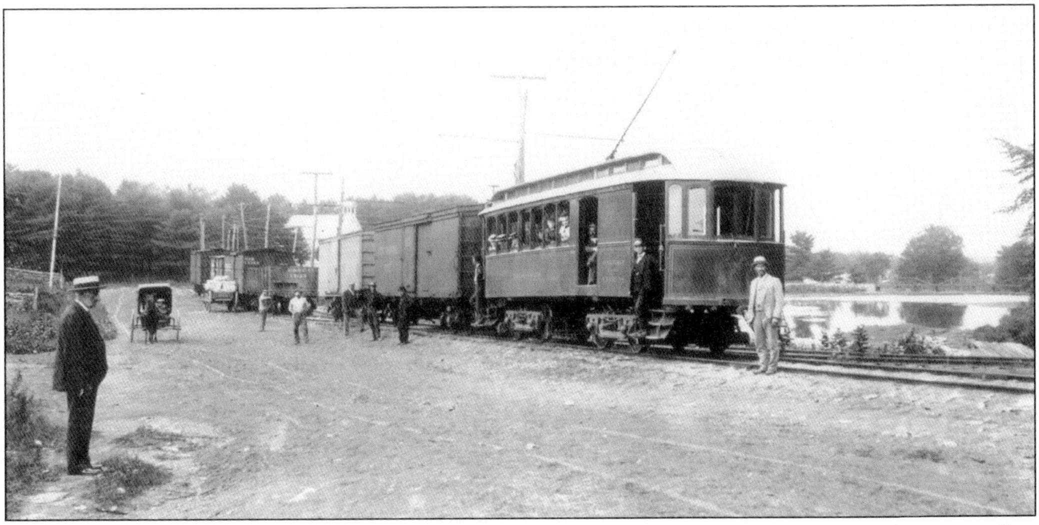

What was a rare sight elsewhere in the country was part of daily life in Milton—an electric trolley hauling six loaded freight cars. Here, the Ballston Terminal Railroad trolley car *A.N. Chandler* heads down what would later become Route 29. St. Paul's Church, which still stands, can be seen in the background. (New York State Archives.)

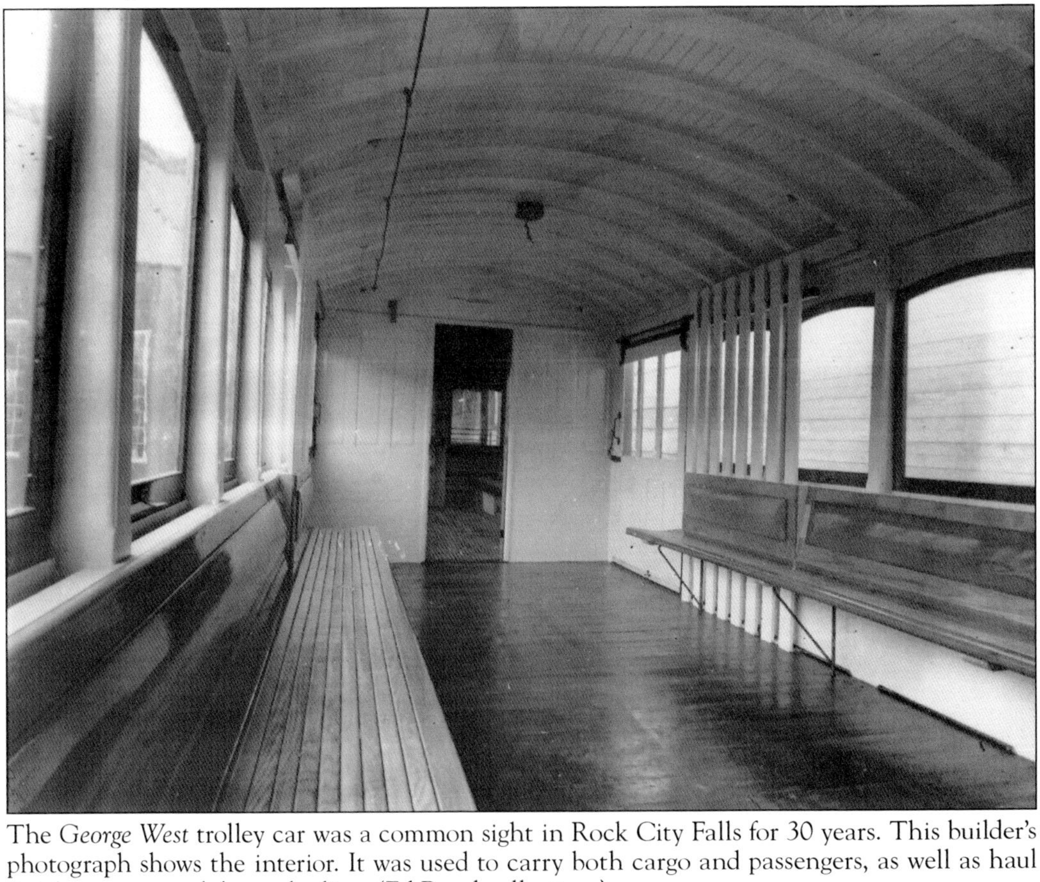

The *George West* trolley car was a common sight in Rock City Falls for 30 years. This builder's photograph shows the interior. It was used to carry both cargo and passengers, as well as haul freight cars up and down the line. (Ed Bond collection.)

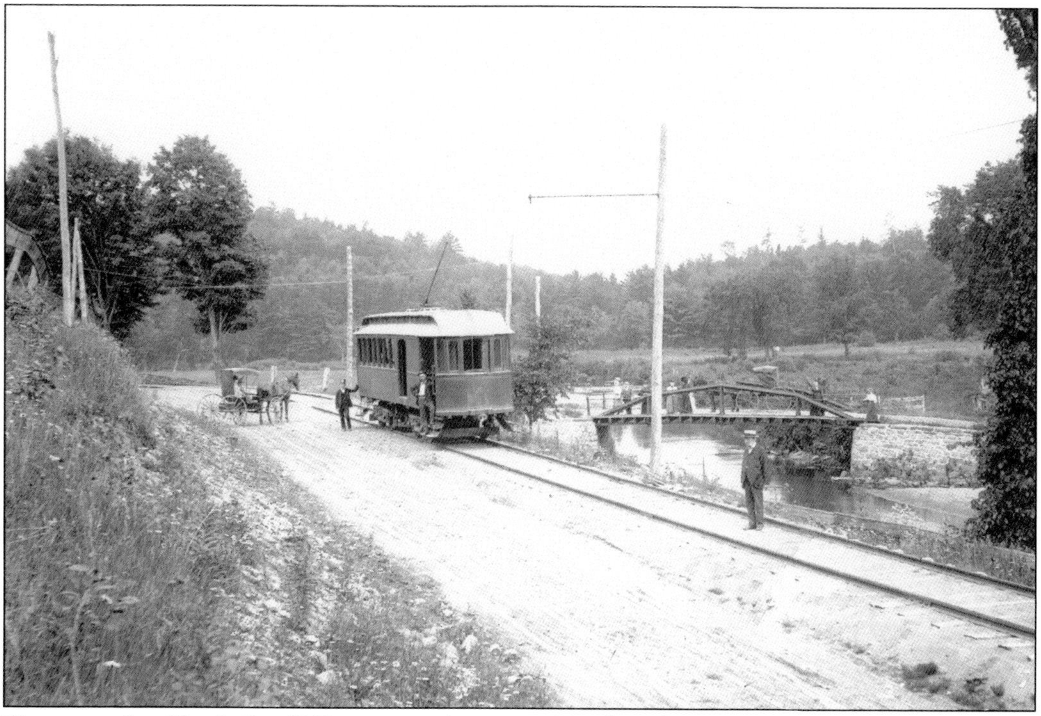

The west side of Rock City Falls was once known as Hatch Mills, site of the first industrial activity on the northern end of the Kayaderosseras. Here, the Ballston Terminal Railroad trolley has just left Rock City Falls and is heading north toward its termination point in Middle Grove. The bridge in the background is near present-day Route 29. (Chris Morley collection.)

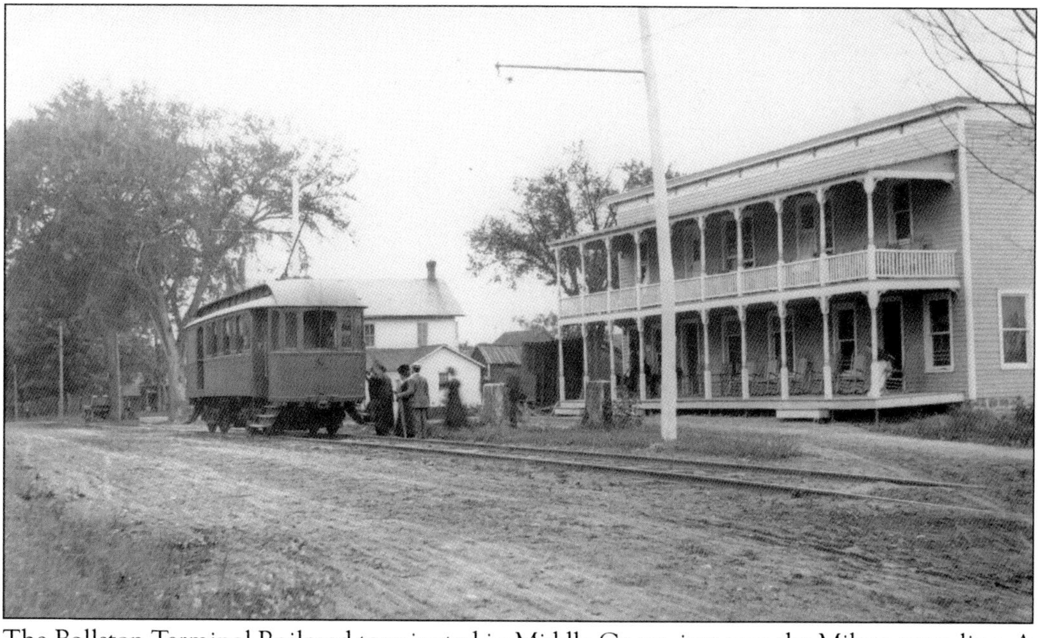

The Ballston Terminal Railroad terminated in Middle Grove, just over the Milton town line. A turnaround track is just out of view on the left. The Middle Grove Hotel served as a waiting room for students and workers heading to Ballston Spa. (Paul and Marilyn Pastore collection.)

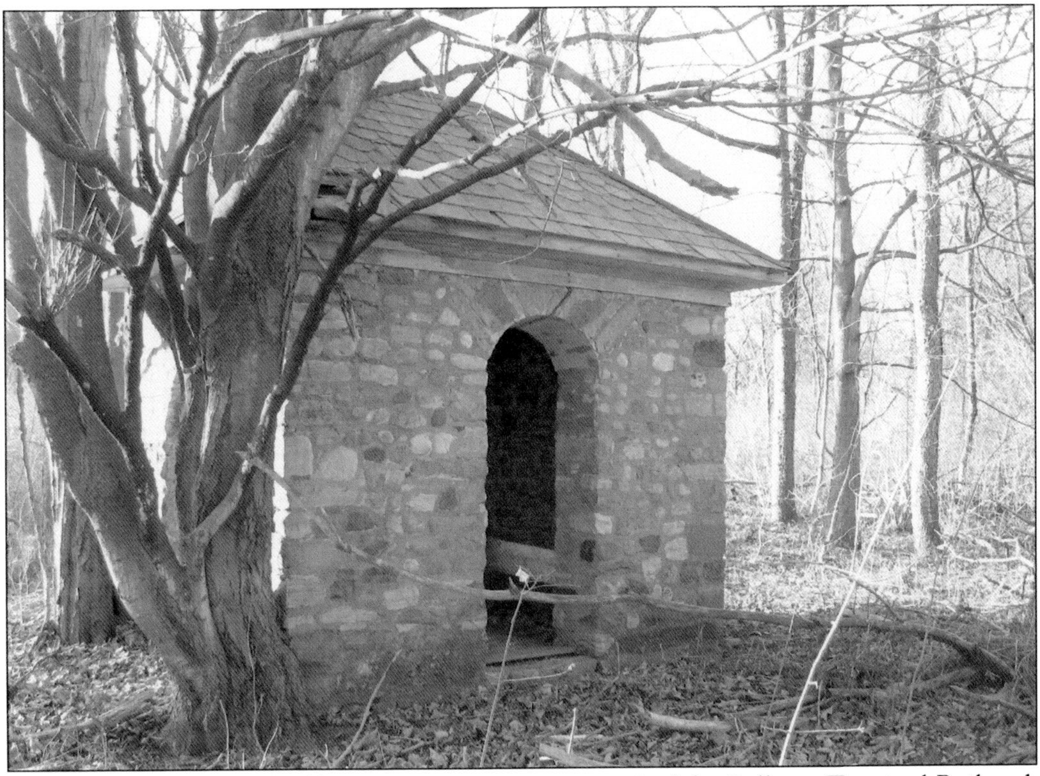

This quaint little stone building was a "passenger station" of the Ballston Terminal Railroad. It was probably built in the early 1900s, although documentation for its history could not be found. Indications of the railroad's right-of-way can be seen just behind the structure. (Author's collection.)

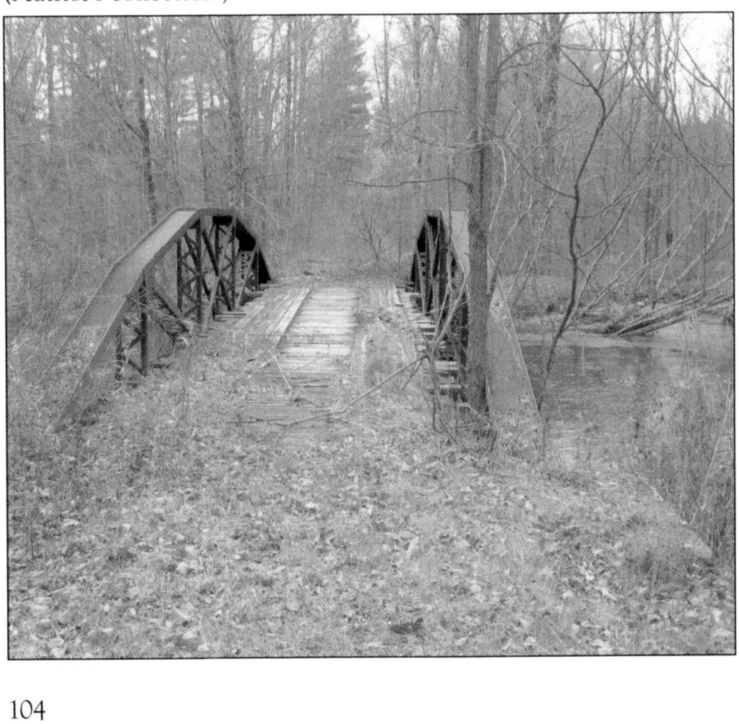

An unused bridge at the end of Heisler Road constitutes the only existing bridge of the Ballston Terminal Railroad. Remarkably, it survived the metal scrap drives of World War II. Beyond the bridge is part of the Boice Town Park and walking trail. At this point, roughly two miles of the trolley right-of-way is still apparent in the undeveloped forest from Rock City Falls to West Milton. (Author's collection.)

Six

Around Town

Although Ballston Spa, Bloodville, and Rock City Falls were the most prosperous population centers in Milton, there were several other important settlements in its history. The earliest was at Milton Hill, located a short distance north of Milton Center on Middle Line Road. Over two dozen families settled there soon after the Revolutionary War, and most expected that it would become the primary village in Milton. A prosperous hamlet emerged that included a district school, two churches, and Elisha Powell's store, the largest general store in the region. However, Ballston Spa's position as the county seat enticed many families to relocate there, and by 1825 Milton Hill had begun to decline.

Just after the Revolutionary War, one of the town's leading men, Gen. James Gordon, built a sawmill and gristmill where the Kayaderosseras crosses Middle Line Road. This area became known as Milton Center and grew into a thriving hamlet with a large tannery, wheel factory, hotels, stores, and churches.

Factory Village, just north of Bloodville, was another settlement based on industrial activity. The Milton Factory was established in 1813, and three paper mills were later added, including the successful National Mill that produced knockdown folding boxes until 1919. It was also the home base of the Ballston Terminal Railroad.

A short distance north of Factory Village was the hamlet of Craneville. Lindley Murray Crane, of the famous Crane family of Massachusetts papermakers, relocated to Milton and purchased a paper mill. There, he invented and sold several types of paper, including paper collars, waterproof paper, and security paper used for printing currency.

West Milton was a consolidation of Clute's Corners and Speir's Corners, hamlets named after prominent general store owners. A large pond near Speir's Corners contained a sawmill and gristmill, while a well-patronized hotel operated nearby. The Pioneer Paper Mill was the largest employer.

Other settlements included Rowland's Hollow, site of a gristmill and quarrying operation on the northeast side of town, and North Milton, a residential area once well known as the site of the Old Stone Church and Bentley Farm.

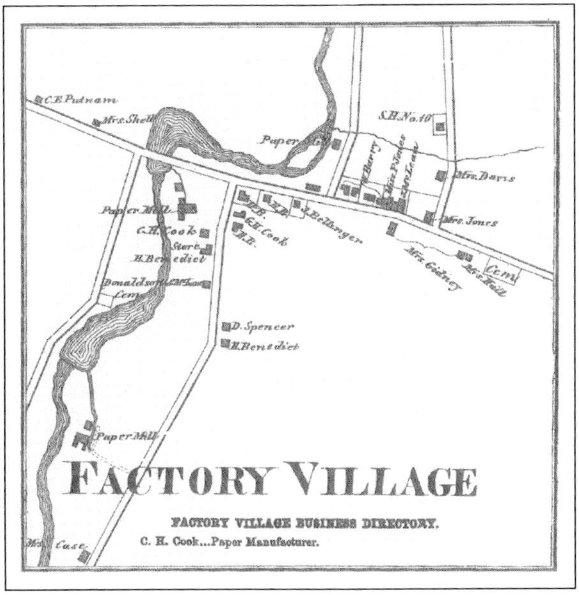

Factory Village, located just north of Bloodville, was the site of one of Milton's earliest settlements, then known as Merrick's Mills. A Mr. Merrick established a c. 1800 factory where the future National Mill thrived for decades at the southwest corner of the hamlet. Before 1850, Chauncey Cook, David Derrick, and Lindley Crane established other paper mills along Kayaderosseras Creek. (Author's collection.)

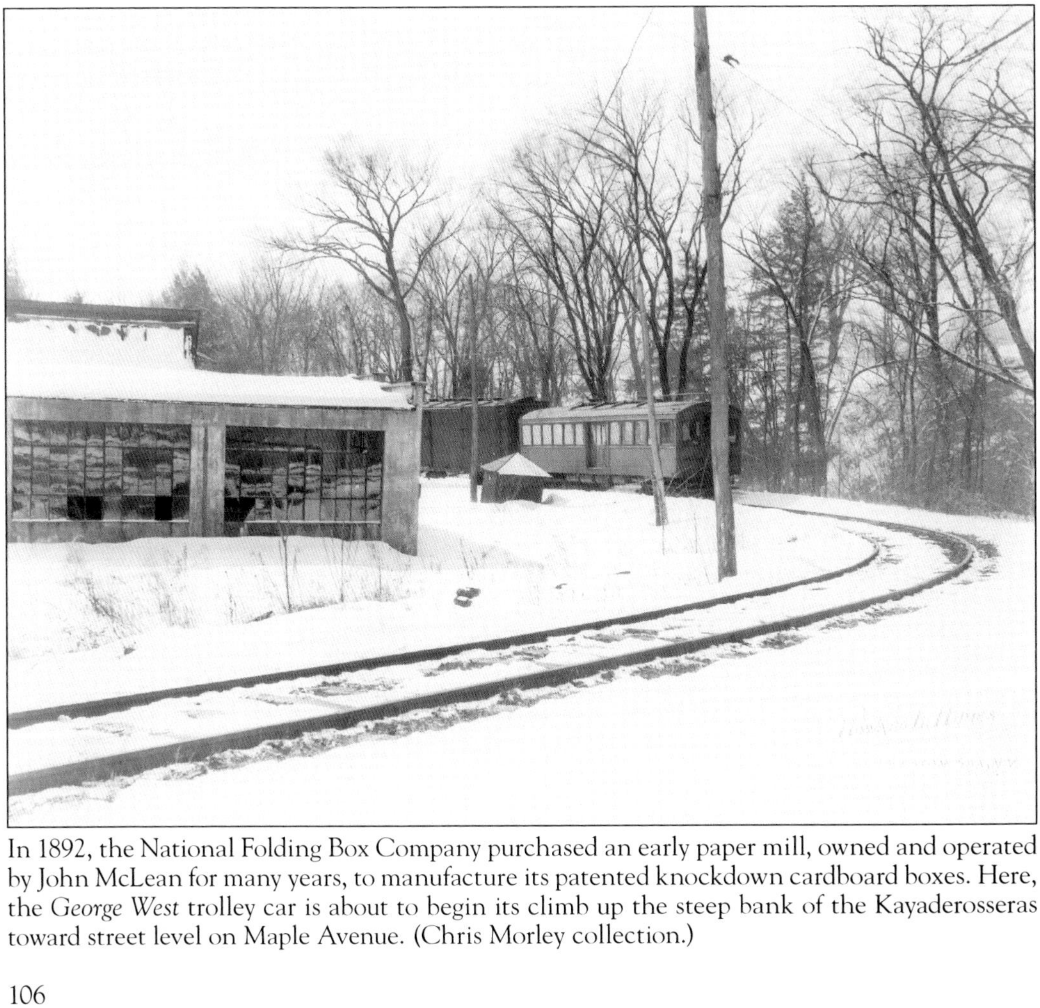

In 1892, the National Folding Box Company purchased an early paper mill, owned and operated by John McLean for many years, to manufacture its patented knockdown cardboard boxes. Here, the *George West* trolley car is about to begin its climb up the steep bank of the Kayaderosseras toward street level on Maple Avenue. (Chris Morley collection.)

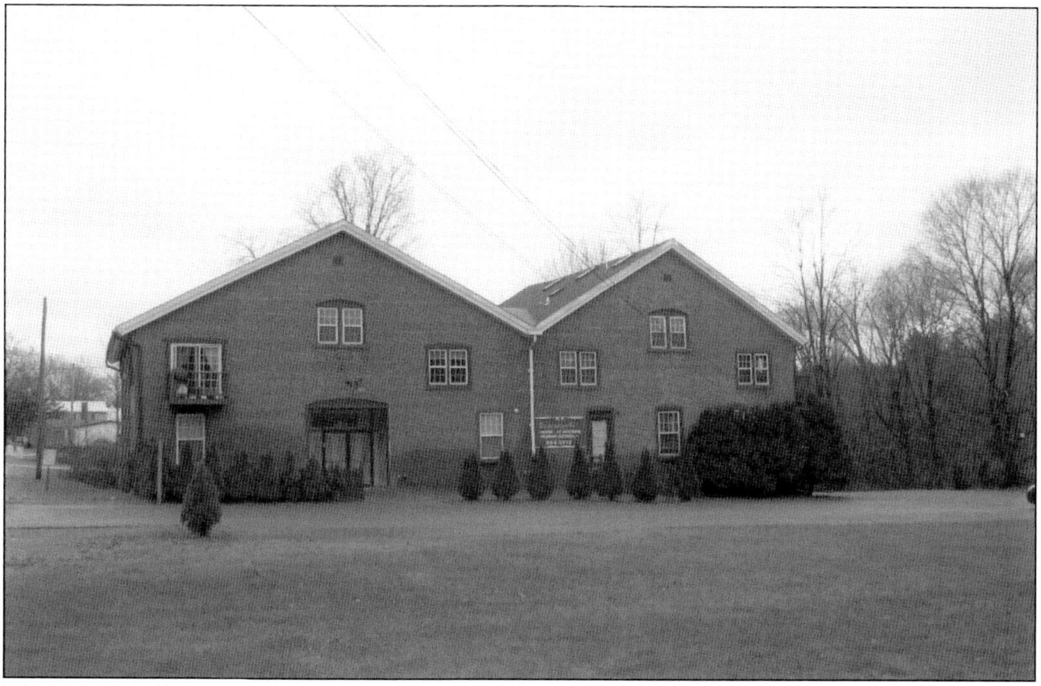

The Cook mill, used for years to manufacture paper for collars and cuffs, was converted into a powerhouse in 1896 to provide electrical current for the new Ballston Terminal Railroad. A carbarn was constructed nearby to house the two trolleys at night. (Author's collection.)

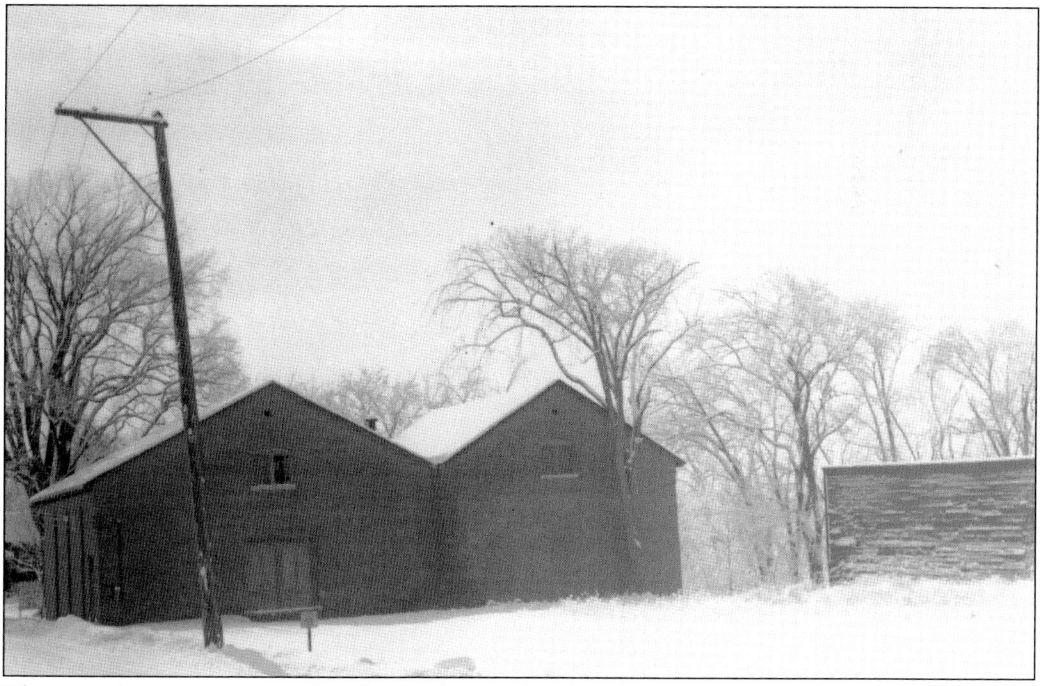

The powerhouse survives to this day as a business and apartments, but the carbarn, just visible on the right, did not last long after this photograph was taken. (Saratoga County Historical Society at Brookside Museum.)

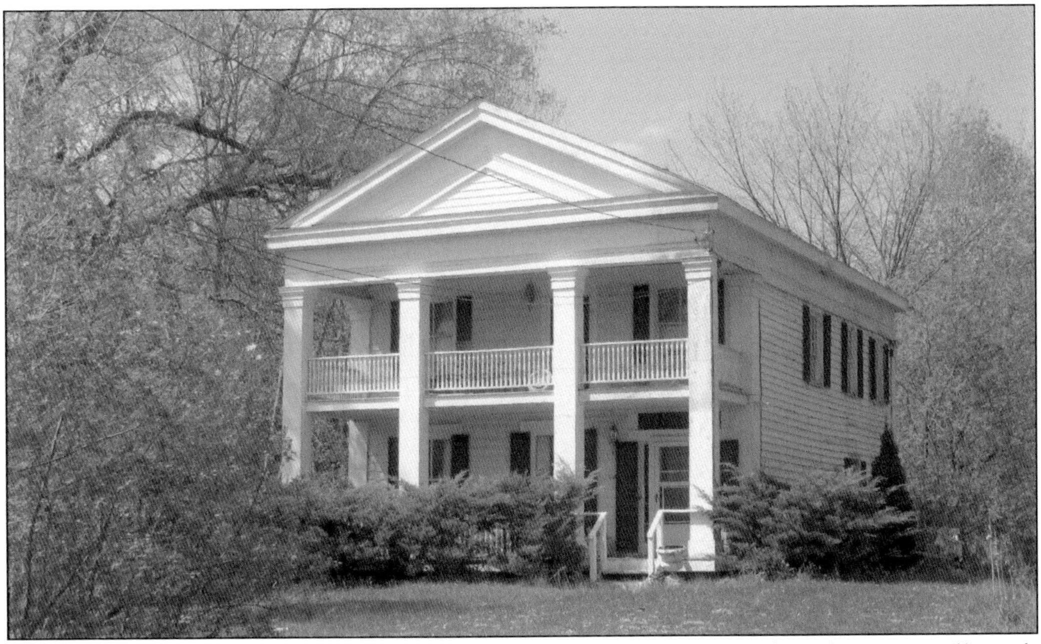

In 1845, Lindley Crane relocated from Dalton, Massachusetts, and purchased a paper mill north of Factory Village. He used some of the riches from his mill to build this mansion across the street. After the mill shut down, it reportedly served as a house of ill repute but has since been renovated for use as a residence once again. (Author's collection.)

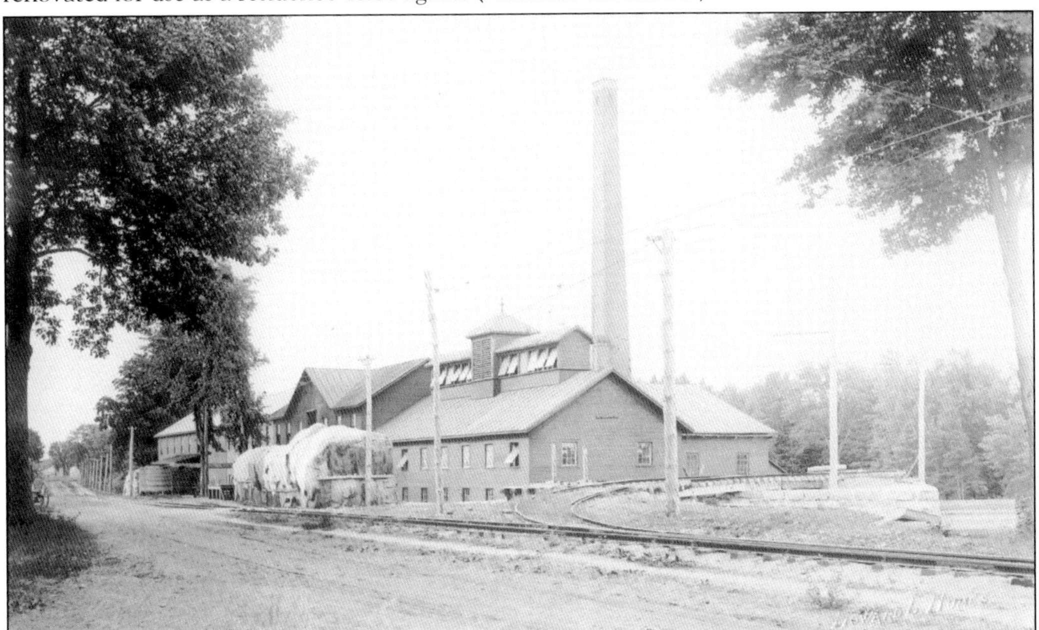

After Lindley Crane retired due to poor health in 1874, George West purchased his paper mill for $55,000, renamed it Eagle Mill, and converted the machinery to manufacture manila paper. It was served by the Ballston Terminal Railroad beginning in 1898. After almost 80 years of operation as a paper mill, it burned down in 1917 and was not rebuilt. (Saratoga County Historical Society at Brookside Museum.)

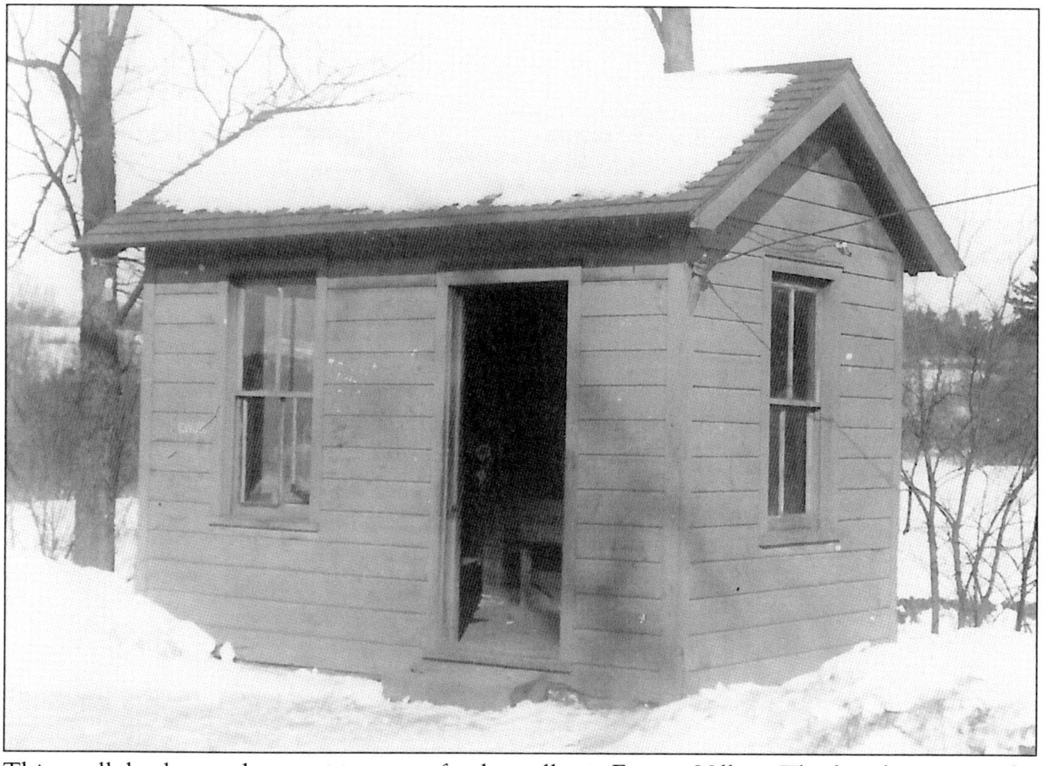

This small shack served as a waiting room for the trolley in Factory Village. The faint lettering to the left of the window is "ENYR," short for the Eastern New York Railroad, the successor to the Ballston Terminal Railroad. The frozen Kayaderosseras is down the bank. (Chris Morley collection.)

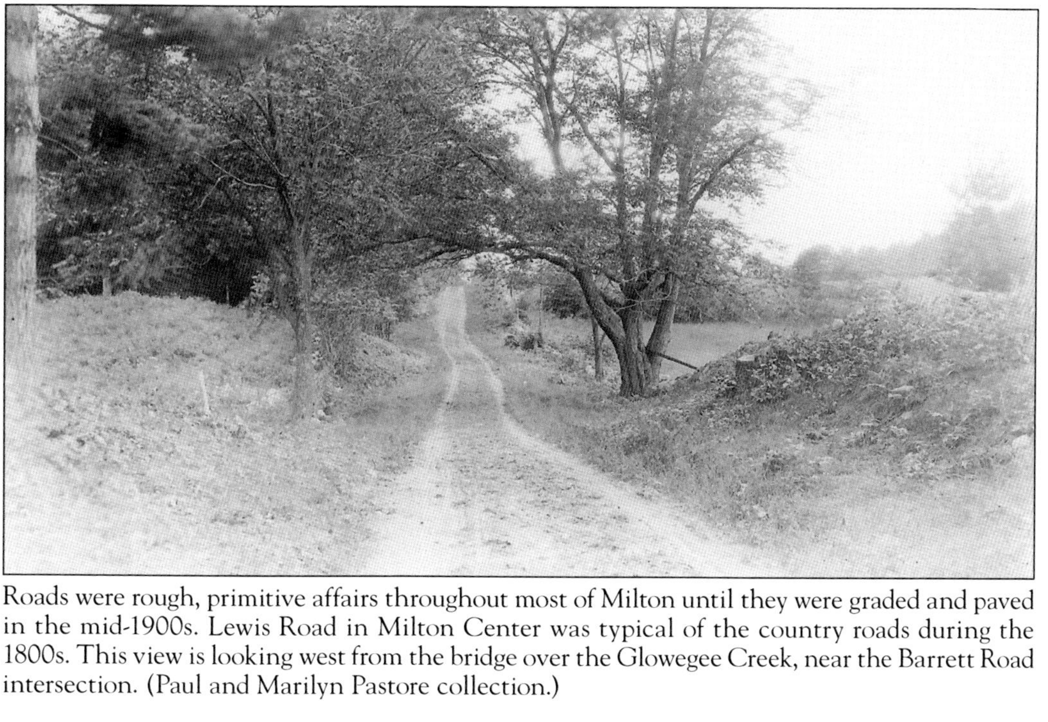

Roads were rough, primitive affairs throughout most of Milton until they were graded and paved in the mid-1900s. Lewis Road in Milton Center was typical of the country roads during the 1800s. This view is looking west from the bridge over the Glowegee Creek, near the Barrett Road intersection. (Paul and Marilyn Pastore collection.)

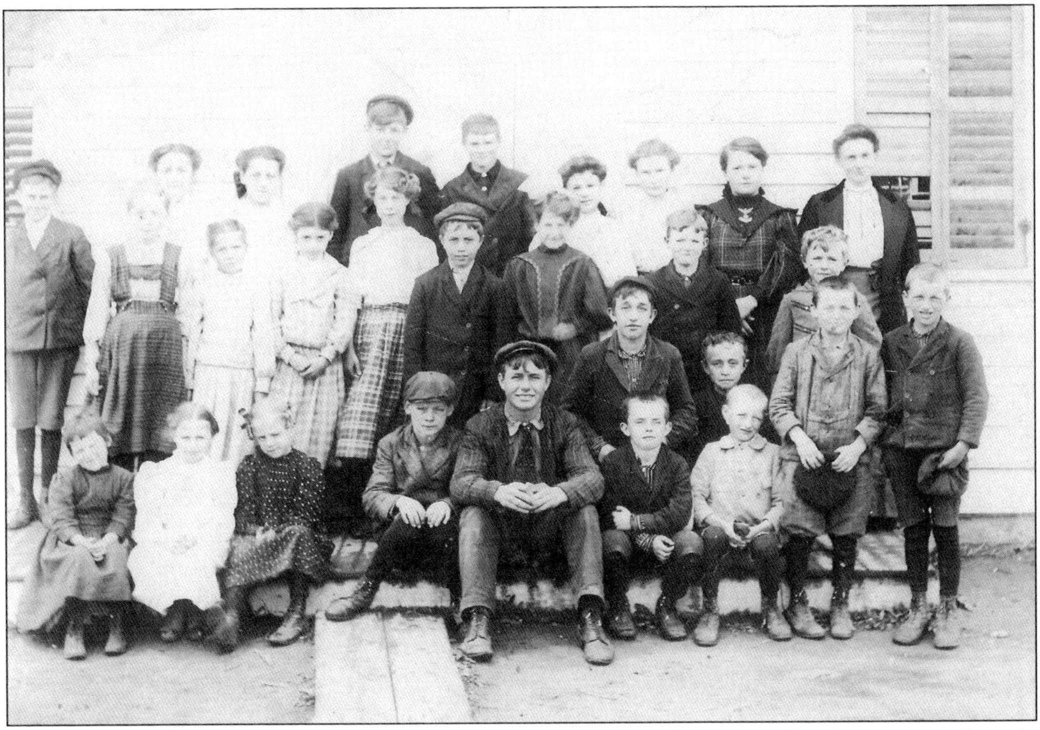

Although Milton Hill was one of the oldest settlements in the town of Milton, it was largely abandoned once Ballston Spa was made the county seat. However, there were enough residents to maintain a school into the 1900s. School No. 3 was located on Middle Line Road, between Barrett and Galway Roads. Anna Shane was the teacher (top right). (Paul and Marilyn Pastore collection.)

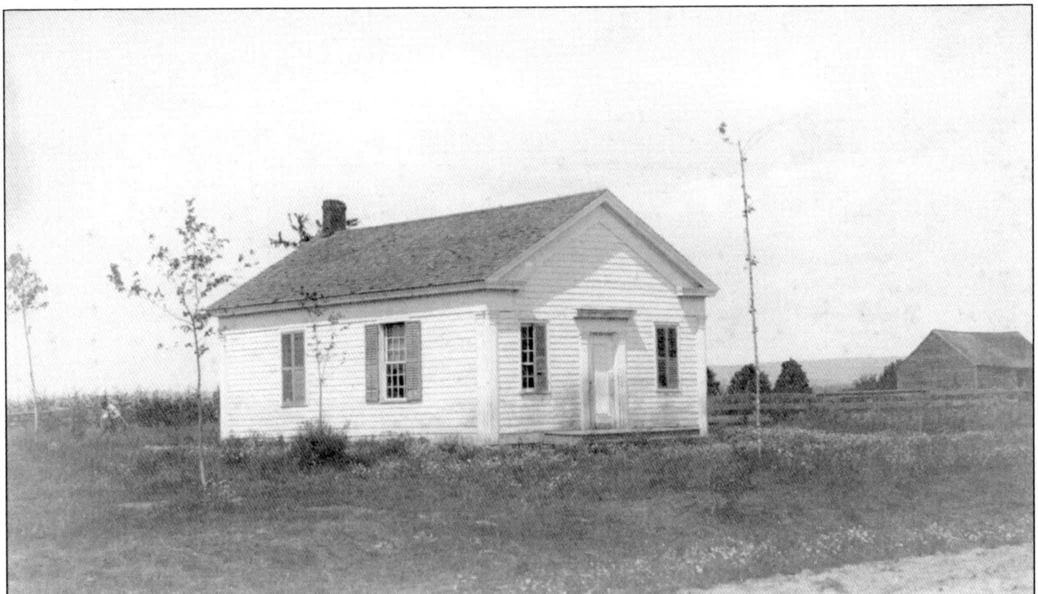

School No. 3 at Milton Hill is one of nine school buildings in town that have survived since all schools were consolidated to Ballston Spa, Saratoga, and Galway. Today, it is a residence. (Town of Milton Historian.)

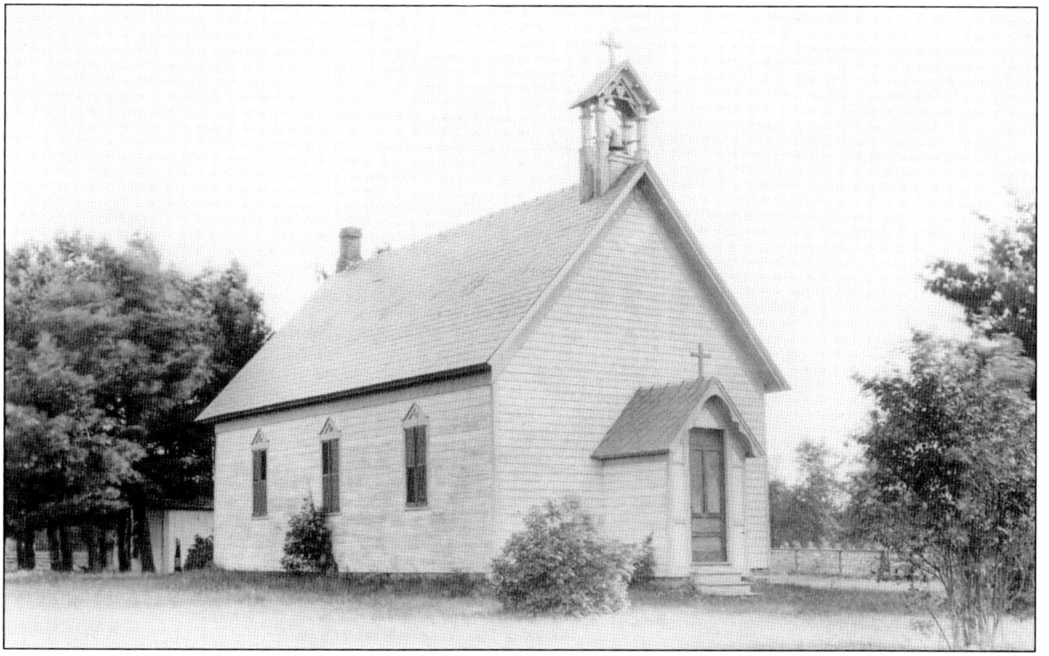

The short-lived St. James' Episcopal Church of Milton Hill was organized in 1796. The parish suffered from a lack of funding and was torn down in 1849. However, in 1880, Rev. Walter Delafield spearheaded the establishment of a new St. James church. It was built on land donated by Samuel Massey, proprietor of the nearby hotel, just west of the Milton Center Corners on the south side of the road. (Town of Milton Historian.)

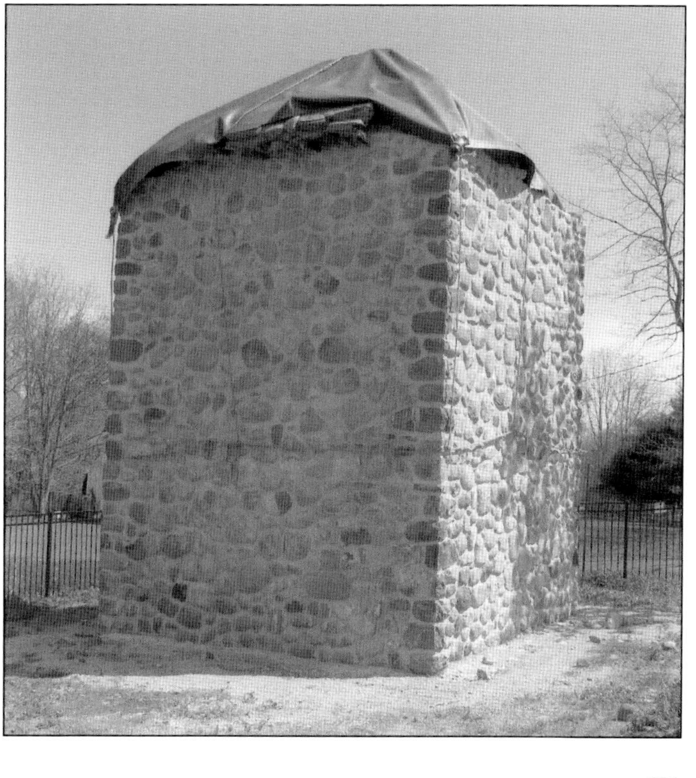

This unusual water tower was built to service the well-known Rose Hill farm, which was originally established in 1806 by James Thompson, one of Saratoga County's first judges. The year of its construction is open to debate, with estimates ranging from the late 1800s to early 1900s. Rose Hill farm remained in the Thompson family until 1923. (Author's collection.)

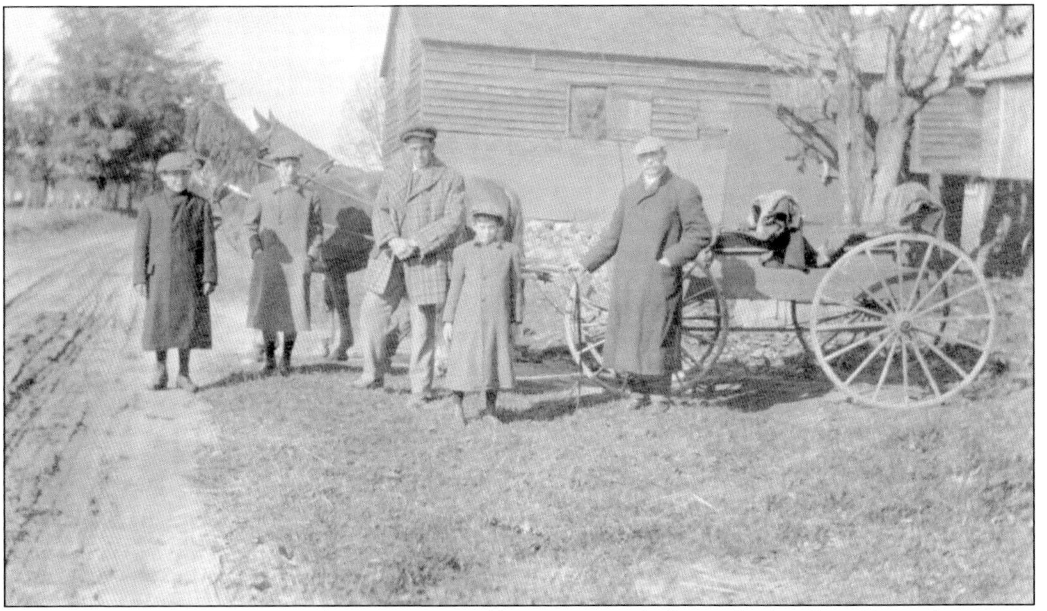

Despite the intense industrial activity in Ballston Spa and along the banks of Kayaderosseras Creek, farming was the primary occupation for most Milton residents until the early 1900s. From left to right are Lloyd Conde, Thurman Conde, John Keeler, Carl Conde, and Charles Conde. They are pictured around 1917 at the Keeler Farm, which was located on Galway Road, a half mile west of West Milton. (Town of Milton Historian.)

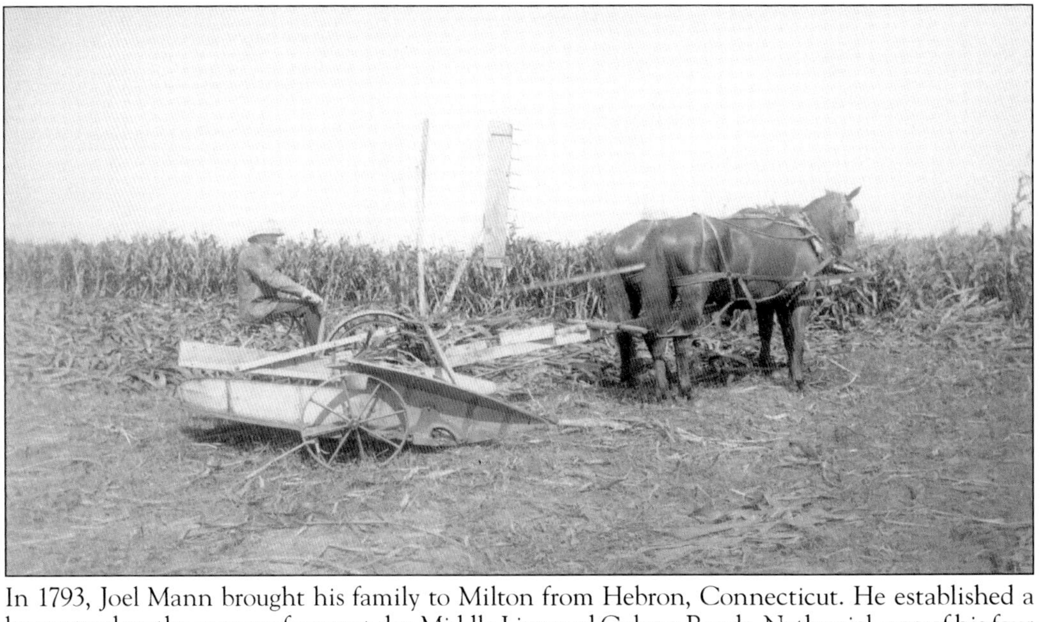

In 1793, Joel Mann brought his family to Milton from Hebron, Connecticut. He established a homestead on the corner of present-day Middle Line and Galway Roads. Nathaniel, one of his four sons, remained here into adulthood, establishing one of the town's longest-lived farms. Pictured is an early harvester cutting corn on the Mann farm. (Town of Milton Historian.)

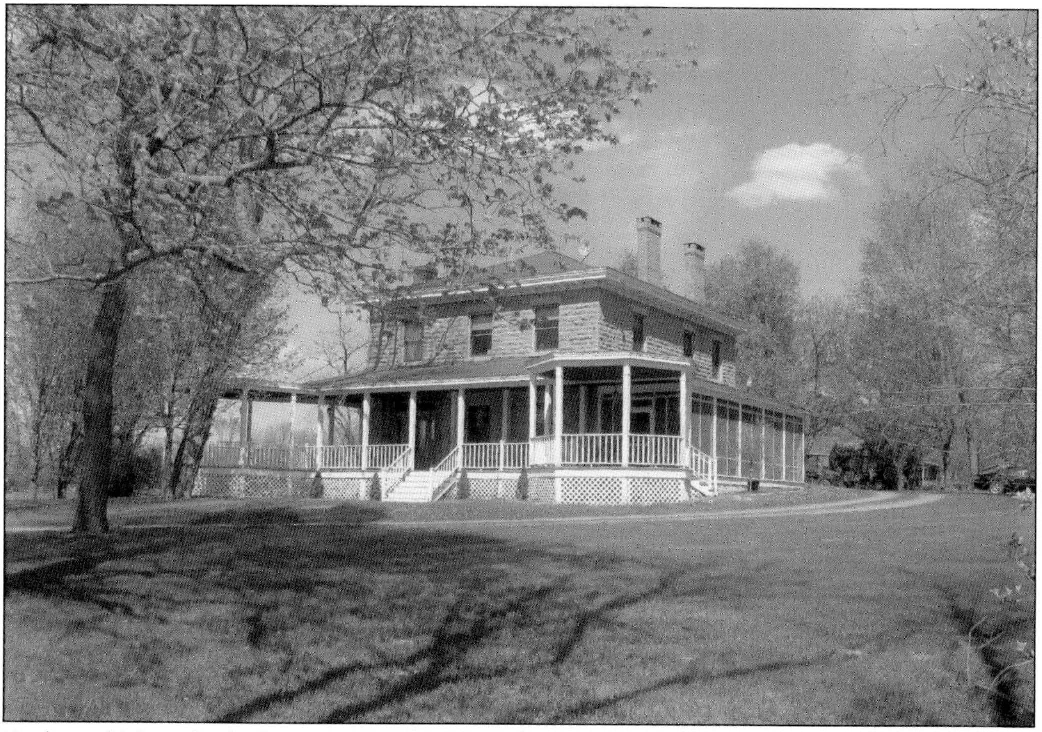

Nathaniel Mann built this stone residence on the corner of Middle Line and Galway Roads on the plot of land purchased by his father. It remained in the family continuously until Conklin Mann sold it to Henry Lewis in 1921. The stone came from the quarries of nearby Rowland's Hollow. (Author's collection.)

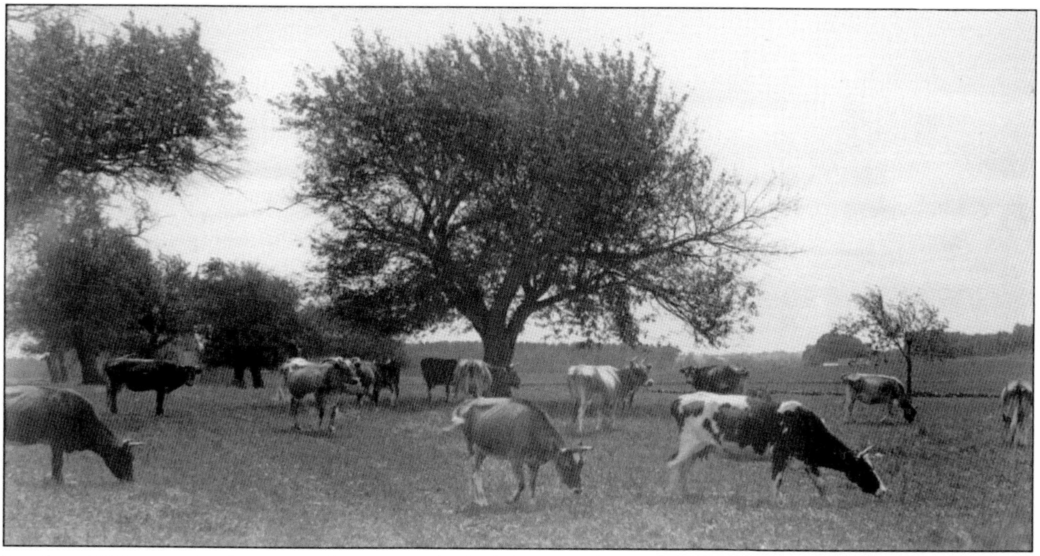

In the 1800s, agriculture in this area shifted from subsistence farming to cash crop farming, primarily wheat. However, competition from the Midwest caused Saratoga County farmers to diversify into other crops and livestock, and thus the dairying industry was born. The first exports from Milton's farms were cheese and butter. Pictured is a herd of cows on the Mann Farm. (Town of Milton Historian.)

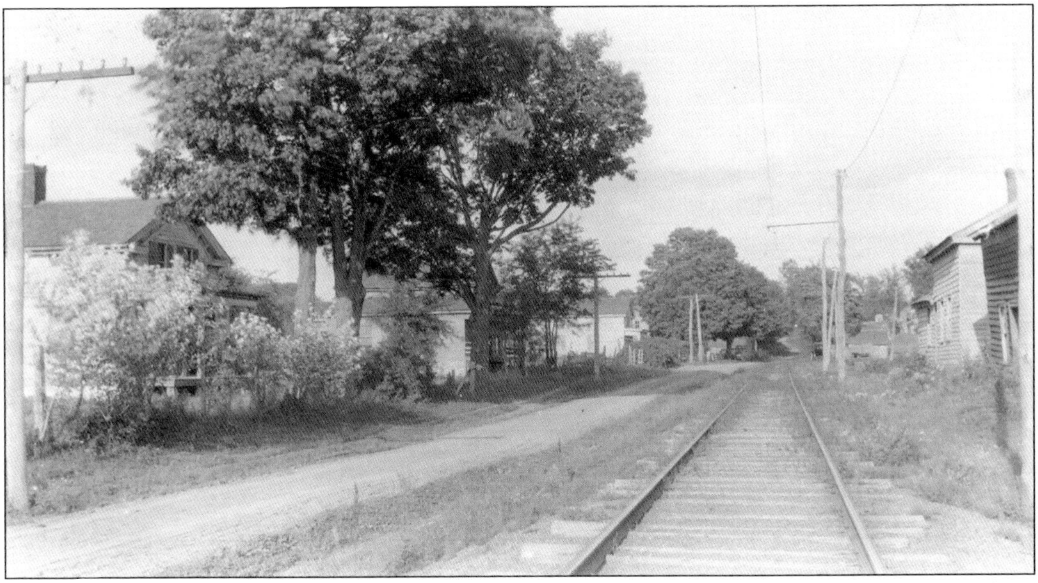

This peaceful scene shows the Ballston Terminal Railroad trolley tracks heading east at Milton Center. By the time the railroad was built in 1896, most industry had been relocated to Ballston Spa. Only the Lewis Sawmill was listed as one of the railroad's customers. (Paul and Marilyn Pastore collection.)

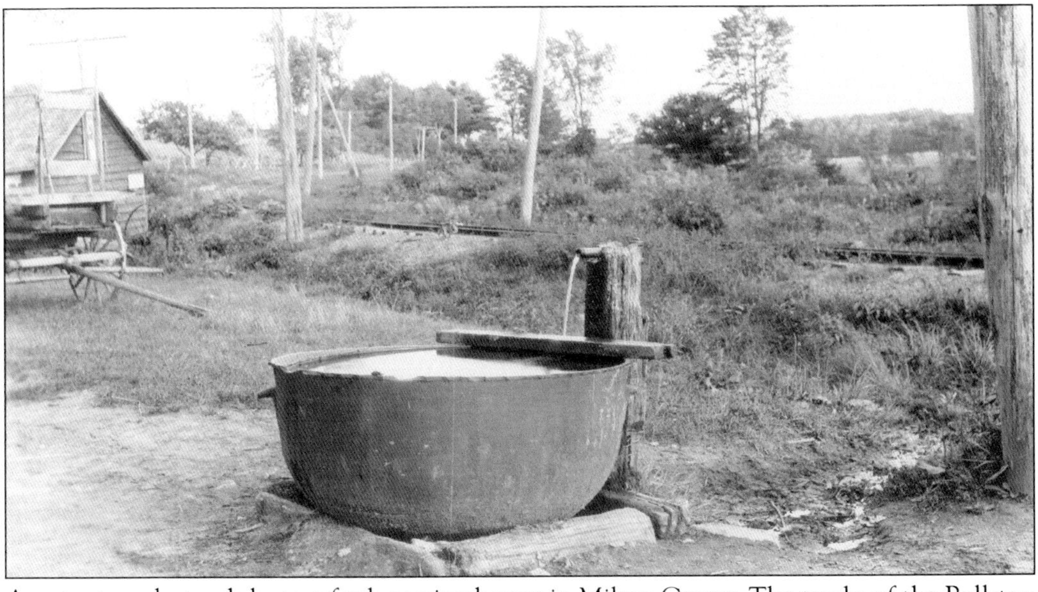

A water trough stands by to refresh passing horses in Milton Center. The tracks of the Ballston Terminal Railroad are in the background. The photographer appears to be facing east on Geyser Road, where the track curved south to follow Rock City Road into Craneville. (Town of Milton Historian.)

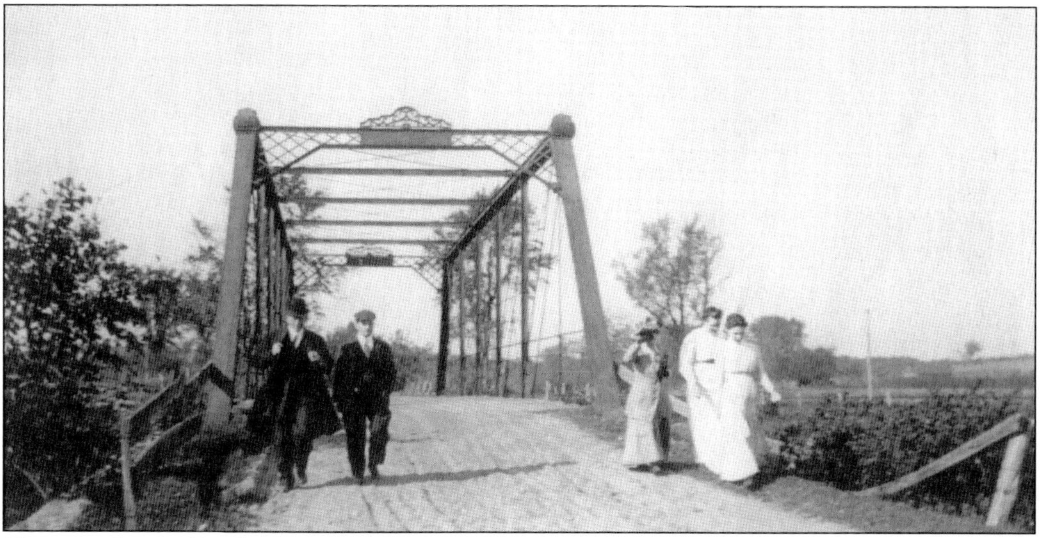

Shown is the road bridge over Kayaderosseras Creek at Milton Center. Middle Line Road was one of the most important thoroughfares in Saratoga County until new county and interstate roads were constructed. (Saratoga County Historical Society at Brookside Museum.)

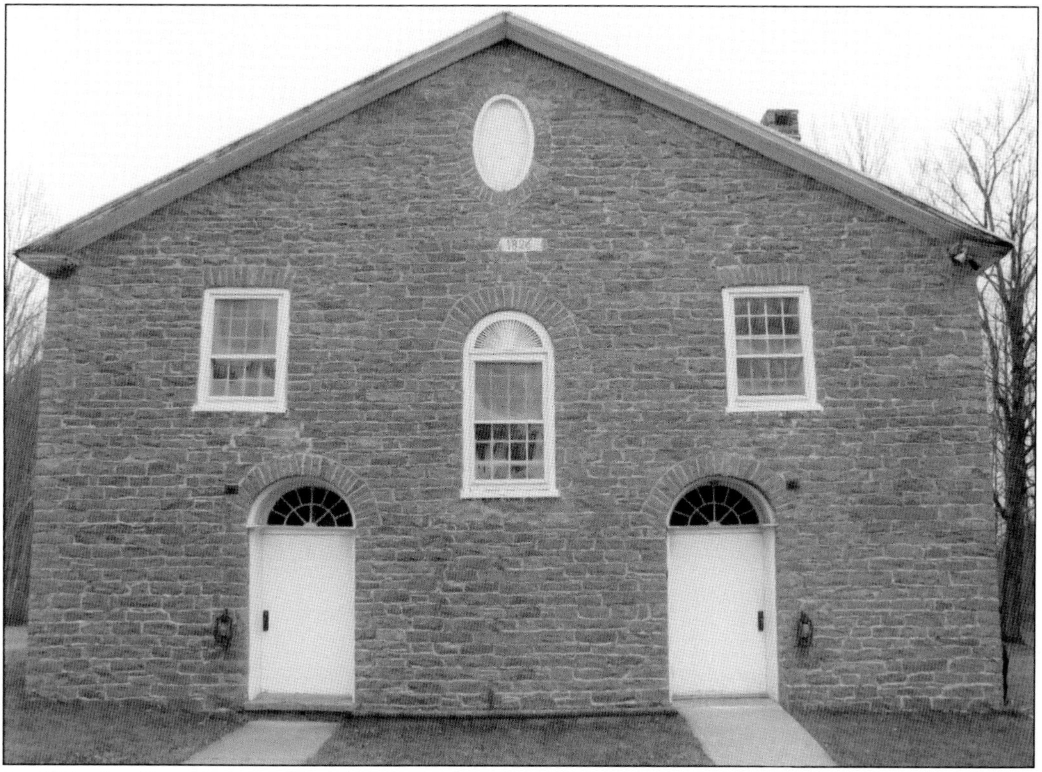

In 1793, the First Baptist Church in North Milton was founded at the home of John and Sarah Bentley, owners of the long-lived Bentley Farm. Meetings were held in individual homes until a wooden structure was built about five years later. In 1826, a stone building was constructed across the street from the Bentley Farm called the Stone Church, one of the oldest continually operated churches in Milton. (Author's collection.)

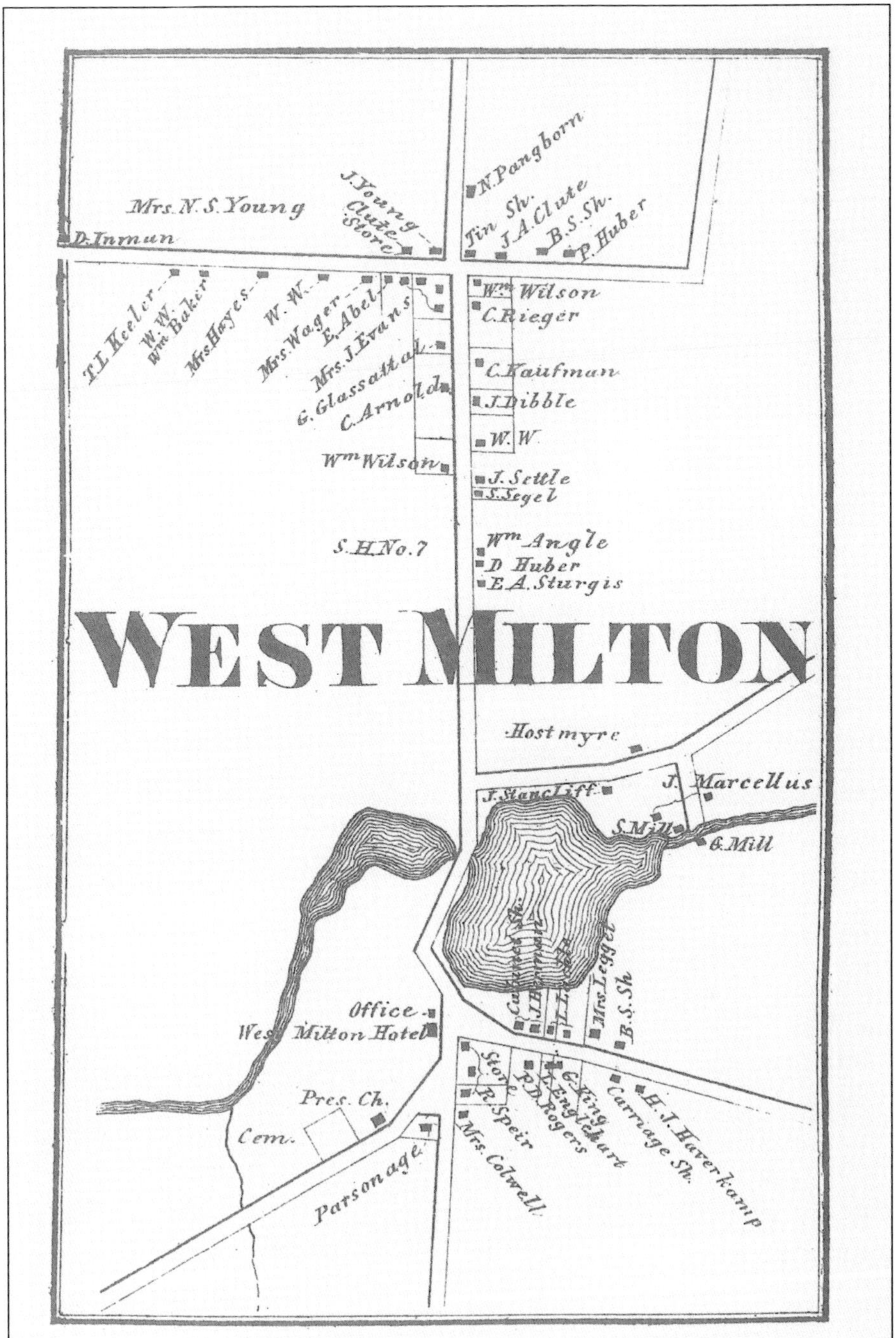

The hamlet of West Milton was separated into two settlements, Clute's Corners and Speir's Corners, named after the two general store owners. Clute's Corners contained a store, schoolhouse, tin shop, and about 30 households. Speir's Corners contained a sawmill, gristmill, general store, Presbyterian church, carriage shop, the West Milton Hotel, and a large pond with two mills. The pond has since been drained, but the banks are plainly visible today. The Pioneer Paper Mill was located a short distance northeast of this map. (Author's collection.)

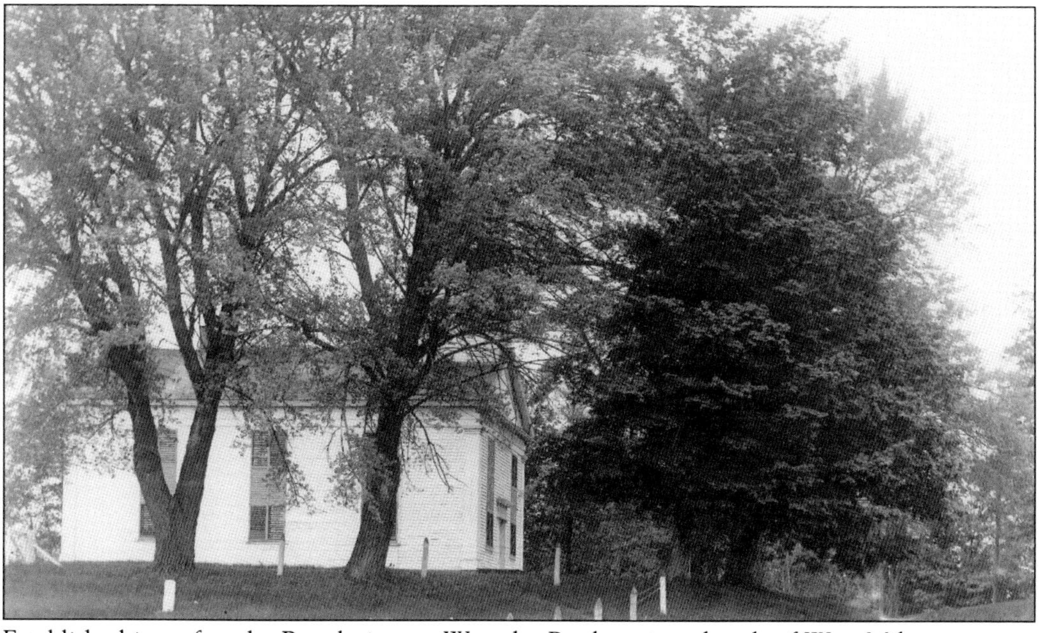

Established just after the Revolutionary War, the Presbyterian church of West Milton was one of the oldest in town, along with the one on Milton Hill. The first building was erected on the John Conde farm but was abandoned in 1840. It was replaced by this building at Speir's Corners in the same year. (Town of Milton Historian.)

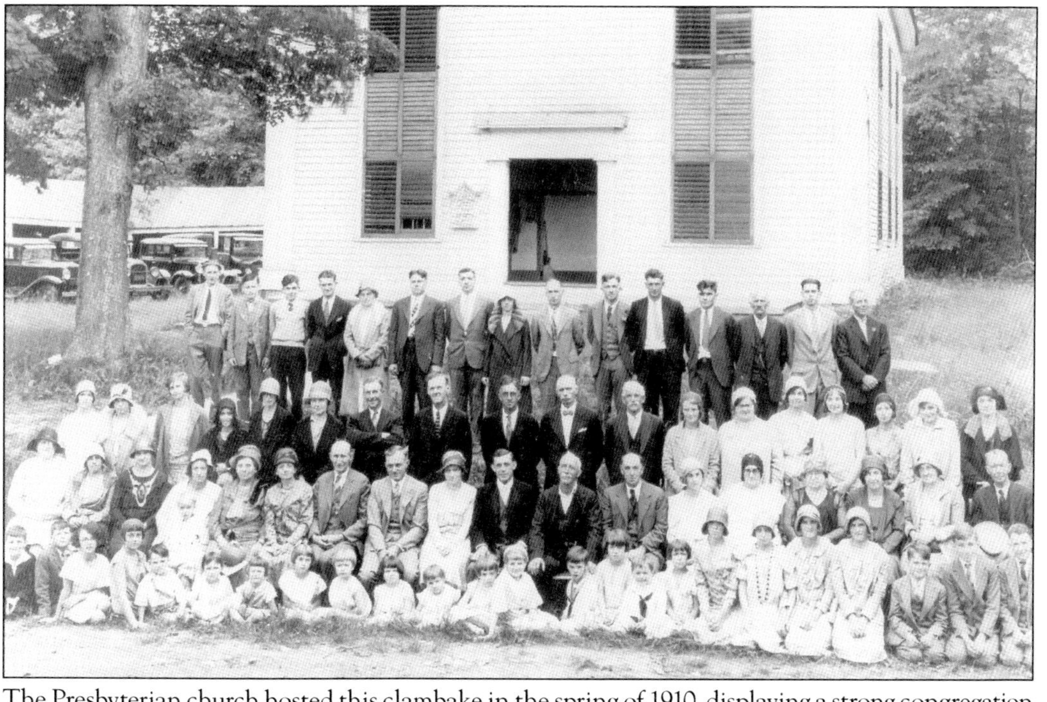

The Presbyterian church hosted this clambake in the spring of 1910, displaying a strong congregation even after the population of West Milton was in decline. However, the closure of the Pioneer Paper Mill and other businesses caused membership to drop, and the building was razed in 1927. (Paul and Marilyn Pastore collection.)

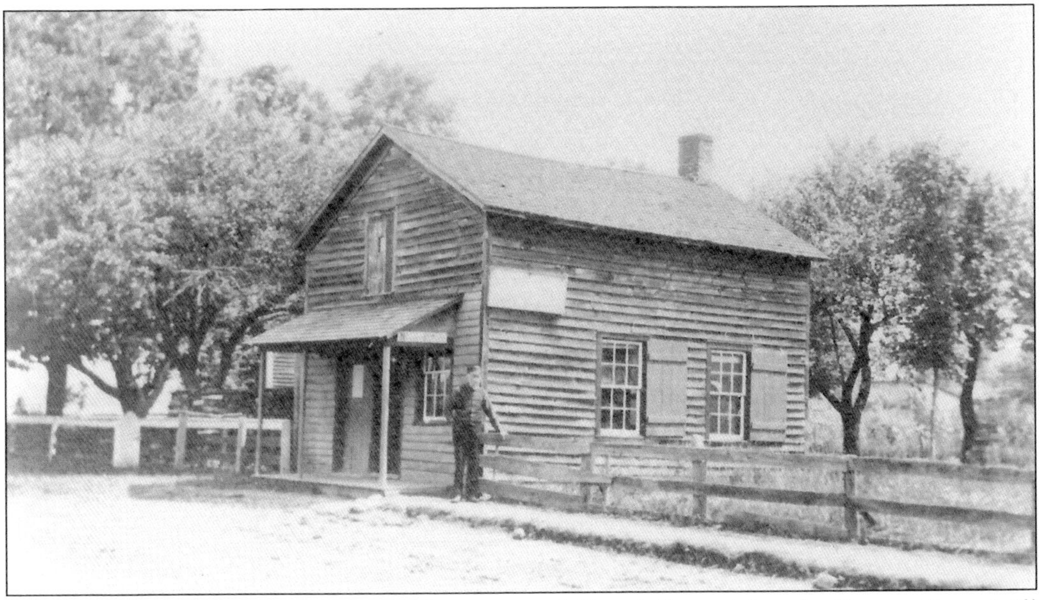

This post office on Crook's Grove Road once served West Milton. After the Pioneer Paper Mill closed, some residents were forced to relocate to Ballston Spa and beyond, which in turn negated the need for a dedicated post office. (Paul and Marilyn Pastore collection.)

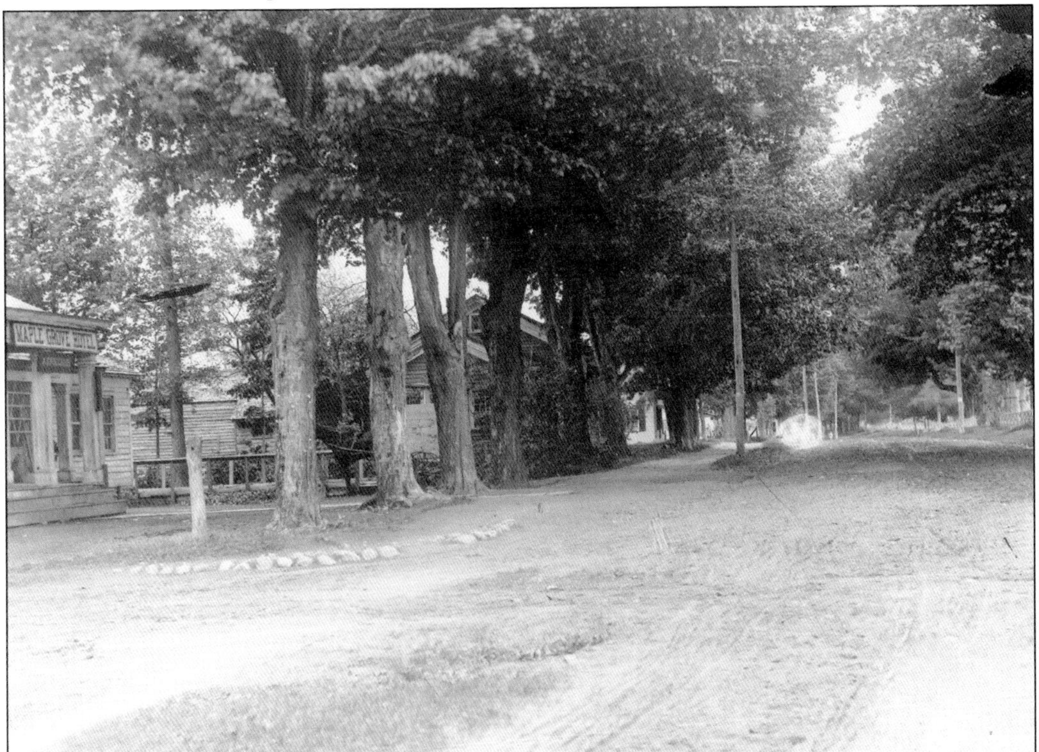

This is the only known view of the short-lived Maple Grove Hotel in West Milton, seen on the far left in the photograph. It operated for a dozen or so years in the early 1900s on the corner of what is now Atomic Project and West Milton Roads. (Town of Milton Historian.)

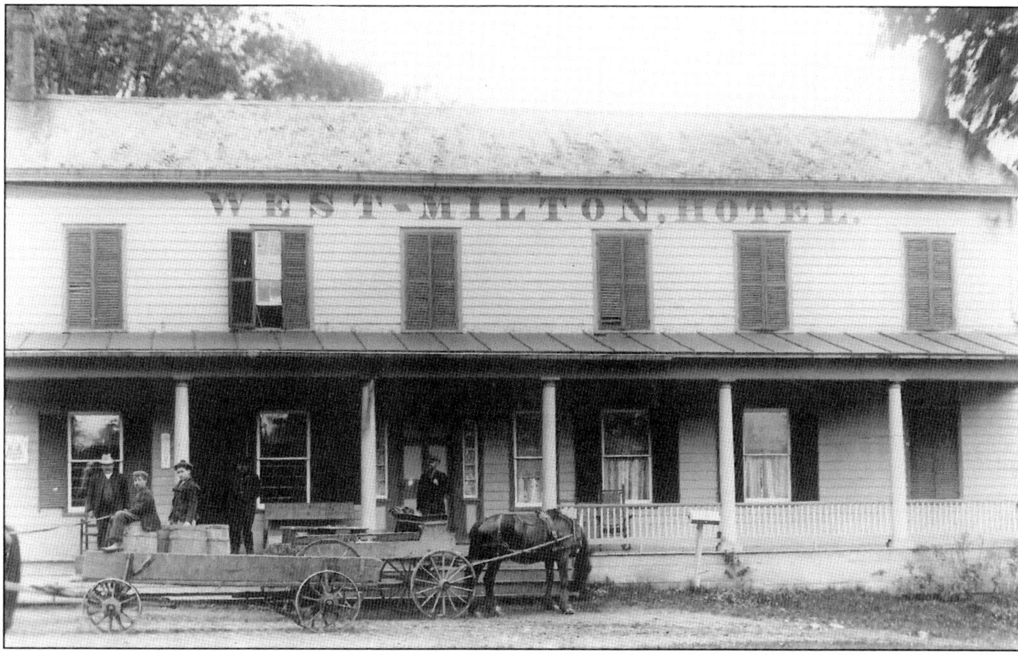

The West Milton Hotel was located on the corner of West Milton and Galway Roads. It was a favorite way station for travelers going west toward Galway or east toward Ballston Spa for over 100 years. This haven of comfort was destroyed by fire in 1918. (Paul and Marilyn Pastore collection.)

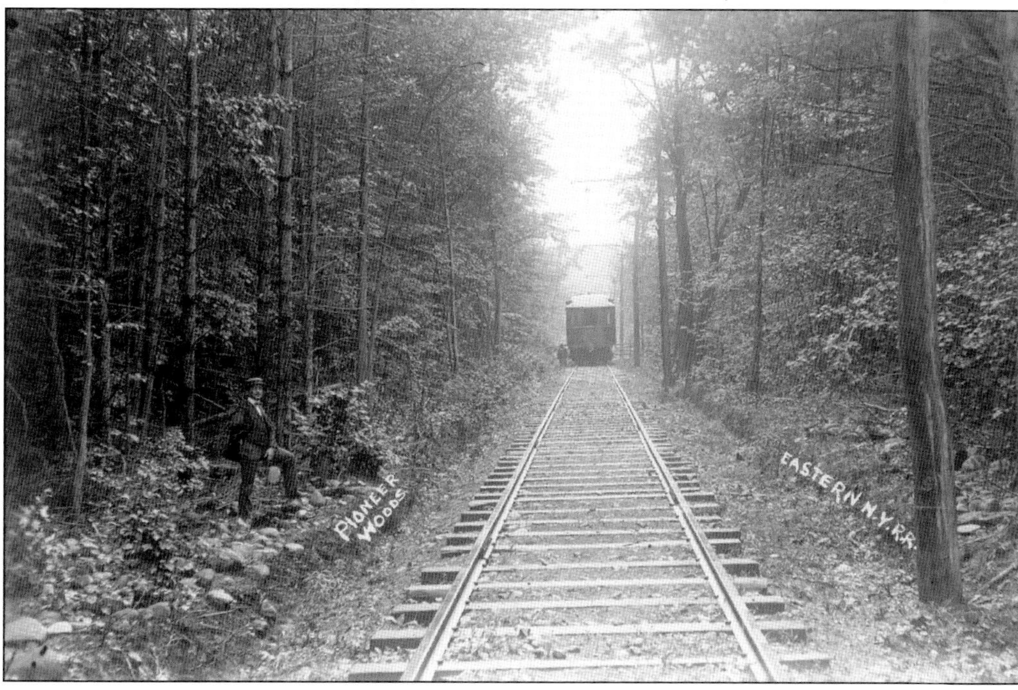

The Ballston Terminal Railroad trolley navigated long stretches of heavily wooded areas throughout the town of Milton. This 1910 image shows it parked along the line between the Pioneer Mill in West Milton and Rock City Falls. Today, this stretch of former railroad bed is a walking trail. (Saratoga County Historical Society at Brookside Museum.)

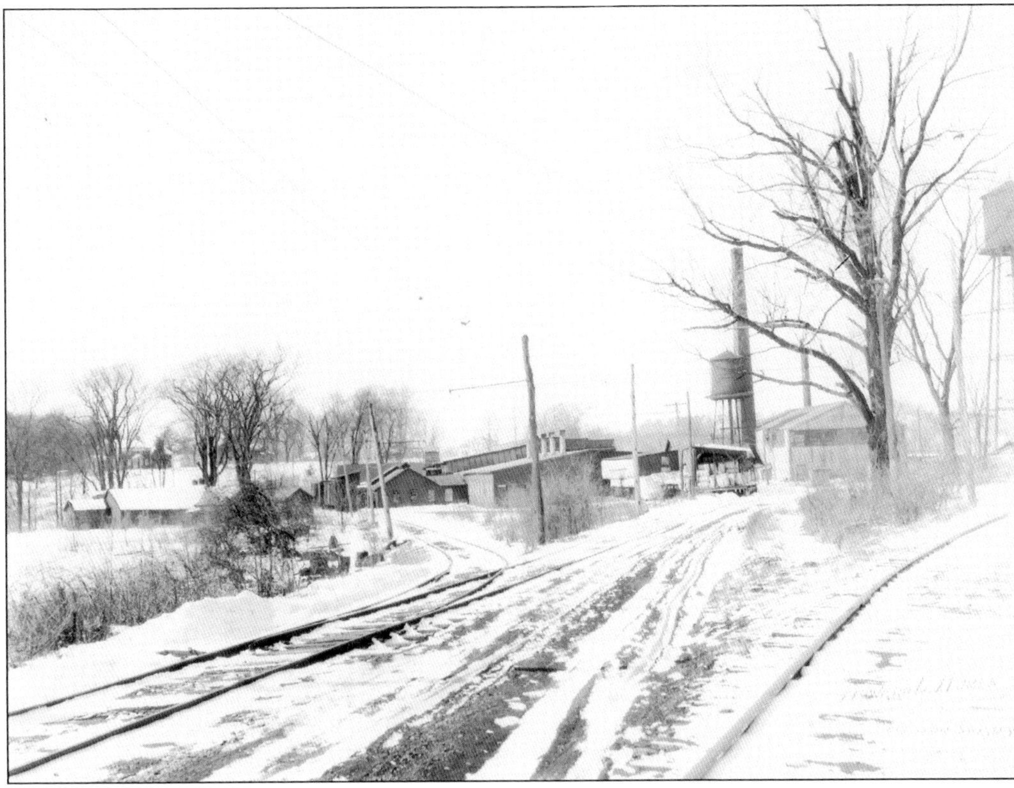

Pioneer Mill was very successful as a paper mill during the 1860s, but an ownership dispute led to its destruction by an arsonist. In 1870, George West purchased the property and had the mill completely rebuilt for the production of manila paper. It was among only three paper mills in the town to survive until the closure of the Ballston Terminal Railroad in 1929. (Saratoga County Historical Society at Brookside Museum.)

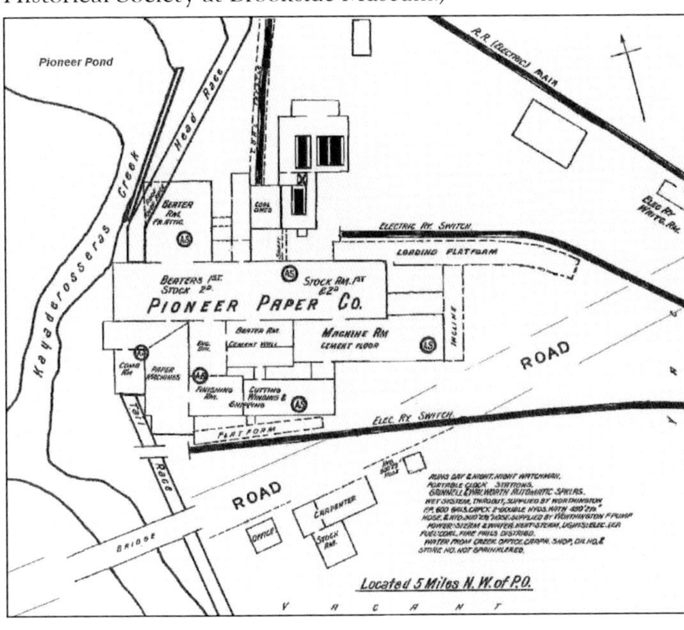

The extensive Pioneer Mill complex was served by two freight car spurs and one coal trestle spur. To give an indication of the size of the mill, the small beater room (center) survived the mill's eventual destruction and is now a residence. The dam, tailrace, and a few building foundations also survive. (Chris Morley collection.)

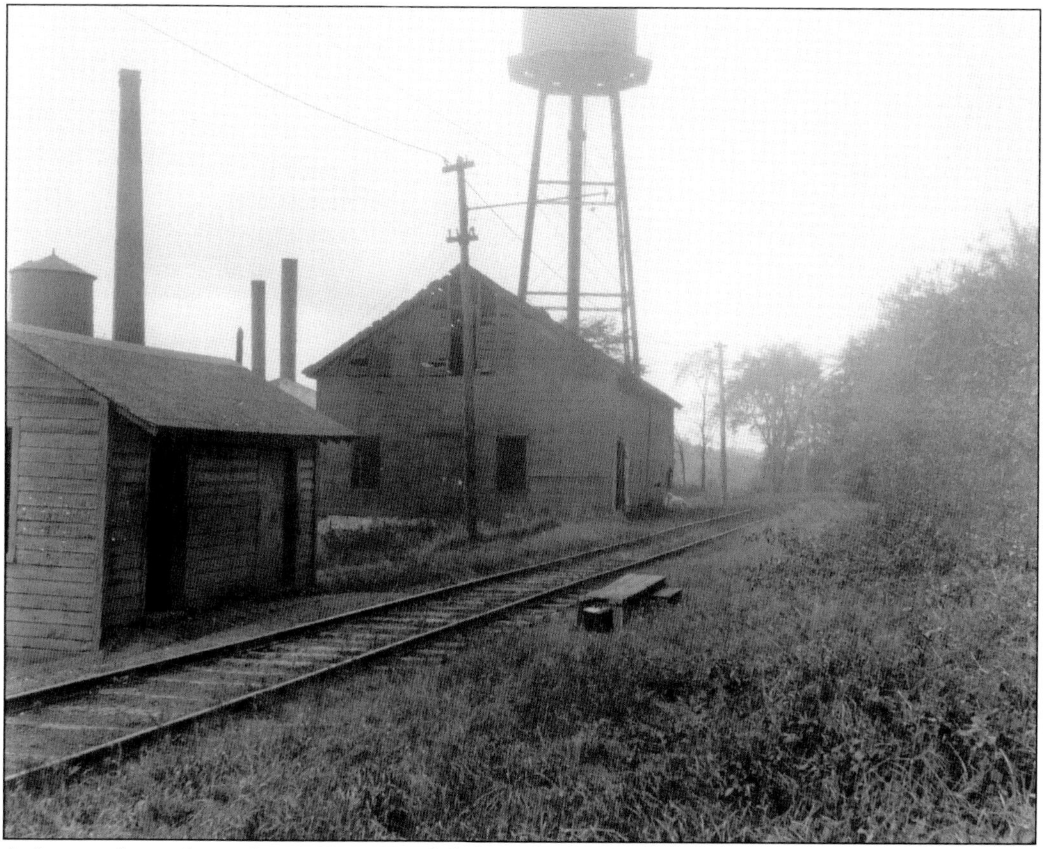

A few smokestacks and water towers of the Pioneer Mill can be seen along the right-of-way of the Ballston Terminal Railroad. Students and workers used the small building on the left as a waiting room for the trolley. (Chris Morley collection.)

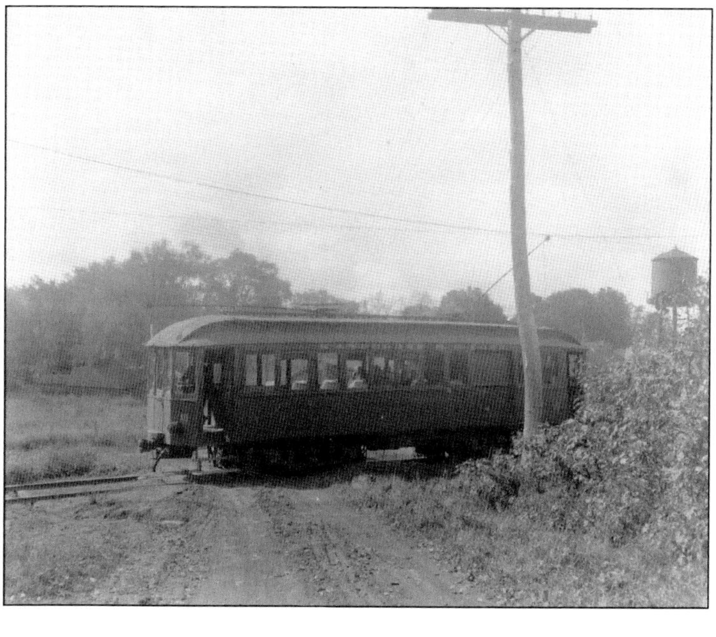

After two bankruptcies, the electric trolley line that served Milton was known as the Kaydeross Railroad Corporation. Here, the passenger trolley is crossing West Milton Road near Pioneer Mill on its way to Milton Center. (Saratoga County Historical Society at Brookside Museum.)

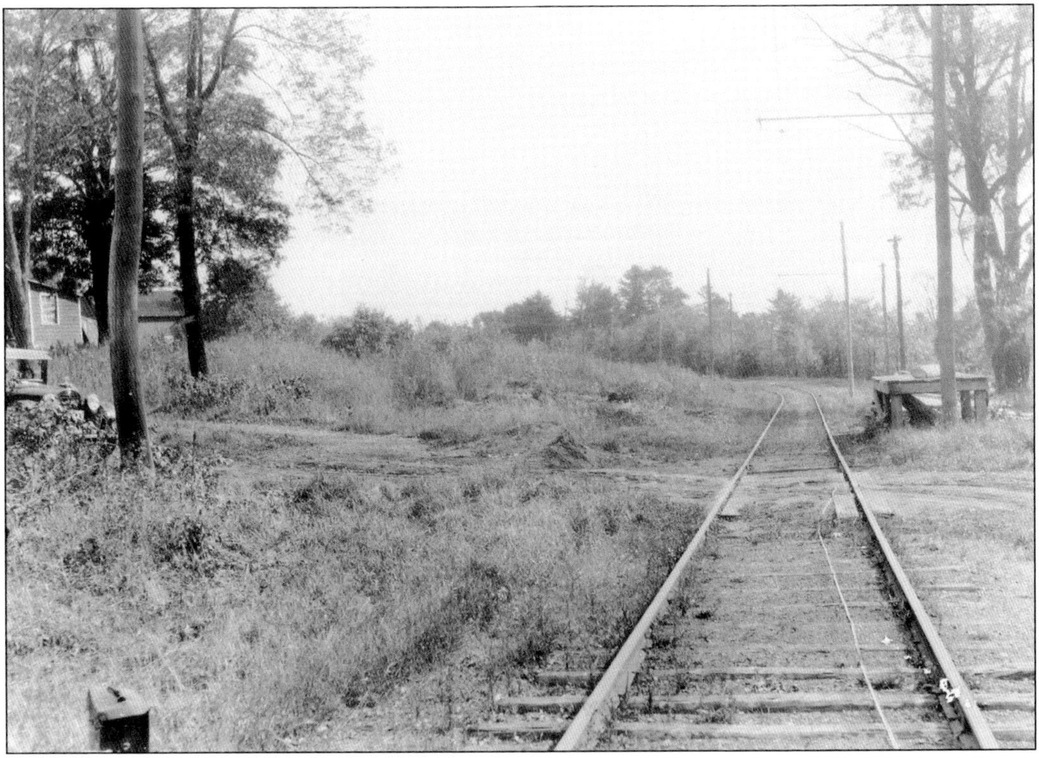

This view of the Ballston Terminal Railroad tracks is looking east over West Milton Road. The next stop would have been at Milton Center. (Saratoga County Historical Society at Brookside Museum.)

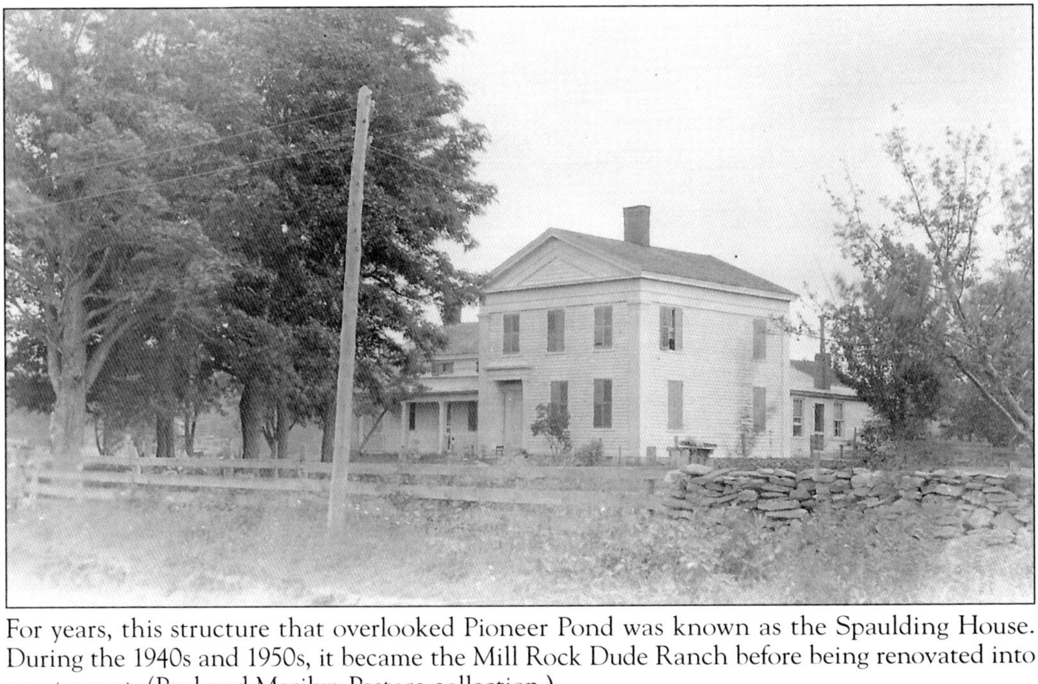

For years, this structure that overlooked Pioneer Pond was known as the Spaulding House. During the 1940s and 1950s, it became the Mill Rock Dude Ranch before being renovated into a restaurant. (Paul and Marilyn Pastore collection.)

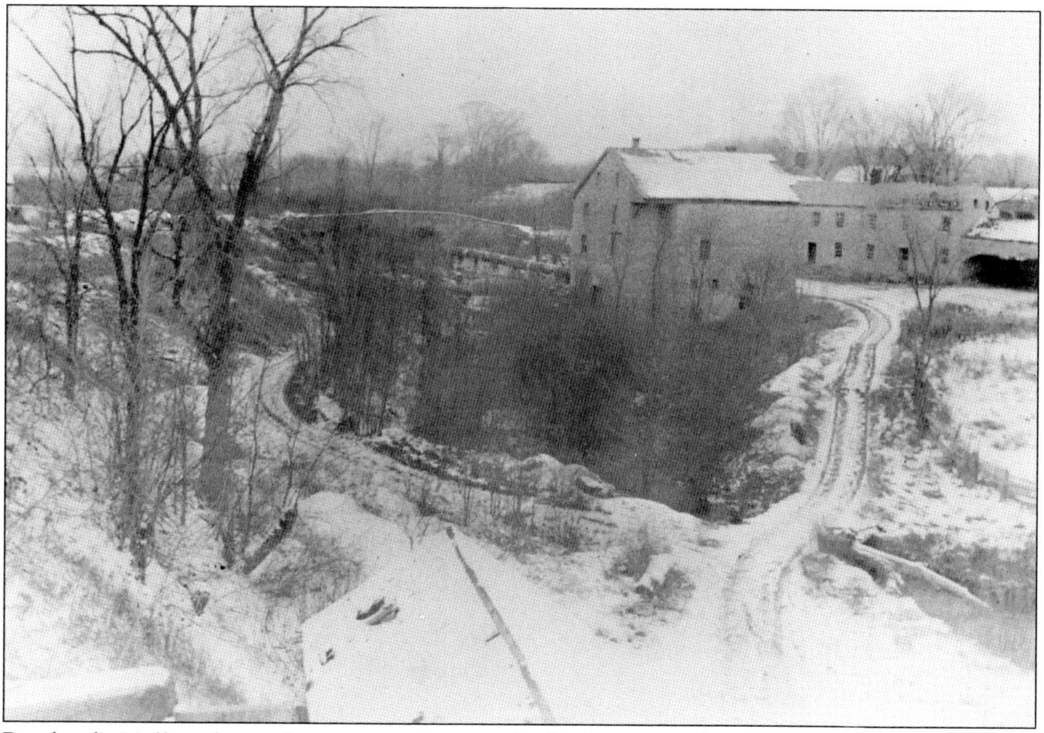

Rowland's Hollow, located at the northern end of Milton on present-day Rowland and Grand Streets, was once a thriving hamlet. In the 1840s, Hiram Rowland established a gristmill that was one of the largest in the county. He also partnered with Chauncey Kilmer in an ill-fated paper mill in Rock City Falls. (Paul and Marilyn Pastore collection.)

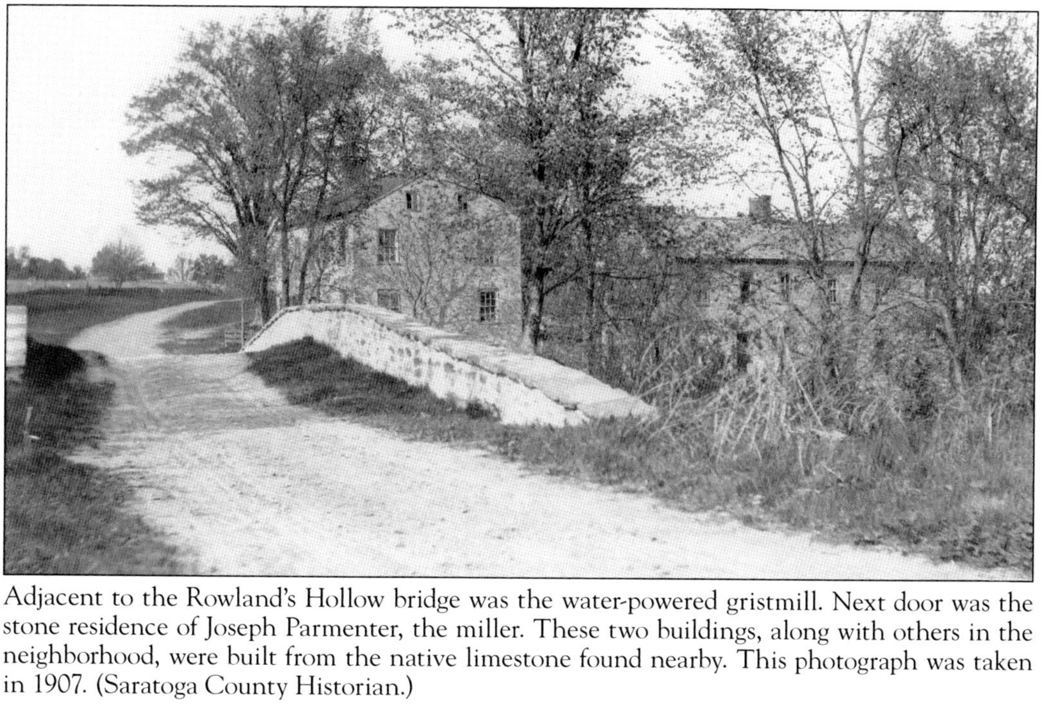

Adjacent to the Rowland's Hollow bridge was the water-powered gristmill. Next door was the stone residence of Joseph Parmenter, the miller. These two buildings, along with others in the neighborhood, were built from the native limestone found nearby. This photograph was taken in 1907. (Saratoga County Historian.)

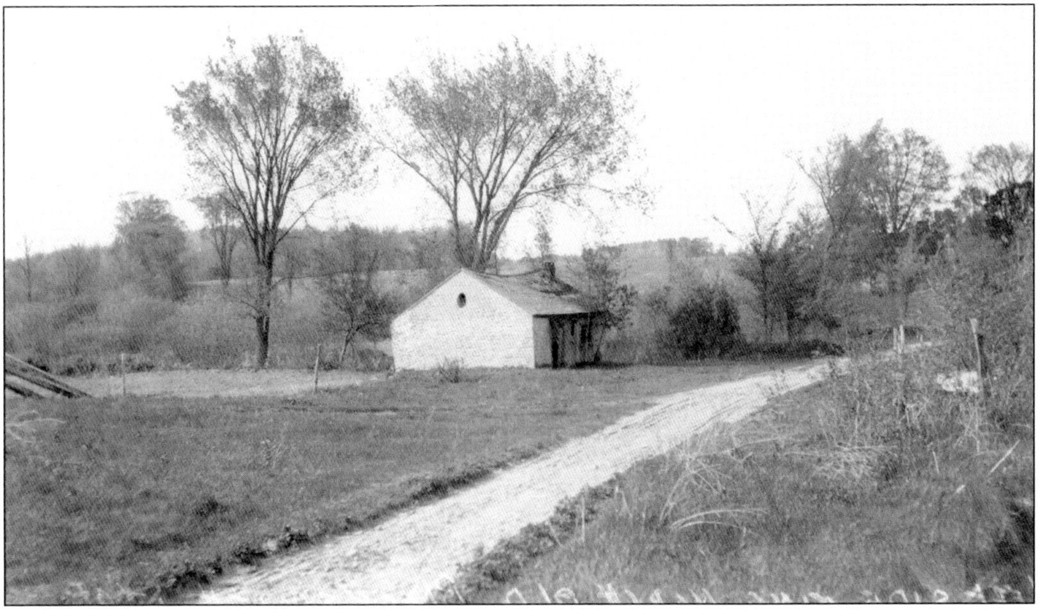

The hamlet of Rowland's Hollow was so extensive that it required its own schoolhouse, a building that survived into the 1920s. In addition to the lime quarry, kiln, and gristmill, there was also a plaster mill, stone quarry, and two mineral springs. The Prince Wing home reportedly was occupied long after the quarries shut down by a family who cut and sold ice from the pond. (Saratoga County Historian.)

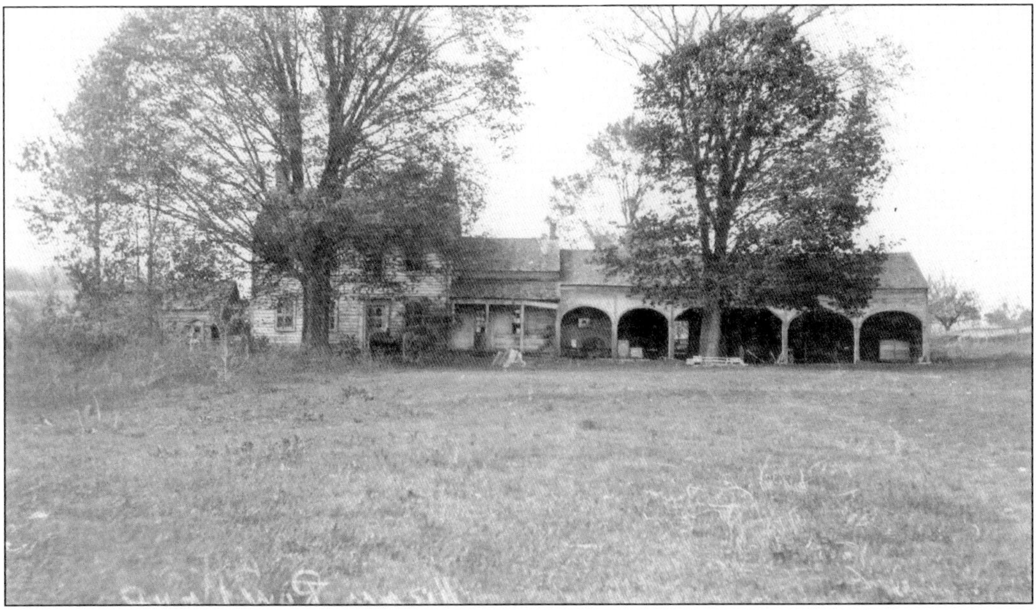

This rambling farmhouse was home to Hiram and Isaac Rowland, who owned the gristmill and sawmill. Meanwhile, Price Wing owned the lime quarry and limekiln, operated year-round by Patrick Leonard. During the mid- to late 1800s, paper mills from Rock City Falls, Ballston Spa, Hudson Falls, and Corinth used the lime produced here to make paper. (Saratoga County Historian.)

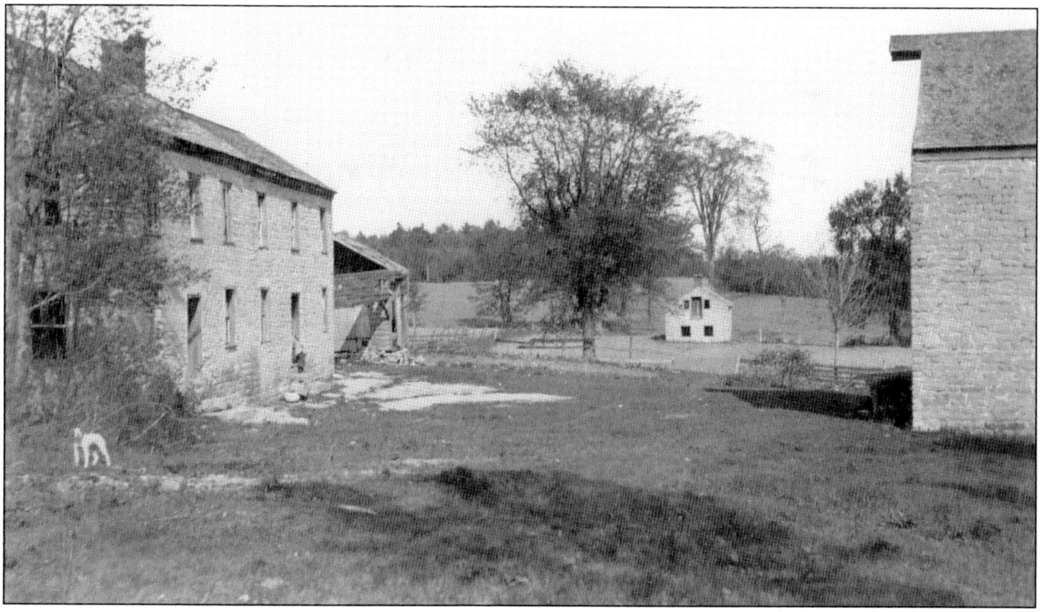

This scene shows the gristmill (left) and the residence of Joseph Parmenter, who operated the gristmill. The blacksmith shop is in the distance. When paper manufacturers figured out how to make paper from wood at the turn of the century, the lime quarries went silent, and the settlement was all but abandoned. (Saratoga County Historian.)

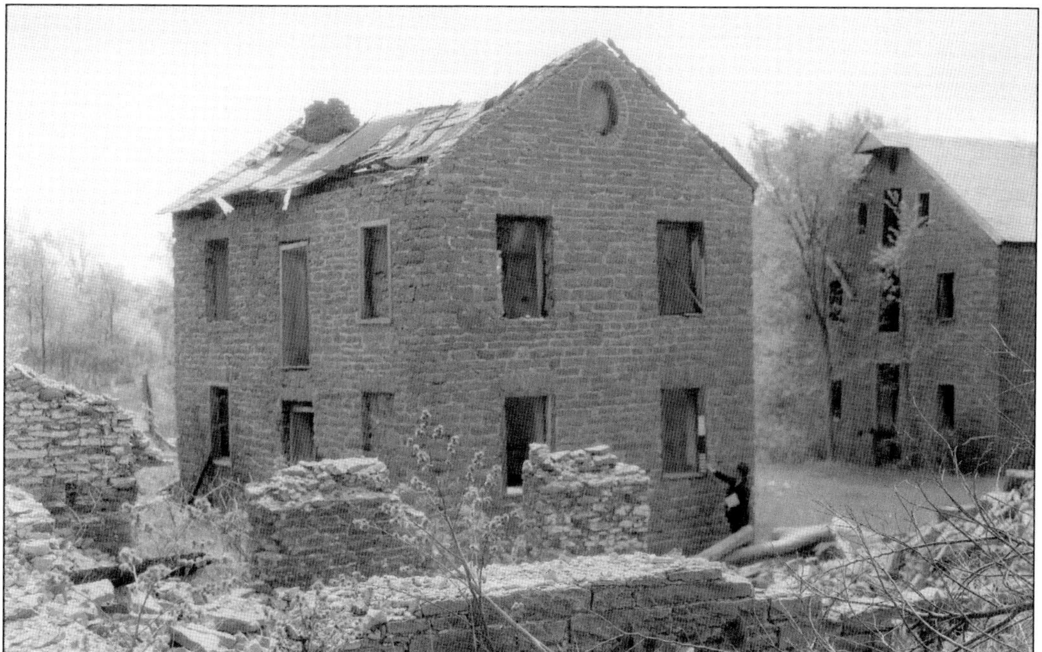

This c. 1940 photograph of Rowland's Hollow shows the durable stone buildings of the miller's residence (front) and gristmill (rear). The land surrounding the hamlet was not resettled after the factories shut down, so some of the buildings survived into the late 1900s, although the ruins have dwindled. (Library of Congress.)

BIBLIOGRAPHY

Blodgett, Royann and Hollis. *Memories: Bicentennial Celebration, Town of Milton*. Ballston Spa: The Bicentennial Book Committee, 1992.

Bulkeley, John. *Leading Men and Leading Pursuits of Ballston and Vicinity*. Ballston Spa: William S. Waterbury, 1874.

Dunn, Violet, Robert Hayden, and Clayton Brown. *Saratoga County Heritage*. Ballston Spa: Saratoga County, 1974.

Grose, Edward. *Centennial History of the Village of Ballston Spa*. Ballston Spa: *Ballston Journal*, 1907.

Horne, Field. *The First Respectable House: Brookside and the Growth of Ballston Spa*. Saratoga Springs: Kiskatom Publishing Company, 1984.

Johnstone, Jan. *Saratoga County Communities*. Saratoga Springs: Saratoga County Planning Board, 1980.

Puckaber, Bernard. *Through the Years: A Pictorial History of the Village of Ballston Spa, New York*. Ballston Spa: Ballston Spa Bicentennial Commission, 1976.

Saratogian, The. *Our County and Its People: A Descriptive and Biographical Record of Saratoga County, New York*. The Boston History Company, 1890.

Spafford, Horatio Gates. *A Gazetteer of the State of New York*. Albany: H.C. Southwick, 1813.

Starr, Timothy. *Lost Industries of the Kaydeross Valley: A History of Manufacturing in Ballston Spa, New York*. Rock City Falls, 2007.

Stone, William. *Reminiscences of Saratoga and Ballston*. R. Worthington, 1880.

Sylvester, Nathaniel Bartlett. *History of Saratoga County, New York*. Philadelphia: Everts and Peck, 1878.

About the Organization

Brookside believes that local history is vital to the growth of communities because it unifies and strengthens communal bonds, fosters exploration and discovery about shared heritage, exercises imaginations, and provides context and inspiration for new goals and growth. Brookside inspires community memory and enrichment by telling the story of Saratoga County through programs and exhibits that are both interactive and engaging. Brookside also promotes a deeper understanding, appreciation, and enjoyment of Saratoga County's past for people of all ages, backgrounds, and levels of interest through educational programs, innovative exhibits, ambitious web programming, personal experiences, and enduring relationships. In addition to being a regional attraction, the museum conducts and publishes research in the field of Saratoga County history through exhibits, programs, publications, and an interactive website. Brookside also fosters research through access to its library and collections and by providing educational programming at the museum, in the community, and online.

Consistent with our mission to preserve history on a local level, this book was printed in South Carolina on American-made paper and manufactured entirely in the United States. Products carrying the accredited Forest Stewardship Council (FSC) label are printed on 100 percent FSC-certified paper.

MADE IN THE USA